Relke confusion, — chans
'Gentile' being 'israelite'.

this use of 'Jews' in far too
fluid.

(see ch 3)

eg p84 — the author onus
that a grn desta of people 70 AD,
the term "gentile" included (even
was restricted to ??) 'Jews' in the
Diaspora!!! Complete rubbish!

Jesus Christ Divided

Solving the Mystery of the New Testament

MICHAEL LAFOND

© Michael LaFond 2014

Do not suppose that I came to bring peace on earth; I came not to bring peace but a sword. For I came to divide a man against his father, and a daughter against her mother, and a bride against her mother-in-law, and man's enemies are his household.

Matthew 10:34-36

Table of Contents

Map i
Preface 1
Introduction 6
The Order of the Pauline Epistles 15
The Journey of Saint Paul 39
When is a Gentile a Jew? 71
Sadducees, Pharisees, and Essenes 89
The Early Days of the Gospel 96
The Man of Lawlessness 114
Fighting with Beasts 132
Trial at Jerusalem 166
A Prisoner for Christ 185
The Gospel of Paul 193
The Gospel of James 220
The Aftermath 233
Afterword 240
Appendices 243
    Details of Paul's Journey from the Epistles 244
    Details of Paul's Journey in the Acts of the Apostles 258
    Proposed Chronology for Paul's Career in Christianity 266
New Testament Apocrypha 269
    Epistle of Paul to the Laodiceans 270
    Didache (Teaching of the Twelve Apostles) 272
    Epistle of Barnabas 280
Acknowledgments 315
Index 317

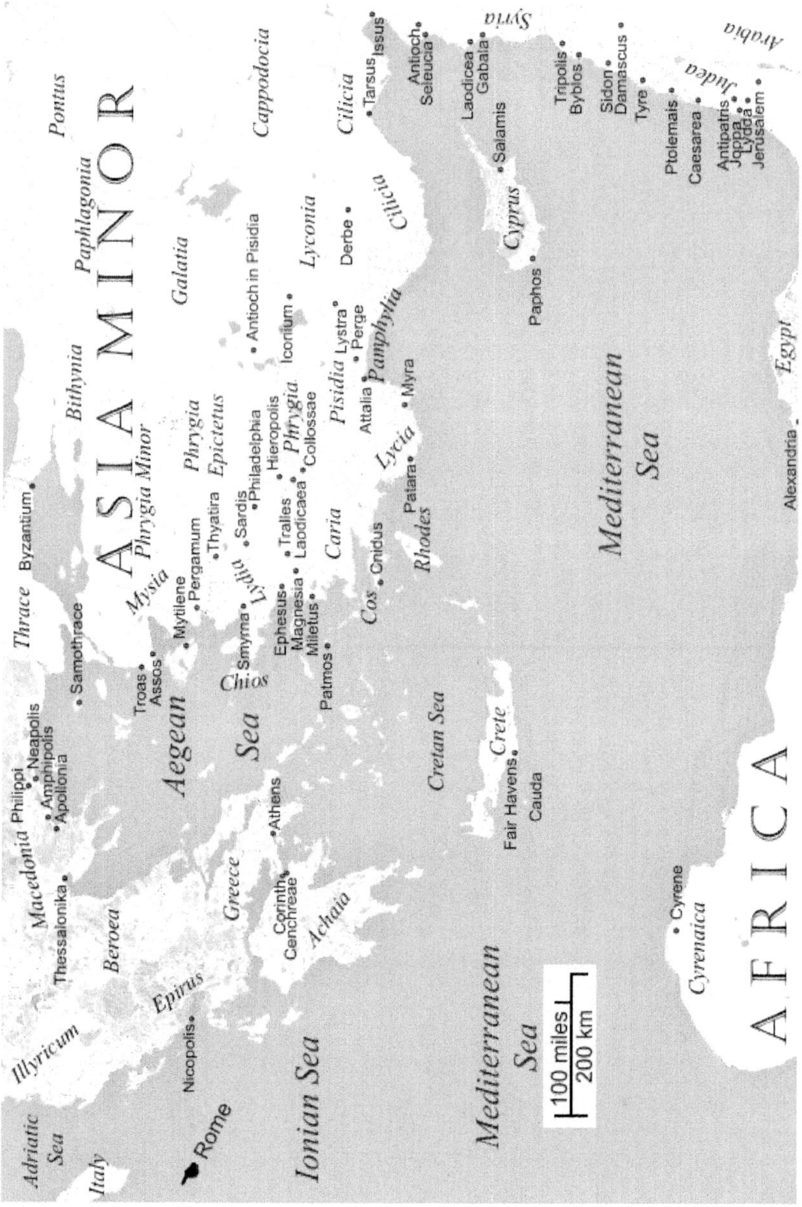
ASIA MINOR
AFRICA
Mediterranean Sea
Mediterranean Sea
Ionian Sea
Aegean Sea
Cretan Sea
Adriatic Sea
Italy
Rome
Illyricum
Epirus
Nicopolis
Macedonia
Thessalonika
Beroea
Philippi
Neapolis
Amphipolis
Apollonia
Thrace
Samothrace
Byzantium
Greece
Achaia
Corinth
Cenchreae
Athens
Troas
Assos
Mytilene
Chios
Mysia
Pergamum
Thyatira
Smyrna
Lydia
Sardis
Philadelphia
Ephesus
Magnesia
Miletus
Patmos
Tralles
Laodicaea
Hieropolis
Collossae
Caria
Cos
Cnidus
Rhodes
Patara
Lycia
Myra
Attalia
Perge
Pamphylia
Pisidia
Lystra
Iconium
Antioch in Pisidia
Derbe
Lyconia
Phrygia
Phrygia Minor
Phrygia Epictetus
Bithynia
Paphlagonia
Pontus
Galatia
Cappodocia
Cilicia
Tarsus
Issus
Antioch
Seleucia
Syria
Laodicea
Gabala
Salamis
Cyprus
Paphos
Tripolis
Byblos
Sidon
Damascus
Tyre
Ptolemais
Caesarea
Antipatris
Joppa
Lydda
Jerusalem
Judea
Arabia
Egypt
Alexandria
Crete
Fair Havens
Cauda
Cyrene
Cyrenaica
100 miles
200 km

Preface

This book is intended to present carefully a piece of the history of early Christianity. The subject of the book alone causes controversy. Scholarship is already impacting how we understand Jesus and the Bible through its interpretations of the evidence. The interpretations are subjective and biased by a false idea that "conservative" judgments, however that may be defined, are somehow more useful or accurate. This book will attempt to avoid those biases and to reconsider the available evidence. The author's background and potential biases are discussed.

The reader should be aware that some of the content of this book is likely to be controversial. This is not unusual for a book on the topic of religion. Almost any book worthy of reading, informative or inspiring on its subject, will present something new and challenging, and when the subject is religion, "new and challenging" will necessarily cause concern to someone. I have endeavored to provide substantial new information and inspiration for debate and contemplation.

The stakes are high and could not be higher. The religious faith of two billion or more persons is being influenced by the opinions of a small number of academics. Some translations of the Bible have already been adjusted on the basis of new scholarship. This is not a conspiracy: the translation of the Bible is a process that necessarily requires decisions about which primary texts are authoritative and which readings are more accurate or true to the original. Without reservation, translation sometimes demands a scholarly judgment about the original purpose and meaning of the text, of the ideas and events described, and even of Jesus himself.

This book is primarily concerned with the emergence of Christianity and the formation of the New Testament historically. We are going to address the story of the early Church with a fresh approach. Most, if not all, religions retain vital stories about their beginnings— how the divine transmitted wisdom and power to humans. These stories provide a rationale or justification for the practices and the beliefs.

Today, all forms of Christianity share the same story for the earliest period. Jesus was divine or divinely guided from birth, with supernatural powers and accompanied by many miraculous signs. Around thirty years old, Jesus took on apostles and followers, who were mostly thick-headed with rare moments of inspiration. Jesus preached in an indirect manner that he was the Messiah, knew he was the Son of God, and voluntarily submitted to humiliation, torture, and crucifixion in order to save the world. After the death and resurrection, Jesus soon ascended from the earth to reside in heaven, sending the Holy Spirit to inspire and guide the apostles to create the Church. The early years of the Church were full of miracles, and Christianity spread easily, divinely, although facing some irrational opposition and persecution by some Hellenists, some Jews, and some unwitting Romans. Internally, the Church started out unified, peaceful, and divinely inspired— golden. Later, human inconsistency diluted the influence of the Holy Spirit, causing some degradation in the holy institution. This narrative has been from ancient times a fundamental doctrine of Christianity.

In the 16th century, especially with the Reformation, scholars started to look at the texts in the Bible and especially the New Testament in a more rigorous and objective fashion. The resurgence of natural sciences offered a systematic approach to studying nature and everything in it, including humans. Noble scholars began to apply these principles to many spheres of human knowledge, and even to the holy texts. They learned that the Bible we currently have was not necessarily the original in every detail and that numerous versions existed differing from what we now call the received text. The list of possible originals continues to grow as more texts and fragments are found by archaeologists. By the 19th century, the scientific spirit had inspired scholars to question even the most fundamental beliefs of the Christian narrative, albeit tentatively and diplomatically.

In 1906, Albert Schweitzer wrote the *Quest of the Historical Jesus* in which he concluded that Jesus did not claim to be the Messiah, arguing that Jesus must be understood as an apocalyptic Jewish rabbi from the first century and not as a superhuman. This view has since dominated research into the origins of Christianity, creating a growing dissonance between the Jesus of faith and the Jesus of scholarship.

The driving force behind this approach has been a scholarly conservatism, which attempts to employ the same kind of systematic skepticism that has served the natural sciences so well. In the scholarship of Biblical studies, and other historical studies, conservatism means to avoid dramatic, unsubstantiated claims. Belief is set aside to achieve a level of objective distance. Evidence is reduced to what we can actually know without belief or speculation. Consequently, a conservative scholar must not argue that Jesus was God, because that is an unprovable speculation. In fact, Jesus could not even have claimed to be God, because that would not fit the known facts that show Jesus to be an apocalyptic Jewish rabbi of the first century. Unless, we had acceptable evidence otherwise, which we do not.

Or so we think. Because a major effect of scholarly conservatism has been that much of the evidence has been ignored or adulterated to fit a conservative sense of propriety. This plays out in many ways, such as distancing Jesus and even the apostles from Christianity as we know it. Another example of a scholarly bias is found in dating objects, texts, events, etc., because this often requires a subjective judgment. My favorite example of scholarly conservative bias, because it is so obvious, is that Zarathustra, the founder of Zoroastrian religion, is routinely placed by many scholars in the seventh century BCE, although the best scholars in this area, including Mary Boyce, have placed him in the 17th century BCE or before based on language and culture. I am not going to argue that case here because it is off subject, but the reason for the perpetuation of this one-thousand-year error is that the earliest datable archaeology is the first Persian empire in the later sixth century BCE. So, the "conservative" dating for Zarathustra, making the minimal claim, does not put much time between him and the Persian empire.

In Christianity, we see dating with the opposite tendency for the same reason of conservatism. Texts and objects that might impact the story of Christianity are dated more distantly from the events in order to prevent the dramatic impact they imply— the texts and objects are subjectively dated either much earlier or much later than Jesus and the apostles. Similarly, many of the texts, by tradition or even internal statements, have been identified with important historical persons, but the conservative approach is to doubt the potentially important attribution in order to nullify the consequential implications, precisely because the implications might have a disturbingly dramatic impact. In this manner, scholarly conservatism preserves a calm and unquestionable simplicity within a bubble of self-imposed ignorance, in spite of the fact that very little in history is really that simple.

In this book, we will seek to risk error in the opposite direction. Redefining conservatism, I will suggest that the texts and traditions are accurate unless better evidence shows that they are not. By bringing in more evidence, we will find that the complications actually clarify the story and carry the narrative in new, exciting— ahem— more sober and less dramatic directions.

It is natural and generally wise that the reader should wonder about the biases influencing the author. Any worthy author— and I endeavor to be worthy— will seek to suppress and overcome their natural biases to present the truth without prejudice. Of course, some residual bias is almost inevitable, but I am hopeful that someone reading this book will not be able to judge with confidence my religious or philosophical background, because I have presented the evidence faithfully and argued with candor for the sake of reason alone.

Still, I feel that the reader deserves to consider how my views may have colored the picture as I have drawn it. My early education was as a Roman Catholic, which I practiced faithfully for all of my childhood and adolescent years. I gradually opened myself to the great variety of approaches to the Christian tradition. Eventually, however, I rejected all denominations. I opened myself to other religious traditions, and I have found tremendous value in most of them. I remain a Christian by philosophy, but I do appreciate many other philosophies too, especially Judaism and Buddhism. Since I do not reject any particular religious approach, my openness led me to study anthropology at the University of Arizona. My approach is scholarly, philosophic, and scientific. I studied Greek on my own, and the translations are mine except where otherwise indicated. This book was borne out of twenty years of effort and one simple idea: the texts and traditions must be evaluated without prejudice. Let us see where they take us.

Introduction

Was Jesus sane? Could Jesus be sane and believe in Christianity himself? Currently, scholars avoid the dilemma by distancing Jesus and the apostles from Christian beliefs. This book will take a different approach, acknowledging that Jesus was both sane and Christian, according to the society and culture of his time. Jesus belonged to the Nazoreans, who were organized, awaiting the Messiah, and who had a developed Christology. Saint Paul wrote letters demonstrating the already established Church, but scholars disparage those letters as forgeries in a circular argument. The New Testament evidence can be accepted within a cultural context, which will reveal a religious and political struggle for the soul of Judaism and the Church. This book will start with the earliest Christian textual evidence, the letters of Saint Paul, as a foundation to reveal surprising details in the history of the early Church.

This book presents startling revelations from the New Testament texts that have been hidden in plain sight for almost two thousand years: (1.) that Saint Peter and Saint Paul became enemies; (2.) that according to *some* early Christians, Jesus was both the Messiah and the Antichrist, but not God nor the Son of God; (3.) that James, the brother of Jesus, rejected the original teaching of Jesus in order to further his own claim to be the Messiah; (4.) that the apostle Paul actually failed more than he succeeded during his lifetime; (5.) that Christians were instrumental in the First Jewish Revolt; and (6.) that Jesus did claim to be both the Son of God and God.

    This book started for me as a personal quest to discover the real Jesus Christ, which necessarily transformed into an attempt to reevaluate the evidence. While I admire the work that has been done in recent years about the historical Jesus, I feel that some of the conclusions of the current scholarship have overlooked important facts and evidence. Perhaps, this has been a natural result of focusing on the answers rather than the questions.

The most important question about Jesus Christ is the question that everyone thinks but no one asks. Many errors in our overall understanding of Jesus directly proceed from the avoidance of this question: How could Jesus believe he was God and still be sane? The question may make us uncomfortable; yet, this is not a small matter but the key to understanding the historical Jesus and the beginning of Christianity.

The reason for the success of Christianity has been nothing less than the brilliance and wisdom of Jesus himself. His words are startling and astounding, but also reflect a clarity and directness of thought that impresses even nonbelievers. It is not an exaggeration to say that Jesus may well have been the sanest person to have ever lived. Much in Christian ritual and doctrine that is objectionable is forgiven precisely because of the impact of reading the words of Jesus Christ.

Because Jesus of the Gospels was so clearly sane and in control of his own mind, it becomes nearly impossible to rationally accept that he believed that he was God. And this is now influencing every serious historical book about early Christianity. Presently, scholarly assumptions assert that Jesus could not have said nor believed that he was a supernatural being, and New Testament scholars have done everything that they can to distance Jesus from the Divinity.

Moreover, modern scholarship does not even give the apostles credit for believing in the divinity of Jesus Christ, but those ideas are blamed on nameless and overly pious successors. The most influential modern thinkers have devised theories that the disciples of disciples transformed Jesus into a demigod, out of passionate faith, by developing doctrines about him long after he was gone. The doctrines, ideas, and descriptions—found in the New Testament and other non-canonical Christian writings— deifying Jesus and exalting the Resurrection are called "high Christology" by scholars.

The paradigm of current scholarship insists that high Christology was the result of exaggerated piety working steadily, slowly, over decades. In patently circular logic, high Christology is itself deemed sufficient evidence to date the traditional texts as much later and to ascribe them to different, unknown authors, thus distancing the ideas in time from Jesus. According to modern theories, the requirement of time to develop such a theology makes Jesus, Peter, and Paul immune to Christian belief.

However, this book will show a much simpler and more encompassing solution to the puzzle: The reason that Jesus could be sane and yet believe that he was divine is that his culture permitted such beliefs. By definition, a person who reflects the norms of their own society is sane.

Of course, first century Jews held many beliefs that we might find strange; moreover, some sects were stranger than others. Certainly, Jews of the first century believed in demons, gods, magic, and miracles. Many Jews, and we can easily believe that they were in the majority, fully expected God to overcome the Romans and to reestablish the sovereign nation of Israel. Some highly educated Jews, especially those few with a Roman education, probably did not believe in such superstitious ideas; but most Jews, including many who were highly educated in Jewish traditions, did expect an apocalyptic climax to the problems of Israel. Even the great author Philo of Alexandria demonstrates a profound spiritual faith, although his treatment of scripture is mostly allegorical. We should not be surprised that Jesus would be a faithful Jew also.

It is not, however, sufficient to say that Jesus did not fall outside the norms of his time and was, therefore, sane. His sanity and clarity have withstood the examination of many times and many peoples throughout the whole world. Also, the mere possibility of the miraculous would not alone convince Jesus, given his intellect, that he was the Messiah and even God. It would have required the sustained active support of events and his community to convince a sane person of such great intellect that he is something so very special. Jesus must have received powerful and convincing forms of support from his contemporary world and within his own experience. He must have been recognized from an early age as a special person. The doctrines of his sect must have called for a human representative of God on earth, and important persons must have reinforced intellectually within Jesus the idea of his selection by God. Events signaled to Jesus and his community that something significant was happening, and its meaning was known according to their shared myths.

Understanding Jesus in this way, as a product of the culture of a specific community, groomed through an educational process, in a time when such beliefs were common, explains much. Anyone who had experienced exactly what Jesus had experienced, with experiential proof of his own ability and power, would have believed the same about themselves; in other words, Jesus could not have reasonably thought otherwise, because he was the Messiah and Son of God according to his culture and faith.

There are actually many examples to which we might point in order to demonstrate that this has occurred in many cultures at many times. Some Roman emperors were declared to be gods within their own lifetimes. Egyptian pharaohs were incarnations of gods. Every ancient king was in fact considered to be above all other men and worthy of obedience, which implies an exalted, god-like status. Saints are held to be miraculous intermediaries in the Catholic Church, and the Pope is the Vicar of Christ. The Dalai Lama is the incarnation of the Buddha of Compassion. None of these examples are merely the result of single person's egomania; rather, each of these is an example of a special member of a community achieving special recognition, reinforcing an exalted position within their society, in order to fulfill a need of the social organization. In the same manner, we can expect that Jesus Christ was elevated to high position within his own Jewish sect.

This, of course, presupposes that a certain group existed in the first century that could produce someone like Jesus Christ. If Jesus Christ really existed as he was described among early Christians, then necessarily a community also existed that was able to conceive and foster his mission. Therefore, this begs a most important question: which group was capable of producing a Jesus Christ?

Of course, the Gospels are very clear that Jesus was a Nazorean, and we know from the Church father and bishop of Salamis Epiphanius that several sects with names similar to that existed before and after Jesus, and one of these included disciples of the early apostles. The most common interpretation of Nazarene or Nazorean, and other variations, explains the name as derived from the town where Jesus lived, Nazareth; however, a few Gospel references clearly refer to Jesus as a member of a group rather than simply as an inhabitant of a town. Of course, we do not have to choose, because the Nazareans might well have lived in Nazareth.

Naturally, any group that cultivated a Messiah would be ready to believe in him. Having their prayers answered, with the appearance of the Messiah, we should expect to see the group celebrate, gathering in numbers to share in the good news. Of course, the group must have already developed a theology that defined the role of the Messiah, and we should also expect Jesus, as the Messiah, to echo their beliefs and, in doing so, we should expect him to be well received. Interestingly, however, we know from the Gospels that few Nazareans accepted him initially, probably indicating that he did not echo their expectations completely. We should note that the ability to be so discerning to reject Jesus as a potential Messiah requires that a thoroughly developed set of ideas and expectations, i.e., a well-developed Christology, already existed before Jesus.

A well-developed Christology also suggests the possibility that the group had an established structure and organization, with ready authorities in a hierarchy holding sufficient power to approve or disapprove of Jesus as the Messiah. All human organizations have their internal politics and internal conflicts. We should therefore expect that a Messiah, Jesus Christ, would have to be something of a politician, capable of establishing his authority by gaining the consensus of the organizational hierarchy and the membership as a whole. Although we may not like the image of Jesus Christ as a politician, I would submit to you that many of Jesus' retorts to trapping questions within the Gospels have the slippery quality of an astute politician avoiding a pitfall.

We do have evidence that the Church was highly organized from our earliest texts, the letters of Saint Paul; but these parts and even whole letters are arbitrarily invalidated as forgeries and ignored by nearly all scholarship precisely because they suggest highly developed thinking and social structures. Obviously, invalidating evidence opposed to a theory, and then citing the lack of evidence as proof of their conclusion, is circular reasoning at best. Moreover, a better explanation of the evidence we have, including the letters of the New Testament, exists in viewing the miraculous birth of Christianity as a cultural phenomenon.

Within a context of radical apocalyptic Judaism, Jesus might well have been the Messiah, meaning the successor to King David. What, however, if the Messiah were less than completely successful as a politician? Some of Jesus' teachings could have been too radical for some or not radical enough for others. Consider the challenge of the proliferation of minor sects and the many rabbis and even messiahs described by Epiphanius: It could not be easy to attempt to unify a people as diverse and far-flung as the Jewish people in the first century. I am suggesting that this was exactly the case in the mission of Jesus Christ, and I intend to present much evidence regarding the nature of Jesus' mission and of the conflicts that subsequently arose. Most of all, we will gain new insight and intimate knowledge of Jesus Christ and the foundations of the Christian tradition.

The idea that there were conflicts in the early Church is not new, and I owe much of my confidence to the many scholars who have discussed the idea in the past. Indeed, while much within this book will appear new to some, much of it is not; perhaps, it only appears to be new because I am taking the ideas more seriously and developing them further. Many great insights by scholars and lay authors have languished, because they were viewed in isolation and then ignored as controversial. By bringing the ideas together with others, the reader will see that many unusual ideas actually prove quite reasonable in the proper context.

Unfortunately, I am also opposing some closely held positions among modern Christian historians and theologians, which places a heavy extra burden on my reasoning. For example, Christianity of all persuasions has seen it convenient to maintain the idea of an initial golden age, free from the petty conflicts and squabbles that have plagued Christians since shortly after the apostolic age. According to popular Christian doctrine, human instability and error accumulated after the deaths of the original apostles, subsequently producing conflicts and heresies, as the influence of the Holy Spirit waned within the Church. Of course, this position, while accurately depicting human frailty, has nonetheless always been a pious fiction. Judaism itself was not monolithic and neither was the Christian religion that proceeded from Judaism. We have only to read the canonical texts to note that early Christianity struggled in defining itself right from the beginning, even from first days of Jesus' mission.

Consequently, I will not be shy in setting aside unreasonable assumptions or superstitious reasoning. Some readers will undoubtedly complain that I am too skeptical and realistic about some facts, and others will find me too accepting and superstitious. That is as it should be, because I will endeavor to understand persons of ancient times from their own cultural biases. My approach is historical, but also anthropological. Therefore, I choose not to prejudge from religion, culture, or time, but to search for timeless truth. I will not adhere to any doctrine nor dogma, unless it is found in the evidence itself. Everything is up for question. I hope to serve the reader dispassionately and faithfully.

It would take many books to fully explore Jesus Christ and the phenomenon that was early Christianity. In this book, we are going to start logically with the earliest Christian texts, the Pauline Epistles. Because the Letters of Saint Paul are the earliest texts, they naturally should be closer to the original understanding of Jesus Christ. This is a different approach from the usual, because we are going to leave the Gospels mostly to the side. I think that this is justified because, although the events occurred earlier, the Gospel texts are later, much edited, composite documents, which collect traditions from disparate and perhaps competing groups of believers. As such, the Gospels cannot always tell us which was the original tradition and which was later, nor why conflicting traditions have been retained. The letters of the New Testament, especially those of Paul, are texts that contain the single (for the most part) and distinctive point of view of their respective authors.

Starting with the Pauline letters engages the historical narrative about sixteen years after the Resurrection, at the moment when converting the gentiles to Christianity was suddenly taken up in earnest. In treating with the writings of Saint Paul, I will also touch upon the other letters within the New Testament and especially compare with the Acts of the Apostles, written somewhat later.

It is striking that so little appears to have happened in Christianity in sixteen years prior to Paul's mission to the gentiles. The battles that we are joining in Paul's epistles are the kinds of issues that one would expect at the very beginning of the Church and not more than a decade later. We have nearly nothing as evidence of what has been happening in this earlier gap of years, although our texts, including Paul's letters, suggest battles with Jewish authorities in Judea, including persecutions. To answer this question even speculatively, concerning why Christianity had been so arrested in its early development, we will have to focus first upon Paul, his mission, and his relationship with the Jewish Christians, examining the questions and the surprising answers about the development of the Church and the background of the Christian religion.

This book is structured in the same manner and order that I followed in my research: I started with the Pauline letters. First, without expecting to be successful, I attempted to find an order to the epistles by analyzing the information Paul offers in describing the concurrent events. Quite accidentally, this turned out to actually be possible. Then, with this new information, I sought to discover the itinerary of Paul's missions. Again, this was surprisingly possible. I began then to compare this information with Acts, noting the similarities and the differences, and I discovered that a narrative was being reconstructed that had not been obvious before. Then, I went back and I reconsidered some of the ancient presumptions, even to the meaning of certain words. Returning to the narrative, I could understand the story in more detail, and I began to see how the other letters of the New Testament fit into that same historical reconstruction. Along the way, I discovered some shocking coincidences, and the uncomfortable fact that there existed in that early formative time not one gospel, but two competing visions of Jesus Christ.

The Order of the Pauline Epistles

We begin our quest starting with the letters of Saint Paul. This chapter will circumvent theories about which of Paul's letters are authentic by addressing the letters directly. The letters themselves permit the reconstruction of a definite order through the internal details that Paul provides. Once the order is proven, forming a definite and harmonious narrative of Paul's journey, the idea that any of these letters does not proceed from Paul becomes extremely unlikely.

The oldest Christian texts are the fourteen letters of Saint Paul. Older than even the Gospels, these fourteen texts provide us a window into the earliest Christian doctrine and practice. However, the letters lack clarity for modern readers, because we are deprived in large part of the context behind the letters.

The letters of Saint Paul are found in the New Testament after the Acts of the Apostles. They are arranged in order according to length with longest first and shortest last, except for the Letter to the Hebrews. Consequently, the chronological order of the Pauline letters has been unknown and subject to speculation and educated guesses. This disorder, along with certain reasonable but incorrect assumptions, has helped to conceal the real story behind the letters.

Attempts to place the letters in order and within a rough context using the Acts of the Apostles have for the most part failed; not surprisingly, because Acts is not in the modern sense, an historical document. This text has a religious and political agenda, glossing conflicts and difficulties in the early Church in order to serve the legend of the perfect Church. The legend of the Church having a golden age has been an important doctrine, offering believers confidence that the Church has been guided by the Holy Spirit, by God himself. Even an uncritical observer, however, can detect the contradictions within the narrative of Acts, and we can learn much from understanding its concoctions.

Knowing that this text is not entirely accurate, it would be better not to rely upon Acts in interpreting the letters of Paul. Yet, we have until now lacked reasonable alternatives; we had no other solid historical evidence to provide support for any other conclusions. This assessment, however, has always been mistaken; surprisingly, it has always been possible to build an historical context from Paul's letters themselves, without relying on the Acts of the Apostles. Unlike the Acts of the Apostles, the letters of Saint Paul are documents contemporaneous with the events, and both the author and the hearers were in the midst of the situations described. Therefore, the letters are naturally truthful and they are supremely authoritative; they are the best possible source we could imagine. So, before we look to any other source— adding speculations, errors of bias, and problematic inferences— we should glean every possible unvarnished detail provided by Saint Paul himself.

Our method will be simple, therefore: Firstly, we shall order the letters using the significant information provided in each letter. Paul writes to his communities including salutations from those he is with to those who will hear the letters, naming both whom he is writing to and whom he is with. He also includes news and administrative directions to his followers, and he discusses his past, his plans, his successes, and sometimes even his failures. From all of this data, it becomes a simple matter to logically arrange the letters in sensible order according to Paul's discussion of the situation. Secondly, following the order of the letters, we will be able to reconstruct a coherent narrative and understand why Paul was writing and to what purpose. Finally, we will be in a better position to compare our findings to the other texts in the New Testament, including the Acts of the Apostles, and to determine what other information is useful for filling out the story. In doing so, we will be able to achieve a deeper understanding of Paul's mission and how Christianity came to be what it is.

The epistles of Paul follow a defined structure, demonstrated in nearly all of them. The letters begin with a greeting, followed by a prayer of thanksgiving, one or more homilies in the body of the text, and ending with a parting salutation. The greeting is sometimes quite formal and it usually consists of three parts: a sometimes elaborate identification of the author, an often complex or even poetic identification of the audience, and a formula of benediction. The prayer of thanksgiving follows, and it flows into the homilies as seamlessly as possible. The homilies address contemporary issues of importance, generally flowing into one another and finally entering into the parting salutation. The parting salutation may contain an elaborate blessing, a personal greeting or acknowledgment of the hearers, and a formula of benediction to end the letter called a "doxology."

This structure is not inviolable, but from Paul's consistent adherence we can surmise that it was clearly an already well-established formal genre, perhaps imitating formal Greek letters. Supporting this conclusion is that the other letters of the New Testament also resemble this structure, although with much less formality. The consistency of Paul's letters suggests that this style of letter already had some currency with those whom he corresponds and that public letter writing between communities was already a common feature of Judaism, at least in the Diaspora.

Within his letters, Paul often greets persons by name and places authority on his messengers, some who presumably carry the letters in question. He sometimes mentions his own location indirectly, and sometimes he discusses other churches. These details may occur anywhere in the text, but usually they are contained in the parting salutation. Through a systematic examination of places and persons named and the content of the message, we will determine where Paul was and where he was going and when, carefully reconstructing a coherent narrative of his career as an apostle of Christ.

As an aid to the reader, I have listed important details that Paul provided about his missionary activities from all of his letters in Appendix 1. For the sake of clarity, the data are ordered chronologically as I have reconstructed the order of the letters. Here is the list of the letters arranged by my conclusions regarding the evidence:

Saint Paul's Letters (in chronological order)

1 Thessalonians
2 Thessalonians
1 Corinthians
Galatians
2 Corinthians
Romans
Hebrews
Titus
1 Timothy
2 Timothy
Ephesians
Philemon
Colossians
Laodiceans (apocryphal)
Philippians

Laodiceans is included in the list for the sake of completeness, because I believe the extra-canonical text, now only preserved in Latin, to be genuine and not pseudonymous, meaning a pious forgery. It may have been left out of the New Testament at an early date to achieve the magical number fourteen, replaced by the later addition of Hebrews, and also because it is tiny and contains nothing obviously significant. Most scholars and even many ancient Church fathers have rejected this letter as pseudonymous, but without strong arguments or evidence, although it was included in some copies of ancient Latin Bibles.

I will demonstrate that the above ordering of the letters is correct, with some minor caveats, starting with the earliest letter and working methodically to the last, developing the chronology of each letter relative to the others. It is natural that the reader will wonder if other orders are possible. Of course, any number of improbable scenarios is possible, but we should believe the simpler, more reasonable explanation. By the end of the discussion, I believe it will be clear that this order is not only the simplest, the most reasonable, and the most probable; but it is the correct one.

Before we begin our detailed examination of the Pauline letters, it might serve us to refresh our memory from Paul's own summation of his missionary activity that he wrote in Galatians and other letters: Paul had been a Hebrew born of Hebrews, an Israelite of the tribe of Benjamin, circumcised on the eighth day, adhering to Mosaic law as a Pharisee. He was a practitioner of Judaism, which he does not define, although he equates religious zeal with persecuting the Church.[1] That last point— zeal in Judaism assumes persecution of the Church— is extremely interesting and important for our later discussion of his mission.

    Paul had a revelation of Jesus Christ at Damascus. He immediately went away into Arabia for some mysterious purpose. He then returned to Damascus. After three years, Paul went to Jerusalem for the first time as a Christian, and he stayed only fifteen days. He then proceeded with his missionary activity into the regions of Syria and Cilicia.[2]

    Then, *during* a total of fourteen years, Paul went to Jerusalem a second time and had a confrontation with some unnamed apostles and with Cephas,[3] whom we commonly know from Greek and Latin as Peter,[4] and with James, the Lord's brother. Paul returned to Syria. Cephas, however, when visiting Antioch, followed the demands of

---

[1] Gal. 1:13; Philip. 3:5-6.

[2] Gal. 1:15-21.

[3] Aramaic for "rock."

[4] From the Greek and Latin for "rock."

others who came from James concerning purity of fellowship. Paul confronted him openly and called him a hypocrite.[5]

Because Paul speaks so directly and specifically about his history as a Christian in Galatians, we can easily deduce from the details that all of his epistles in the New Testament are the product of his missionary work after the confrontation with Cephas in Antioch. We know this because Paul gives a full accounting in Galatians of his Christian career up until the time that he preached at Galatia, including the confrontation with Cephas, but does not refer to lands west of Cilicia. Therefore, all of the communities addressed by the other letters, being west of Cilicia (excepting the Letter to the Hebrews) and unmentioned in his recounting of his time before preaching in Galatia, are later in his journeys. Paul does offer a few additional details regarding his earlier work in other letters, but this recounting will suffice for now as an introduction to the missionary journey described by the letters.

1 and 2 Thessalonians

Scholars have long been virtually unanimous that 1 Thessalonians is Paul's earliest epistle followed by 2 Thessalonians, although some have argued that 2 Thessalonians is pseudonymous. Temporarily putting aside the dispute over 2 Thessalonians, from the internal evidence alone we have good reason for considering these two letters as earlier than the other letters.

First, in both of these letters, Paul indicates that he is writing jointly with Timothy and Silvanus (also known as Silas).[6] Paul is treating Timothy and Silvanus as equals in the greeting, but we know from the other letters that he considered himself to be a father in the faith to Timothy, at least. The status of coauthors that Paul gives them in the letter indicates not only that the Thessalonians knew Timothy

---

[5] Gal. 2:1-14.

[6] 1 Thes. 1:1; 2 Thes.1:1.

and Silvanus, but that these two had played a strong role in evangelizing the community at Thessalonika.

Secondly, we should focus on the fact that Sylvanus is with Paul. Paul refers to Silvanus only one other time in all of his other letters, when he says that Silvanus and Timothy had preached the gospel together with him in Corinth.[7] As we shall see in the details of these letters, Paul is preaching at Corinth now, so this is the time to which he refers in 2 Corinthians. Although we cannot know from Paul's silence a reason for the disappearance of Silvanus from his later discourse, the fact that Paul does not mention Silvanus beyond this part of his journey probably indicates that some sort of split occurred. We can also see that Timothy, Silvanus, and Paul very likely preached the gospel at Thessalonika and Corinth relatively close in time. This corresponds well with the fact that Paul, Sylvanus, and Timothy were driven out from Antioch together not long before preaching in Macedonia.[8]

When Paul reassures the Thessalonians that the dead are not lost in Christ, he confirms to us that they have not been Christians long enough to have witnessed many deaths in their community.[9] It is surprising that the Thessalonians appear to be ignorant of basic Christian teachings concerning the Resurrection of the Dead. Both their inexperience and their ignorance of basic Christian dogma attest that the Thessalonians were extremely recent converts.

Paul says that the Thessalonians have been an example to all of Macedonia and Achaia and even beyond.[10] Considering the short time that the Thessalonians have been Christians, this would strongly suggest that Paul is writing from somewhere near Achaia. The coincidence of Silvanus being a co-author in the two Thessalonian

---

[7] 2 Cor. 1:19.

[8] 2 Tim 3:11; 2 Thes. 2:15.

[9] 1 Thes. 4:13-18.

[10] 1 Thess. 1:7-9.

letters and also named as preaching with Paul at Corinth, but not being mentioned in regard to other communities, also argues strongly that Paul wrote both letters from near Corinth, when Silvanus accompanied him.

That Paul wrote from Corinth is further supported when Paul says that he had stayed alone at Athens,[11] from where he sent Timothy to the Thessalonians, because Athens was just north of Achaia, between Corinth and Thessalonika. Timothy must have returned quickly to Paul in southern Greece to bring him news of the Thessalonians, news that prompted the first letter. Whoever carried the first letter to Thessalonika, probably Timothy again, must have reported to Paul additional information, prompting an immediate second letter. This explains the precisely equivalent situations within the two letters (some manuscripts treat these as a single letter) and the lack of references to other, newer communities. Therefore, Paul wrote to the Thessalonians twice from Achaia, very close in time, probably within days or weeks, while preaching the gospel in southern Greece.

Of course, if Paul was just then preaching the gospel in southern Greece when he wrote the Thessalonian letters, and the Thessalonians are an example to the Corinthians, then these letters with certainty must predate the Corinthian letters, because the Corinthian letters refer to Paul's time among them and presume that the Corinthians were already Christians.

Suppose that we can show that other letters are later than 1 Corinthians? Those letters naturally would also have to postdate 1 and 2 Thessalonians. In this manner, carefully and in succession, by proving that one letter must be earlier or later than others, we can build a chronological chain in order to restore the true order of the letters, thereby reconstructing a context for them.

Although 1 Thessalonians enjoys wide acceptance as being prior to 2 Thessalonians, the evidence for this is more subtle and subjective. First, 1 Thessalonians contains many details about Paul's

---

[11] 1 Thess. 3:1-2.

missionary activities, especially at Thessalonika itself, while 2 Thessalonians offers none. This suggests that 2 Thessalonians followed on 1 Thessalonians so soon that little had changed and there was little to tell. Had 2 Thessalonians been first, it should have contained the news about Paul's missionary activities. Furthermore, the second letter is very short and unadorned in comparison with most of Paul's letters, which would be expected in a quick follow-up because the general situation has not changed. Also, Paul's extended explanation about his reason for sending Timothy so soon makes far more sense if he wrote 1 Thessalonians first and only a short time before. Therefore, we have little reason to challenge the traditional order, and some good reasons to trust it.

Obviously, I am accepting 2 Thessalonians as a genuine letter from Paul based on the tradition, and the content and the context support this conclusion. Most importantly, the inclusion of an apologetic explanation for sending Timothy again gives this letter outstanding credibility, because apologies and excuses weaken the appearance of Paul's authority to readers. Moreover, the alternative is that a pseudonymous author had an extraordinarily creative and convoluted imagination, which I count as an improbable and strained explanation.

The principal argument against the authenticity of 2 Thessalonians is the high Christology, referring to the well-developed doctrine and deification of Christ. The high Christology, however, is entirely natural to Paul's theology. Paul often speaks of Christ as God, such as when he states that "we are Christ" or "we are all in Christ." What else could he mean except that Jesus Christ was a divinity? This is not to say, at this point, that Paul was a Trinitarian, but neither have we eliminated that possibility.

1 and 2 Corinthians

As discussed above, 1 Corinthians must be later than both of the letters to the Thessalonians, because Paul wrote those letters while he was first evangelizing in Achaia. We need only to show that the remaining letters were later to establish the place of 1 Corinthians in the chain of events. However, there was another letter to the Corinthians that we do not have, although we know about it because of 2 Corinthians 5:9. Nothing else is known about this lost letter.

First, we should note that in 1 Corinthians Paul again addresses some very basic issues in Christian life, which says that here also not much time has passed since Paul evangelized them. Especially, he discusses marriage and sex, as well as food issues. These basic questions of daily life could not have been ignored long; therefore, Paul has not traveled long from Achaia before writing to the Corinthians.

Paul did not teach the Thessalonians basic dogma and he did not teach the Corinthians about daily life, strongly begging the question: what did his preaching did consist of? Later, we may be able to make some positive statements on this subject; however, for now we should just note that Paul's preaching was extremely limited. Therefore, as we should suspect, he did not require much time to evangelize. Paul corroborates this view in 1 Corinthians when he indicates that it is time for the Feast of Unleavened Bread,[12] and then he writes that he will stay in Ephesus until Pentecost because of an opportunity to preach the gospel.[13] This means that Paul expected to need less than seven weeks to evangelize the new community. This corresponds well with the apparent minimal nature of his instruction.

Paul says the Corinthians should follow the instructions that he gave to the Galatians regarding the collection for the saints.[14] This collection was a major project that Paul discusses in many of the epistles, and here Paul writes about it for the first time. Paul reveals here that he discussed the collection at Corinth and dispatched someone to Galatia from there, allowing the Corinthians to know Paul's instructions to the Galatians. The absence of any mention of the

---

[12] 1 Cor. 5:8.

[13] 1 Cor. 16:8-9.

[14] 1 Cor. 16:1.

collection in the Thessalonian letters indicates that Paul had not begun the collection before reaching southern Greece,[15] and Paul verifies this later in 2 Corinthians, writing that Achaia had more time than Macedonia to produce their gift for the saints— the Corinthians have had since last year to work on their collection.[16] This further certifies that both letters to the Corinthians were later than both of the letters to the Thessalonians.

In 1 Corinthians, Paul is at Ephesus saying that he will travel to Macedonia and, in 2 Corinthians, Paul is in Macedonia explaining how he came there from Ephesus. Therefore, we can see that Paul wrote 2 Corinthians within a couple of months after 1 Corinthians, during the summer of the same year. Second Corinthians also indicates that Paul had been in Achaia, beginning the plans for the collection, at least six months before, but it could not have been too much more than six months. This timing becomes very important because Paul gives us a concrete benchmark, by stating that he received his revelation of Christ fourteen years before.[17] This benchmark dates 2 Corinthians close in time to Galatians, where he also mentions the fourteen-year timing.

Paul tells the Corinthians in his second letter to them that he is about to come to them for a third time. We only have evidence, however, for one previous visit to Corinth at this point. This problem is cleared up if Paul went northwest to Illyricum[18] from Corinth after his first visit and then passed through Corinth a second time, the easiest path by ship, before reaching Ephesus.

---

[15] 2 Cor. 8:1-11.

[16] 2 Cor. 8:10.

[17] 2 Cor. 12:2.

[18] Rom. 15:19.

Galatians

Now we are ready to address Galatians, although a little out of order, because Paul wrote Galatians between 1 and 2 Corinthians in the late spring or early summer. Because Timothy is not aware in 1 Corinthians that Paul was detained at Ephesus,[19] it seems likely that Paul sent Timothy by land east to Galatia carrying this letter from Ephesus. Apparently, he had told Timothy to meet him in Corinth but he was afterwards delayed in Ephesus, which is why he expected the Corinthians to see Timothy first. The reason that we should believe that Paul was at Ephesus when he wrote Galatians is because of his reference to the Galatians and the collection in 1 Corinthians, implying that at the time of writing 1 Corinthians, he was still positive about the Galatians' faith.[20] The content of the Letter to the Galatians, however, shows that he has become disillusioned.

In Galatians, as we have mentioned, Paul summarizes the important events of his career until the time of his preaching to the churches of Galatia, until the confrontation with Cephas at Antioch. Paul recounts his Christian mission in Galatians arguing that he has never depended upon certain persons in Jerusalem for the authority to preach.[21] As support for his argument, Paul insists that he has not been to Jerusalem much at all, thus demonstrating his independence from certain persons there. He recounts his last visit, stating that he went to Jerusalem again, for only the second time in fourteen years.[22]

This understanding of Galatians 2:1, that Paul means he has been a Christian for fourteen years at the time of his writing, requires some discussion. Traditionally, this pericope has been translated as "then *after* fourteen years again I went up to Jerusalem with Barnabas taking with me also Titus;" the word "after" seemed to be needed in

---

[19] 1 Cor. 16:10.

[20] 1 Cor. 16:2.

[21] Gal. 1:13-2:14.

[22] Gal. 2:1.

our modern languages in order to logically connect the previous verse to the following. However, the Greek word, διά, means "through" or in referring to time "during," and it does not mean "after" anywhere else in Greek literature. Therefore, this is a highly suspect translation, creating a new and unique understanding of the word for this one purpose. Scholars have long known that this translation is weak, but there was no clear alternative that made sense, given the chronology of the Acts of the Apostles and our traditional assumptions about the nature of Paul's mission. Fourteen years just seemed too short of a time for Paul to found and build all of those congregations from scratch. We have already seen, however, that Paul required less than seven weeks, and not years, to establish a church.[23] Therefore, if we set aside the traditional assumptions about the chronology, we can take Paul at his word.

Perhaps, this translation of the Greek word, διά, might be justified as a mistake made by an ancient scribe, but there is no evidence or even a plausible speculation of how such an error happened. Adding to the desire to blame a scribe is the fact that the modern literal translation "then through fourteen years again I went up to Jerusalem with Barnabas taking with me also Titus;" sounds clumsy in our modern languages. But it was not necessarily clumsy in the ancient Greek. Moreover, if we just parenthesize "through fourteen years"— the original document would not have included any punctuation— we arrive at the sense befitting the context of the argument in Galatians: that Paul is stressing how relatively little time he had spent in Jerusalem over the length of his Christian career in order to show that he was independent of certain persons in authority there.

It is also important to reiterate that the time frame that Paul gives in Galatians 2:1 is his entire time as a Christian since his first revelation of Christ until the time of the letter itself. This understanding of Paul's statement corresponds well with the order of the letters and

---

[23] 1 Cor. 16:8-9.

the chronology we are building from them, because Paul is still in his fourteenth year from his original revelation when he writes to the Corinthians the second time.[24] Moreover, we can see now that this is the only reading that makes sense, because Paul could not have spent fourteen years in Syria and Cilicia and have visited Jerusalem the second time in his fourteenth year but then still be in his fourteenth year on his second visit to Macedonia writing 2 Corinthians. Therefore, Paul wrote Galatians in his fourteenth year from his revelation of Christ, between the letters 1 and 2 Corinthians.

The fact that Paul does not at all mention the collection in the Letter to the Galatians tells us that he already considered the project a failure there. Perhaps, he had given up on the Galatians as apostate, for he does not begin nor end this letter on a strong positive feeling of love that he does in his other letters.

That Paul does not mention the Galatians in relation to the collection in 2 Corinthians is also strong evidence that he had already given up on their part by the time he wrote that letter. This places 2 Corinthians shortly after Paul wrote to the Galatians, although still in Paul's fourteenth year as a Christian, as he says.

A previous letter to the Galatians written from Corinth about the collection probably existed, as he mentions in 1 Corinthians,[25] but it is lost. Paul does not mention a previous letter to the Galatians; but it is difficult to imagine him sending verbal instructions on the important matter of the collection without also sending a personal communication as well.

Romans and Hebrews

In 2 Corinthians, Paul was in Macedonia planning to return to Corinth for a third time and he hoped they would do well with the collection. In Romans, Paul says the collections of Macedonia and Achaia have

---

[24] 2 Cor. 12:2.

[25] 1 Cor. 16:1.

been completed.[26] This strongly implies that Paul wrote Romans in Achaia and not long after 2 Corinthians.

Paul commends to the Romans Phoebe, who is a deaconess at Cenchreae, a town near Corinth in Achaia.[27] Paul mentions her first in passing along greetings and says that he is sending her to the Romans, which suggests that he is near Corinth, at Cenchreae in Achaia where she ministers. Also, Paul states that Erastus is the city treasurer,[28] and later in 2 Timothy Paul informed his coworker that Erastus remained in Corinth,[29] a coincidence which corroborates strongly that Paul was writing Romans at or near Corinth.

Closely to be associated with Romans is the Letter to the Hebrews, a very unusual letter. Many, if not most, scholars think that it is not a letter at all but a homily, and most think that someone other than Paul wrote it. There are some good arguments for these ideas— the Greek is different and the ideas are unusual when compared with the other letters. My answer to these objections is that Paul is writing to a very different community for a very different purpose. Paul wrote all of the other letters to Greek-speaking communities or to his Greek-speaking lieutenants, composing them or dictating them, naturally, in Greek. Hebrews, on the other hand, can only be addressed to a Jewish Christian community, probably Jerusalem, and as such, Paul would have composed this letter in Aramaic. Later, a scribe translated the letter into Greek for the sake of Greek Christians. This also explains why Hebrews is found out of order at the end of the collection of Paul's epistles— although it is longer than some of the others— because it was a late addition to an already existing collection. As to the unusual nature of the ideas, this is not the simple preaching that the Greek communities received, but a scholarly, even priestly, justification of

---

[26] Rom. 15:26.

[27] Rom.16:1.

[28] Rom. 16:23.

[29] 2 Tim. 4:20.

Jesus Christ as the Messiah of the Jews and the head of a new priesthood. Hebrews is Paul's gospel for the Jews as Romans is Paul's gospel for the Hellenes.

Scholars have believed Hebrews to be a homily because it lacks much of the structure of Paul's other letters. Specifically, Hebrews lacks the introductory greeting and thanksgiving prayer. On the other hand, the concluding salutations and the discussion of his plans in Hebrews 13 show definitively that this was originally a letter.[30] Perhaps, the translating scribe felt embarrassed by the manner that Paul addressed the Jews in greeting them— probably because he was either too harsh or too meek— but the letter was too rich and eloquent for the translator to discard it completely. Without the usual greeting and thanksgiving, the letter is now in fact truncated artificially into a homily.

This letter should be coupled with Romans partly because Paul is with persons from Italy. There is a slight possibility that I am mistaken in the timing and that Hebrews belongs just prior to 1 Corinthians, since Paul apparently had met many from Rome during his first visit to Corinth, as we see in the concluding salutations of Romans. This is also mentioned in Acts. On the other hand, coupling this letter with Romans makes more sense, because Paul states he will return to Jerusalem soon. This probably means that Paul is in Achaia and the collection is ready— the same situation found in Romans. Paul promises to bring Timothy with him soon but, as we shall see presently, he does not bring Timothy. Paul's subsequent actions would not correspond with his statements in Hebrews, if the letter preceded his second circuit around the Aegean. Therefore, the community that Paul addressed was almost certainly Jerusalem, just prior to his return with the collection.

Since Romans and Hebrews were probably composed at nearly the same time in Achaia, an ordering with Romans being prior to Hebrews makes a bit more sense. Paul says that he will bring Timothy

---

[30] Heb. 13:19-24.

with him, if Timothy comes in time. If, however, Romans, in which Timothy sends greetings, followed Hebrews, then Paul must have promised casually and then reneged, because we later find that Timothy did not accompany Paul but stayed at Ephesus.[31] This is something Paul would not and could not do because, as we see in 2 Corinthians,[32] failure to fulfill even the least commitment would cause great discredit on his mission. Had something of such importance arisen that he would risk discredit by not fulfilling his word, we should expect some mention in later letters, but we find no such mention. Therefore, it seems very likely that Romans predated Hebrews by a little bit, and Timothy did not return in time to travel with Paul to Jerusalem.

Titus and 1 Timothy

The epistles Titus and 1 Timothy are so similar in style and content that we should address them together, because they obviously address a common situation. The Letter to Titus is shorter and less detailed than 1 Timothy, but the similarities are nonetheless striking. Paul addresses Timothy as his "loyal child in the faith" and Titus as his "loyal child." In the greeting, Paul blesses both of them in almost exactly the same manner. In 1 Timothy, Paul attacks certain false teachers and false doctrines,[33] and he tells Titus the same.[34] He instructs both Titus and Timothy on establishing elders including bishops.[35] He instructs them both on proper comportment for leaders and brothers and sisters. The fact that Paul is offering by means of a letter this important instruction on apostleship, suggests that he believes that he may not see them again. Paul ends both letters with a near identical benediction. Therefore, we can clearly see the parallels between these two letters,

---

[31] 1 Tim. 1:3.

[32] 2 Cor. 1:15-2:1.

[33] 1 Tim. 1:6-7.

[34] Tit. 1:10-11.

[35] Tit. 1:5-9; 1 Tim 3.1-9.

which demonstrate that Paul wrote them for the same purpose in a similar situation and very close in time.

Timothy was not able to return to Paul before he left for Jerusalem with the collection for the saints, and Paul was at the time of writing 1 Timothy either en route or already arrived in Judea. Titus on the other hand was left at Crete, which was on the way to Judea from Achaia, so we should expect that Paul wrote from somewhere east of Crete.

All the remaining letters describe Paul in prison at Rome. Titus and 1 Timothy cannot be later than Paul's imprisonment at Rome, because Titus deserts Paul upon his imprisonment.[36] Therefore, the letters Titus and 1 Timothy are obviously earlier than the remaining letters.

A reason to place Titus and 1 Timothy closer and not farther in time from 2 Timothy and Ephesians is the confluence of the details that are shared. Of course, Timothy is in Ephesus, but also in Titus 3:12 Paul mentions Tychicus for the first time, who Paul treats as an apostle in 2 Timothy and Ephesians. Furthermore, the traditional material of the Acts of the Apostles says that Paul faced trial in Jerusalem on his last trip there, while the Letter to Titus shows Paul requesting a lawyer in Titus 3:13 and asking for the apostle Apollos. Therefore, Paul probably wrote Titus and 1 Timothy in Jerusalem, immediately before he was tried and convicted.

Between Titus and 1 Timothy, the priority is not obvious. Although the many parallels listed above place these two epistles in a common milieu, the wording of the content is not identical. This suggests that the two letters were composed separately, although probably within a week of each other. My feeling is that Paul wrote Titus first in order to explain his hasty departure from Crete, which appears to have been unexpected, and to give instructions for Titus in his absence— primarily that Titus should remain at Crete to finish their work. This suggests that very little time has passed. Then, in

---

[36] 2 Tim. 4:10.

1 Timothy, Paul gives far more extensive instructions regarding apostleship, which may indicate that he has become more pessimistic about his own future. He finally names— which he has been up to now noticeably reluctant to do— two who have opposed him,[37] Hymenaeus and Alexander, saying that he turned them over to Satan. If he had written to Titus later, we should expect Paul to warn Titus about the same two enemies; the fact that he does not is significant evidence in favor of the priority of the shorter letter.

2 Timothy and Ephesians
Second Timothy is patently later than Titus and 1 Timothy, because Paul is now imprisoned at Rome and Titus has forsaken Paul. On the other hand, 2 Timothy is clearly earlier than Colossians, Laodiceans, and Philippians, because, among other reasons, Onesiphorus was forced to search for Paul in Rome, showing that he did not know Paul's location.[38] We will discuss further reasons for placing these two letters earlier than the remainder when we deal with those other letters.

In 1 Timothy, Paul specifically directed Timothy to remain at Ephesus, so we should in fact expect Timothy to be there until Paul sends for him. In 2 Timothy, we see Paul doing exactly that— requesting Timothy to come to him at Rome. Paul also says that Timothy is aware that all in Asia have turned against him,[39] and this implies that Timothy is in Asia where he could know that. Paul sends greetings to the household of Onesiphorus,[40] who is in Rome with Paul and who we learn was with Timothy at some time in the past at Ephesus.[41] Paul greets the household of Onesiphorus a second time at the end of the letter and, in this same pericope, Paul sends greetings to

---

[37] 1 Tim. 1:19-20.

[38] 2 Tim. 1:17.

[39] 2 Tim. 1:15.

[40] 2 Tim. 1:16-17.

[41] 2 Tim. 1:18.

Prisca and Aquila. Paul wrote about them in 1 Corinthians, when he was at Ephesus, saying they had a church in their house.[42] Paul's mention of them in 2 Timothy, therefore, further implies that Timothy is at Ephesus.

There is, however, one statement of Paul's in 2 Timothy that may be confusing. Paul says that he is sending out Tychicus into Ephesus.[43] In the usual English translation, this sounds like Timothy must be at some third location, especially when we realize that the likely bearer of this letter is Tychicus himself. The answer, I suspect, is that Paul is here using the traditional phrasing that expresses the bestowal of apostolic authority, because the meaning of "apostle" is "one who is sent out" with authority. So Paul means that he is assigning Tychicus to work as an apostle at Ephesus, because Paul needs Timothy at Rome.

The Letter to the Ephesians would be difficult to place without its close association to 2 Timothy, because it provides few details about Paul's situation. Paul is in prison but he does not say where or why. Paul sends Tychicus, but without 2 Timothy we would not know when or why. We know, however, that 2 Timothy and Ephesians were sent together at the same time, not only because of the similarity of the situation, but because other possibilities are not sensible. If Paul had sent Ephesians before 2 Timothy, then Timothy is still at Ephesus and Paul would certainly have greeted Timothy in the Letter to the Ephesians. But he does not. If Paul had sent Ephesians after 2 Timothy, then Timothy would be with Paul, and Paul would have certainly sent regards on his behalf to the Ephesians. But he does not. Therefore, 2 Timothy and Ephesians were sent together, Ephesians being a letter for public reading and 2 Timothy remaining a private letter to his coworker in the gospel.

---

[42] 1 Cor. 16:19.

[43] 2 Tim. 4:12.

Philemon, Colossians, and Laodiceans

With the Letter to Philemon, we have another case of Paul sending a direct personal letter along with a community letter, or rather, in this case, two community letters, Colossians and Laodiceans.

Laodiceans is extremely short and does not offer much information, which is probably why it was left out of the New Testament maintaining the number of Paul's epistles, after the addition of Hebrews, at the magical fourteen. This letter does indicate that Paul is in prison[44] and that Paul asked the Laodiceans to exchange letters with the Colossians.[45] Both of these statements corroborate what is said in the Letter to the Colossians, promising that this is the missing twin letter. We can be skeptical, but we have no solid reason to doubt its validity.

It is clear that Paul wrote both Colossians and Philemon (and therefore Laodiceans) after 1 Timothy and Ephesians because Timothy is with Paul while Paul is in prison.[46] Although Paul does not say where his prison is, he must be in Rome because the context is so similar to Ephesians: Paul is suffering for the Church[47] and he is sending Tychicus with the letters.[48]

We can easily see that Colossians was sent together with Philemon because of the confluence of details from the two letters. Timothy is with Paul.[49] Epaphras, who ministered at Colossae, is with Paul and sends greetings to Philemon.[50] Mark, Aristarchus, Demas, and

---

[44] Laod. 6.

[45] Laod. 19.

[46] Col. 1:1; Col. 4:10; Phile. 1.

[47] Col. 1:24.

[48] Col. 4:7-8.

[49] Phile. 1; Col. 1:1.

[50] Col. 1:7.

Luke send greetings to the Colossians and to Philemon.[51] Onesimus, who is Philemon's slave and the main subject of the Letter to Philemon, is one of the Colossians.[52] This is sufficient to show with great confidence that these letters were sent together.

Philippians

We only have to establish that the one remaining epistle, Philippians, is later than Colossians in order to complete the chronological order. Paul is still with Timothy[53] and still a prisoner at Rome.[54] Therefore, this letter is at least later than Ephesians and 2 Timothy. Furthermore, because Paul says in Philippians that he will send Timothy, it is unlikely that Colossians and Philemon followed Philippians. Few of the other details can help us to determine if Philippians is earlier or later than the Letter to the Colossians, except one especially significant one: Paul tells the Philippians three times that he is dying.[55]

To the Colossians, Paul had significantly omitted that he planned to come to them, suggesting that he knew he would not be able to visit them. He also did not tell the Ephesians that he would visit them. This is something that Paul does say often to the communities in his letters, so that its absence in these letters may be seen as significant. It means that Paul probably knew he would not leave Rome from the time that he arrived there or even before. The fact that his situation does not change much in his last letters, all from Rome, shows that only a short time passes until he dies, probably a couple weeks. In these letters, there is a definite progression: in Ephesians, Paul is a prisoner; in Colossians, Paul is suffering greatly; and in Philippians, Paul says he is dying. It is true that Paul tells the Philippians that he hopes to

---

[51] Phile. 24; Col. 4:10-14.

[52] Col. 4:9.

[53] Philip. 1:1.

[54] Philip. 1:12-13.

[55] Philip. 1:19-25, 2:17, 3:10.

come to them, but it is also clear from his other statements that this is a vain hope. Furthermore, the fact that Paul, while he is ailing, intends to send even Timothy away probably means that his fate is sealed, and his trusted companion will be of better use elsewhere. From this serious turn of events, progressing from bad to worse, it follows that Paul wrote Philippians last of all.

Now, we have established by the internal evidence a definite order of the epistles of Paul. This is important because no other source can carry the same authority regarding Paul's mission as Paul himself. If other sources differ with Paul, even the Acts of the Apostles, we will have to defer to Paul's own words.

Some scholars have argued to invalidate some of Paul's letters based on content to support specific theories, discrediting those with more advanced doctrine (2 Thessalonians, Hebrews, Ephesians, Colossians) or those describing an advanced Church organization (Titus, 1 Timothy, 2 Timothy). Also, scholars consider as evidence the writing style and vocabulary, analyzing through a comparison against the "real" letters of Saint Paul, to discern some evidence of forgery. These manipulations were valid only as long as the letters had no real historical context. Once a context has been established, however, this extreme action of disallowing the evidence is no longer tolerable. The letters, chronologically arranged by internal details and connections, can now be clearly seen as integral members of a unified collection. Events progress from letter to letter. No longer can 2 Timothy be separated from Ephesians or from Colossians or from Philippians, because these letters are clearly interrelated. Further, the mere fact that they are so interrelated— especially because this interrelation has been hidden from earliest times by the arbitrary ordering in the New Testament— makes it impossible to separate any of these letters from their author, Saint Paul.

This is not to say that no part of Paul's letters is suspect. Specifically, I think we can consider highly suspect certain problematic passages that float from one place to another in different collections of

Paul's letters. Especially questionable are those passages stating that women should not speak in Church, because Paul praised Phoebe as a deaconess and Junia as an apostle, roles which obviously give them speaking authority. Yet, clearly none of the letters can be entirely discarded wholesale, because they together present a sensible and coherent story, which only becomes clear once we restore the original chronological order.

The Journey of Saint Paul

From the letters as reorganized, the journey and career of Paul can be reconstructed with new accuracy. Comparisons with the Acts of the Apostles demonstrate many points of agreement and some significant points of disagreement with Paul's letters. Paul's letters comprise a record of a very short period of time, about two years, from Antioch until Rome. The short time period makes clear that Paul's opposition did not consist of different groups over a long period of time, but rather the same group pursuing him around the Aegean Sea. Peter, Barnabas, and others from James battled against Paul's mission to the gentiles.

We shall now reconstruct Paul's journey and the outline of his story from his letters. Luckily for us, Paul was generous with information about his history, providing us with many details about his life.

Paul was an Israelite, probably according to the conventional meaning that he believed himself to be a descendant of Abraham, Isaac, and Jacob.[56] He also says that he is of the tribe of Benjamin, a Hebrew born of Hebrews, and circumcised on the eighth day.[57]

Paul says that he is a Pharisee in regards to the law. Certainly, we should not argue with Paul about his own mind, but he must be referring to a time prior to his conversion to Christianity; for, the arguments of his letters no longer demonstrate the same veneration for the law expected from a Pharisee. Undoubtedly, therefore, Paul is speaking of his past in Judaism.

---

[56] Philip. 3:5-6.

[57] Ibid.

Paul also says that he was a persecutor of the Church,[58] which he equates with being zealous as a Jew, at the same time as he claims to have been blameless under the law.[59] This is a very interesting statement, because Paul is hinting, perhaps unintentionally, that he believes the Jews are justified according to Mosaic law in persecuting Christians.

Paul admits that he was well known as a persecutor of the Church before his conversion— but not in Israel— because the churches there did not know him by sight.[60] Then he received his famous revelation,[61] which probably occurred at Damascus,[62] but he could also have been elsewhere. However, Paul claims that he had risen to high office, and his permanent residence seems to have been Damascus. In the Dead Sea Scrolls, Damascus held a prominence nearly equal to Jerusalem as a seat of the Jewish religion, an exiled community which sought to reform the religion into a new everlasting covenant. The sect from Damascus, the Essenes, became one of the three major parties of Judaism. Consequently, Paul may well have been an Essene, although he prefers to call himself a Pharisee. This is reminiscent of Flavius Josephus, who called himself a Pharisee while reserving his highest praise for the Essene sect, revealing a rather conflicting affinity with a competing party.

We should note that evidence suggests the Church was originally formed primarily from Essenes, like John the Baptist. The apostles appear to have already been followers of John.[63] The Synoptic Gospels, unlike the Gospel of John, make plain Jesus' relationship to

---

[58] Philip. 3:6; Gal. 1:13.

[59] Philip. 3:6.

[60] Gal. 1:22-24.

[61] Gal. 1:15-16; 2 Cor. 12:2.

[62] Gal. 1:17.

[63] John 1:35-41

John, and thus to the Essenes, by describing Jesus' baptism by John. Moreover, only Pharisees, Essenes, and Christians accepted the prophetic books, unlike the Sadducees and Samaritans who did not, which points to the probability of a common origin. Essenes might well have been a subset of the Pharisaic philosophy which split off from the main group but in some contexts sharing the same name as they shared a common heritage.

Paul, upon receiving the revelation, went away at once into Arabia.[64] Paul does not say what he did there. This is very curious indeed, because this statement, in the context of Paul's argument that he was equal to those from Jerusalem, implies that Christianity had something to do with Arabia, even more so than with Jerusalem, which was the more obvious location for the central authorities of the Church to be found. Paul is adamant that he did not derive his apostleship from Jerusalem, and his whole purpose in recounting his activity as a Christian in Galatians is precisely to refute that accusation.

In this light, Paul's response to his revelation acquires a surprising significance. His immediate departure into Arabia at this critical juncture, and Paul's denial of the influence of Jerusalem, suggests that Arabia held greater authority for Christians than Jerusalem. Yet, we have no information about what was in Arabia that could confer such authority; so, whatever drew Paul there and could have endowed him with authority to the Galatians, in his opinion, the secret remains intact. However, we must speculate that important leaders of the Church had taken refuge out of reach of the Jewish authorities in Judea, and Arabia would have been a likely refuge. This is not at all far-fetched, because Paul's conversion occurred during the time of intense Jewish persecutions of the Church, as Paul confesses to the Galatians. We will remember that John the Baptist had maintained his ministry on the eastern bank of the Jordan, in "the wilderness," and his imprisonment and execution was at the Arabian outpost Machaerus

---

[64] Gal. 1:17.

on the border of Moab.[65] The sect of John and Jesus, the Nazarenes, as enemies of Herod, would have been very welcome in the Arabian capital city of Petra. This was a likely place for Paul to find exiled Nazarene leaders— out of reach of Jewish and Roman authorities; but close enough to return quickly if the situation changed in their favor. Paul, as a highly-placed Jewish leader from Damascus, would have naturally sought others of similar caste.

Another factor which points to the importance of Arabia is that Paul from the beginning considers himself a Nazarene equal in authority to even Peter, James, John, and others in Jerusalem. While he does show the pillars respect, he does not bow to their authority. To some small extent, there is even evidence to suggest that Peter and James agreed that Paul was similar in authority to themselves in that they accepted him without much time to evaluate his abilities as an apostle, and they negotiated with him on the crucial issue of circumcision. Their ready acceptance of his authority suggests that Paul had both knowledge and credentials.

In calculating Paul's time in Arabia, we have to guess roughly, but the evidence suggests that he was there for an extremely long time. Paul's total time from his conversion revelation to death in Rome was near fifteen years, including the fourteen years plus until writing 2 Corinthians and allowing several additional months completing the collection, traveling to Jerusalem from Corinth, a couple weeks under trial in Jerusalem and then his imprisonment in Rome. From Antioch to Rome, including twice around the Aegean and a stopover in Crete, would have been about two years. He may have spent a year in the area of Syria and Cilicia, possibly up to two years, before he was persecuted at Antioch and forced overland to Galatia. We have a definite time period for his mission in Damascus, which Paul measured as three years. Consequently, subtracting the time for his missionary activity, Paul seems to have spent around eight years in Arabia!

---

[65] *Antiquities of the Jews.* Flavius Josephus. Book XVIII, Chapter V.

After Paul's long and mysterious sojourn into Arabia, he returned to Damascus.[66] It is interesting that Paul makes a distinction between Damascus and Arabia, probably indicating that Damascus was now under Roman rule. After three years in Damascus, Paul escaped by being let down in a basket from a window in the wall.[67] This would have been an interior wall of the city with windows (exterior city walls would not have windows, because exterior windows would weaken the wall and the defense of the city), probably separating the Jewish section from the rest of the city. The ethnarch, a title likely denoting the governor of a ghetto—almost certainly a Jewish official, answering to the ruler of the city—[68] attempted to seize Paul, forcing him to flee. By mentioning that the ethnarch had been appointed under the previous authority of King Aretas (9 BCE– 40 CE), Paul would have shown that the ethnarch was not an authority under Jewish law nor by religious sanction but installed by a foreign ruler of an alien race.

From Damascus, Paul went to Jerusalem, apparently for the first time as a Christian or Nazarene.[69] He stayed fifteen days with Peter and James, the brother of the Lord.[70] The purpose of this visit is mysteriously unstated, but he does claim that he was received and accepted as an apostle by Peter and James, the brother of the Lord. From Jerusalem, Paul went into the regions of Syria and Cilicia, where he seems to have used Antioch as a base for his missionary work in that region.[71]

---

[66] Gal. 1:18.

[67] 2 Cor. 11:32-33.

[68] King Aretas IV ruled 9 CE to 40 CE. However, he had been long dead by the time that this event occurred. Paul mentions that the ethnarch was appointed by him to make a point: he was not running from a righteous authority— not a Church official nor from an official appointed by Jewish law.

[69] Gal. 1:18.

[70] Ibid.

[71] Gal. 1:21.

In response to another revelation, Paul returned to Jerusalem with Titus and Barnabas.[72] He laid before a council of acknowledged leaders his gospel to the nations. Cephas, James, and John gave Paul and Barnabas, but excluding Titus, tacit approval to proclaim to the gentiles.[73] The revelation clearly had something to do with the issue of circumcision, and from Paul's letters we can see that he was strongly opposed to continuing Jewish purity laws.

After an undetermined time, but apparently not long after their meeting in Jerusalem, Cephas came to Antioch. Things went sour quickly, however, when some unnamed persons came from James and convinced Cephas, Barnabas, and other Jews to break off fellowship with the gentiles.[74] From the context, it seems that initially Peter did not realize that the Antiochenes were not circumcised Jews. Paul confronted Cephas as a hypocrite,[75] and the Jews (Jewish Christians) drove him out with Timothy and possibly also Silvanus and Titus from Antioch.[76]

From Antioch, after being expelled, Paul began his extensive missionary journey. The next stop that we know about was Galatia. We can infer this because, when Paul recounted his career in his Letter to the Galatians, he stopped his summary after the confrontation in Antioch, expecting the Galatians to know the rest of the story; he did not need to elaborate further to make his point that he never relied upon Jerusalem for his authority. Also, we should note that in his early days at Corinth, he already counted the Galatians as one of his churches.[77] Therefore, Paul probably went to the churches of Galatia soon after he

---

[72] Gal. 2:1.

[73] Gal. 2:9.

[74] Gal. 2:12-13.

[75] Gal. 2:14.

[76] I Thes. 2:14-15; 2 Tim. 3:11.

[77] 1 Cor. 16:1.

was driven out of Antioch, because Paul expects the Galatians to know what occurred after that point in his career.

Paul chose an overland route, perhaps because it was winter and too dangerous to travel by ship on the Mediterranean Sea. He may have tried a sea route first, but winter travel on the Mediterranean was difficult and dangerous. Apparently, judging by his eventual itinerary, Paul was headed for Macedonia, but his strength failed and he had to stop in Galatia.[78] From Galatia, Paul continued on to Philippi. He likely made other stops along this path, such as at Troas, but we cannot know his exact route. It is interesting, however, that Paul apparently bypasses many cities without preaching the gospel, as he had intended to bypass Galatia before he was forced to stop. Especially astonishing is that Paul avoids mentioning one of the most important cities of the ancient world, Byzantium, although it is nearly directly along his route to Macedonia. Apparently, he knew exactly where he was going and to whom he would evangelize— and to whom he would not.

At Philippi, Paul and his companions were mistreated but clearly successful. From Philippi, Paul goes to Thessalonika, and the Philippians support his mission there.[79] Paul probably made other nearby stops in Macedonia as well.[80] He then went through Beroea to Athens.[81] His message was apparently rejected at Athens, because he does not include this community in 1 Thessalonians 1:9, and because he never mentions them in relation to the collection for the saints. In Achaia, Paul has some success with the Corinthians.[82] It is probably at this point that he journeys westward "around unto Illyricum,"[83] and,

---

[78] Gal. 4:13.

[79] Philip. 4:15-16.

[80] I Thes. 1:8.

[81] I Thes. 3:1-2.

[82] I Thes. 1:8-9.

[83] Rom. 15:19.

after writing a letter to the Corinthians which has been lost to us, he returns to Corinth. Paul decides to gather the gift for the saints, and writes a letter, also lost, to the Galatians, probably sending it with Timothy to Galatia.

Paul is next found in Ephesus, where he writes 1 Corinthians and fights wild animals.[84] An unexpected opportunity to preach the gospel caused him to tarry. We can surmise that Timothy arrives at Ephesus with news from Galatia, prompting Paul to write Galatians then and sends it with Timothy. After the unexpected delay Paul goes on to Macedonia by way of Troas.[85] Although little is said about Troas, he was undoubtedly driven out, because he leaves important personal belongings there, suggesting that his departure was in haste.[86] While Paul was in Macedonia this second time, he wrote 2 Corinthians not long after writing Galatians, fourteen years after his revelation of Christ.[87]

Back in Achaia, he is with "some from Italy,"[88] and he writes his famous letter to the Roman community, which he had not yet visited.[89] He sends Timothy to Ephesus, probably to collect their gift for the saints, and Timothy is arrested.[90] Paul writes Hebrews in advance of his return to Jerusalem. The collection is ready in Achaia and Paul decides not to wait for Timothy. With Titus, Paul travels towards Jerusalem with the collection. While en route, Paul and Titus are separated at Crete, and Paul must leave suddenly.[91]

---

[84] 1 Cor. 15:32, 16:8-9, 16:12.

[85] 2 Cor. 2:12-13.

[86] 2 Tim. 4:13.

[87] Gal. 2:1; 2 Cor. 12:2.

[88] Heb. 13:24.

[89] Rom. 16:25-26.

[90] Heb. 13:23; 1 Tim. 1:3.

[91] Tit. 1:5, 1:16.

Paul then writes Titus and 1 Timothy from some unknown location(s), although it is likely that he was at Jerusalem.[92] He appears a short time later in a Roman prison,[93] where his suffering increases towards death. From a Roman prison, Paul wrote 2 Timothy, Ephesians, Philemon, Colossians, Laodiceans, and finally Philippians. Paul died at Rome due to illness, torture, or even execution.[94]

Just like the narrative within Paul's epistles, the Acts of the Apostles ends with Paul in Rome. This cannot be accidental. It reflects that Rome is where Paul's narrative was known to end by the potential readers of Acts. In Acts, however, Paul is not a real prisoner, but he is allowed to live at a home of his own expense, only nominally under guard, for two years. His status as a prisoner is no more than a technicality. Paul does not suffer, and he surely does not die at this point. The circumstances described in Acts contradict absolutely the suffering that Paul relates in his Letter to the Philippians. This also cannot be accidental. Rather, we should see that the author of Acts had a polemical purpose in writing, and we should be wary of the author's manipulations.

Still, the Acts of the Apostles contains much that can inform us about the early Church and its history. Even the manipulations of the author reveal to us beliefs, myths, and aspirations of the ancient Christians. Their values and cultural biases are wrapped within the fantasy of this author, at least as an ideal to strive for. And even within the artificial narrative, we can find that the author had some basis of fact— Paul actually did end his career in Rome.

The final author of the Acts of the Apostles could not have been Luke, because Luke, a physician, was present in Rome when Paul suffered and died. Of course, he would have known that Paul did not

---

[92] Rom. 16:25; Heb. 13:23.

[93] 2 Tim. 1:17

[94] Philip. 1:19-25, 2:17, 3:10.

live in Rome for two years in comfort and ease. On the other hand, could Luke have contributed to Acts? At times, there are great divergences between the story presented by Acts and that presented by Paul's letters. These divergences are too obvious and too significant to have been created by an eye-witness without outright lying. On the other hand, there are parts of the story that agree so well between Acts and Paul's letters that we know the author of Acts had a knowledgeable source about Paul's career and journeys. The difficulty is knowing where the author was knowledgeable, where he was not, and where he was deliberately obfuscating.

One thing is certain: the author did not know the Letter to the Galatians. The Acts of the Apostles has Paul visiting Jerusalem several times before he ever ministered to the Galatians, obviously contradicting Paul's letter. It appears to be important to the author of Acts to show Paul working closely with those at Jerusalem.

The author probably had been ignorant of other letters as well. The Letter to Titus shows that Paul considered Titus to be important in his work and Galatians describes Titus as working with Barnabas and Paul,[95] but Acts gives him no missionary role at all, although he may be at least mentioned if he is meant by either "Titius" or "Titus Justus." The author obviously did not know that Paul suffered at Rome, so it seems unlikely that the author knew Philippians or Colossians, although he may have changed these facts purposely.

The Acts of the Apostles never describes Paul actually suffering anywhere, although we know from Paul's letters that he suffered much and often for the sake of the gospel. This calls into question whether the author knew 1 Thessalonians, 2 Corinthians, 1 Timothy, and 2 Timothy. The great number of things from Paul's letters that the author left out of Acts— things that would presumably aid the author's purpose of glorifying Paul and his missionary work— probably indicates that the author did not have a collection of Paul's letters to work from. This in itself argues for a very early date for the

---

[95] Gal. 2:1-3.

Acts of the Apostles, because it was not many decades before Paul's letters were shared among most communities.

Yet, in many ways, the author's depiction of events agrees closely with what we know from Paul's letters. Although the author apparently knows nothing about Paul's mysterious sojourn into Arabia, he describes his escape from Damascus[96] almost exactly as Paul describes it himself.[97] Interestingly, however, the author chose a different Greek word for "basket" than Paul used, which supports that he did not work with 2 Corinthians in front of him. From there, he has Paul going to Jerusalem for the first time as a Christian,[98] agreeing with Galatians,[99] but he has Paul preaching in Jerusalem,[100] which would have made him known to a church in Judea, contradicting Paul's statement that he was not known.[101] Next, the Acts of the Apostles has Paul going to Cilicia,[102] which is in agreement with Paul's order of events in the epistles, albeit under markedly different circumstances.

Perhaps, we should be more skeptical of Paul's own accounts. After all, if the author of the Acts of the Apostles had a rhetorical purpose, so too did Paul. However, Paul had more reason to tell the truth accurately, because his own credibility, and that of his mission, was at stake. Moreover, he was writing to communities where he would expect criticism, where his gospel and his authority had already met opposition, and they could easily know the same facts from other sources. Therefore, although Paul may not always tell the whole truth, he certainly would not risk telling anything that was false.

---

[96] Acts 9:23-25.

[97] 2 Cor. 11:32-33.

[98] Acts 9:26-27.

[99] Gal. 1:18.

[100] Acts 9:28-29.

[101] Gal. 1:22.

[102] Acts 9:30.

So, perhaps, after his first visit to Jerusalem, believers did send Paul to Tarsus, and Barnabas did retrieve Paul and bring him to Antioch. The author of the Acts of the Apostles adds many details about events— names, times, conversations, and sometimes even the thoughts and intentions of persons— that we are in no place to question. All we can do to judge the likelihood of such detail is to be guided by the overall truthfulness and accuracy of the author, comparing with what we know from Paul's letters.

The Acts of the Apostles does agree with Galatians in that Paul went to Syria and Cilicia after his first visit as a Christian to Jerusalem. According to Acts 11:27-28, describing the prophecy of a famine, Paul was in Antioch during the reign of Claudius or shortly before. Because of the prophecy of the famine, the disciples decided to make a collection for the needs of the believers of Judea, and Paul and Barnabas were chosen to deliver it to Jerusalem. From Galatians, of course, we know that this trip to Jerusalem did not occur,[103] but it is important that the Acts of the Apostles recalls Paul delivering some kind of collection to Jerusalem. In Paul's letters, we see that he collected from the communities around the Aegean Sea, but the author of Acts apparently does not know of that collection. Consequently, it is evident the author knew that Paul had at some point delivered a collection to Jerusalem, but he either did not know any details about it or he made some changes to the story. From this, we can be quite satisfied that the author of the Acts of the Apostles did not know Paul's letters to the Corinthians or to the Romans.

This is an extraordinary realization, because the author of Acts demonstrated no knowledge at all of Paul's letters. This is very surprising, since his letters quickly became famous enough to have a mention in the Second Epistle of Peter.[104] But how can we explain that the author of Acts does not reference even one of Paul's letters?

---

[103] Gal. 1:22.

[104] 2 Pet. 3:15-16.

Next, continuing with the Acts of the Apostles, Barnabas and Paul, in Antioch, receive a commission by prophecy from the Holy Spirit to go on a mission. They take John called Mark with them and go all through Cyprus, from Salamis on the eastern coast to Paphos on the western end, then they cross into Asia at Perga in Pamphylia. Here John Mark leaves them and returns to Jerusalem for unstated reasons. Paul and Barnabas continue onto Antioch in Pisidia. After a week they are driven out, and they go to Iconium. But they have to flee there as well to Lystra and Derbe in Lycaonia. They pass through Perga to Attalia and finally return to Antioch.

Paul does not give any of these details in his Letter to the Galatians. This is not surprising, however, because his purpose in that letter is only to say that he was not subject to Jerusalem authority. He only mentions Syria and Cilicia and he does not refer to Cyprus, Pamphylia, Pisidia, and Lycaonia (although he does refer to persecutions at Iconium and Lystra in 2 Timothy 3:11), but this can easily be explained because these were all failures. Paul would not want to draw attention to large numbers of failures when his purpose was to defend his mission against hostile factions. Therefore, we should not read much into this small difference between the Acts of the Apostles and Paul's letters. The author of Acts may well have accurately reported this missionary journey of Paul and Barnabas, and Paul's long list of hardships listed in 2 Corinthians demands that he had evangelized many communities that he does not name in his letters.[105]

Back at Antioch, an event occurs which is reported both in Galatians and in the Acts of the Apostles, although there are some significant differences. In Acts, some Christians come from Judea demanding that brothers be circumcised.[106] Paul and Barnabas together

---

[105] 2 Cor 11:23-28.

[106] Acts 16:24.

dispute with them and are appointed to go to Jerusalem to discuss the matter with the apostles and elders.

At Jerusalem, they are welcomed by the church, the apostles, and the elders, and they are sent back to Antioch with Silas and Judas called Barsabbas, carrying a letter from James and the apostles, included in Acts 15:23-29. The letter disassociates James and the apostles in Jerusalem from those demanding that Christians obey Mosaic law. The letter commands, apparently as a compromise, that Christians should conform to the covenant of Noah, which proscribes fornication and the eating of meat which was sacrificed to idols or from strangled animals— the minimal covenant required of believing gentiles.

Paul's account in Galatians is quite different, however.[107] Paul says that he went to Jerusalem on his own initiative from Antioch in response to a revelation. Paul says he went with Barnabas and Titus. The Acts of the Apostles does not know Titus as an apostle, and does not mention him at all in relation to this event. Paul's new revelation must have been his own refinements on the Gospel, since Paul says that, in a private meeting with prominent leaders, he laid out his gospel for the nations (gentiles). He says he did this to avoid "running in vain." This statement could be taken in one of two ways. The most obvious reading is that Paul sought verification that his revelation was valid. This interpretation is likely incorrect, however, because soon after this meeting Paul opposes those from James and even Peter himself, which contradicts the possibility that Paul considered Peter and James superior to himself. Therefore, a less obvious interpretation of Paul's statement must be seen as more likely: that Paul sought to *commune* with the leadership in Jerusalem. He was not seeking approval from a higher authority, but rather he wanted to avoid dividing Christ by sharing his revelation proactively with those whom he considered equals— so that there would not be more than one single understanding of God's will. In the early charismatic Church,

---

[107] Gal. 2:1-10.

communication of prophecies and revelations was necessary to avoid schisms; however, as the decentralized Church expanded through the known world, schisms became inevitable because complete communication became impossible and conflicting revelations arose.

What was Paul's revelation and gospel that he proclaimed among the nations? Paul adds a comment here that, although he laid out his gospel for the nations, Titus who was Greek was not expected to be circumcised except by the false brothers. The connection Paul makes between his gospel and Titus not being circumcised suggests that Paul's revelation included that Christians need not be circumcised. And, in accord with this, Paul goes on to say that those who were seeming to be leaders agreed that Paul should be the apostle to the "uncircumcision" as Peter was apostle to the "circumcision." James, Cephas (Peter), and John, who seemed to be leaders, then shook the hands of Paul and Barnabas.

All was agreed— except that it was not. For when Cephas (Peter) came to Antioch, he dined with gentiles until certain persons came from James, and then he withdrew from their fellowship. Thus, Paul called him a hypocrite. The other Jews and even Barnabas stood with Peter. In Galatians, Paul leaves off his account with the confrontation in order to avoid describing the subsequent result; however, we know that Paul suffered persecution at Antioch and the Jews drove Paul, Timothy, and Silvanus (Silas) out.[108]

Obviously, Saint Paul's version is diametrically opposed to the story in the Acts of the Apostles. It is difficult, if not impossible, to see how the author of Acts could know so much about these events and not know that Paul and Peter had faced off at Antioch. Certainly, Paul had confrontations with Jewish Christians in Antioch before he went to Jerusalem the second time, responding to his revelation. This situation, however, would be more remarkable than others, because it involved public confrontation between the very highest personages in the early Church. Consequently, we cannot believe that the author of Acts did

---

[108] 2 Tim 3:11; 2 Thes. 2:15.

not know the most important facts— that Paul had publicly accused Peter of hypocrisy, and the Jewish Christians subsequently drove him out of Antioch. Therefore, we can only conclude that the author deliberately obscured the conflict.

Of course, this throws into question many representations from the Acts of the Apostles. For example, Paul probably never did agree to a compromise that required gentiles to obey the covenant of Noah, abstaining from fornication, meat sacrificed to idols, and meat from strangled animals. Paul always opposed fornication, but in 1 Corinthians he says there is nothing intrinsically wrong with eating food offered to idols unless it causes spiritual harm by creating guilt or doubt in oneself or confusion in a brother.[109] Paul is clearly unaware of any covenant binding Christians to abstain from meat offered to idols— a requirement that would for all practical purposes force Christians outside of Judea to become vegetarians. Therefore, the account in Acts 15:22-31 simply could not have happened as described. It is a fabrication to replace the uncomfortable truth that Paul and the Jewish Christians were opposed to one another on an important issue. Perhaps, it was meant to suggest a resolution of the split between the gentile and Jewish churches, by presenting it as a previous but forgotten agreement among the highest leaders of the two factions. Nonetheless, Acts is not trustworthy in reporting on conflicts within the Church.

Consequently, we should be skeptical about Acts 15:36-39 where Paul quarrels and splits with Barnabas over John Mark accompanying them. This is such a petty matter and quite out of character for Paul, who often shows a willingness to reconcile with real enemies who have persecuted him. In fact, we know that Paul had far greater reason to split with Barnabas at this juncture.[110] The way the author covers over this fact is very clever indeed: Because Mark is the

---

[109] 1 Cor. 8:1-13.

[110] Gal. 2:13.

cousin of Barnabas, Barnabas appears to motivated by family loyalty as well as Christian brotherhood, both laudable virtues. Paul, however, appears to be somewhat petty, although the story leaves open the possibility that he may have been the one who was justified— we do not know this for sure, but believers have to suspect that he might be correct in his actions. We do know, however, that, by the end of his career and life, Paul was close to Mark and possibly reconciled with Barnabas.[111] What, then, can a simple uncritical reader make of this story as its final value? Ultimately, the story dulls and invalidates any conclusions whatsoever, and the rift between Paul and Barnabas becomes insignificant, because no party is clearly at fault and there were no lasting important consequences. Therefore, the separation between Paul and Barnabas has been explained without connection to the furor at Antioch and without discrediting any important Church official.

The author of Acts has set aside completely any question of conflict among the apostles in such an adroit and clever manner that, in appreciation, we might forget that the account is a string of falsehoods. According to Paul, at Antioch he opposed Peter to his face, and Barnabas sided with Peter. Paul was persecuted and driven out. This is why he is so bitter against Peter, James, and John in Galatians, calling them sardonically "those reputing to be pillars." Paul is so near outright sarcasm here that conformity with the idyllic image of the "virgin Church," free from schism and conflict, is impossible, and consequently many translations of Galatians deviate a little from the Greek text, softening the appearance of conflict between the apostles. But, of course, there was conflict between the apostles, which is exactly what Paul says throughout Galatians. Paul simply does not recognize the Jewish Christian apostles as superior, so he cannot accept his mistreatment at Antioch as justice.

According to the Acts of the Apostles, it is at this point that Paul leaves Antioch, separating from Barnabas, in order to do more

---

[111] Col. 4:10.

missionary work.[112] He travels overland going to communities that he had previously visited, including communities where he was persecuted and driven out. Everything is fine, and those who persecuted Paul are either quiet or gone. Also, the Acts of the Apostles has Timothy join Paul at Lystra, although Paul indicates that Timothy was with him in Antioch.[113] Before working with him, Paul is supposed to have caused Timothy to be circumcised in order to appease the Jews— an action which is absolutely incompatible with Paul's position as expressed in his letters[114] and which ignores the Noetic compromise of Acts 15:22-31, an obvious internal contradiction. Also, as we see from Paul's letters, appeasement was generally seen as an admission that one lacked authority from God— something that Paul could never do.

Paul went to Galatia after being driven out from Antioch; the Acts of the Apostles agrees on this point only with the evidence found in Paul's letters. Paul says that he did not intend to preach there, but he stopped only because of a physical infirmity.[115] Perhaps, his persecution at Antioch left him in poor condition? Nonetheless, Paul does in fact say that he preached among the churches of Galatia at this point, and this contradicts the Acts of the Apostles, which explicitly says that Paul did not preach on this pass (his first trip) through Galatia, "having been forbidden by the Holy Spirit to speak the word in Asia."[116] This is nonsense, of course, because Derbe and Lystra and Iconium are all in Asia Minor near Galatia. If by Asia, the author was referring only to the western coast of Asia Minor, as the author of Revelation does, then Galatia was not in "Asia" any more than Derbe, Lystra, and Iconium. Consequently, either way, this artificial manipulation contradicts what has just been told in Acts 15:41-16:5.

---

[112] Acts 15:40.

[113] 2 Tim. 3:11.

[114] Rom. 2:26-29, 4:9-12; Gal. 2:3, 5:2-12, 6:12-15; Eph. 2:11-13; Col. 2:11.

[115] Gal. 4:13.

[116] Acts 16:6.

The author's purpose here is incomprehensible. There is nothing obvious to be gained by denying that Paul preaches in Galatia at this point. Perhaps, it was known that Paul had preached in Galatia only once, and the author felt the need to create an excuse for Paul to return later—perhaps as an indication of ultimate reconciliation. The later trip to Galatia in the narrative provides the additional opportunity to pass through Jerusalem and Antioch, which Paul's letters show could not have happened. The additional trip does add to the impression that Paul also reconciled his problems with the Jerusalem leadership and the Antiochian church and, therefore, the reader might conclude that the problems could not have been so consequential. Perhaps, providing an excuse for such a later trip and its implications is the purpose behind denying that Paul preached on his first pass through, which would mean that it was widely known that Paul only preached once in Galatia. Another possible reason for denying that Paul preached on this pass is simply to engage the Holy Spirit in the story, who was the real protagonist and hero of Acts. Moreover, this artifice creates a precedent, explaining any known unusual action by the apostles as a consequence of communication with the Holy Spirit.

In any case, the Acts of the Apostles and our inferences from Paul's letters agree that Paul traveled from Galatia to Macedonia. Acts details that Paul went through Troas at this point, which may well have been the case; Paul's letters are silent on his exact route. The Acts of the Apostles and Paul's letters seem to agree on the matter that Paul did not preach at Troas on his first trip to Macedonia, although both suggest that he does so later.[117]

From here on and for a while, Paul's account and that of the Acts of the Apostles show remarkable agreement. Paul and Silvanus (Silas) are persecuted at Philippi, but ultimately they are successful.[118]

---

[117] Acts 16:8-11; 2 Tim. 4:13.

[118] Acts 16:12-40; I Thes. 2:2.

Paul and Silas go westward through Macedonia to Thessalonika.[119] After a brief pass through Beroea, Paul preaches alone at Athens.[120] Then Paul meets Aquila and Priscilla (Prisca in Paul's letters) at Corinth.[121] The Acts of the Apostles also says here that Claudius had expelled the Jews from Rome,[122] and from Romans we do see that Paul had indeed met many from Italy on this first trip to Achaia, allowing him to send so many greetings in his later Letter to the Romans.[123] Silas and Timothy rejoin Paul at Corinth. The Acts of the Apostles does not mention Illyricum, although Paul said that he went there.[124] Next, we find Paul in Ephesus with Aquila and Priscilla.[125] The amount of agreement here with Paul's letters shows that the author of the Acts of the Apostles had a reliable source for this part of the Aegean journey.

At Ephesus, according to the Acts of the Apostles, Paul leaves Aquila and Priscilla in order to travel through Jerusalem, Antioch, and the region of Galatia.[126] This trip could not have happened, because the Letter to the Galatians was written while Paul was at Ephesus or soon afterwards in the short time between 1 and 2 Corinthians. As already discussed, Paul writes in Galatians that he only visited Jerusalem twice, so a third trip through Jerusalem before writing this letter is out of the

---

[119] Acts 17:1-9.

[120] Acts 17:10-34; 1 Thes. 1:8-9, 3:1.

[121] Acts 18:2.

[122] This agrees with the Roman historian Suetonius, although the timing of the events is not indicated. However, it does force a date for this event, Paul's first pass through Corinth, before the death of Claudius in October of 54 AD. Suetonius states that "Chrestus" created disturbances among the Jews prompting the expulsion, and almost certainly he is referring to Christ. This cannot be a coincidence that Paul is facing persecutions and Rome has Jewish disturbances, but Paul has not yet been to Rome. However, the evidence implies that Peter was preaching at Rome at this point, which would explain the tumult among Jews.

[123] Rom. 16:1-16.

[124] Rom. 15:19; 2 Cor. 13:1.

[125] Acts 18:18, 18:26;

[126] Acts 18:21-23.

question. Therefore, an extra trip east through Jerusalem, Antioch, and Galatia presented in the Acts of the Apostles is impossible.

Interestingly, however, in Acts Paul returns, after this little sojourn, again to Ephesus and then the Acts of the Apostles continues from there to parallel Paul's letters, having Paul return to Macedonia and then to Greece. The author of the Acts of the Apostles is clearly knowledgeable about Paul's missionary activity in the Aegean, but he has added an additional trip through Jerusalem. It appears that the author has altered some events and situations to create an impression that the Church was unified in its message and leadership and to hide conflicts. Especially, he invented some additional trips to Jerusalem and to other churches that had rejected Paul in order to show that the troubles Paul encountered were only temporary setbacks, caused by non-believing Jews, and that these difficulties were not evidence of any problem within the believing Church.

Just as Paul's letters to the Romans and to the Hebrews suggest,[127] the Acts of the Apostles says that Paul wants to return east, although Acts names the goal as Syria and not Jerusalem.[128] That the trip was for Syria, however, is contradicted by the fact that Acts, just like Paul's letters, shows Paul intent upon going to Jerusalem and having no purpose at all in Syria. Perhaps, the discrepancy shows the Holy Spirit guiding events in spite of the intentions of humans.

In any case, Paul does travel east. But "a plot by the Jews" causes Paul to return through Macedonia to Philippi, Troas, Assos, Mitylene, Chios, Samos, Miletus, notably avoiding Ephesus, Cos, Rhodes, and Patara.[129] Since Paul is silent on this part of his journey, we cannot dispute Acts much here. This itinerary is so extensive, however, that Paul would have broken his promise to the Hebrews to come soon and also to bring Timothy, because Timothy is journeying

---

[127] Rom. 15:25; Heb. 13:23.

[128] Acts 20:3.

[129] Acts 20:1-21:1.

with him in the Acts of the Apostles. Of course, we know from 1 and 2 Timothy that Timothy was at Ephesus when Paul was arrested at Jerusalem and subsequently taken as a prisoner to Rome. Therefore, he would have had to deliberately leave Timothy behind at Ephesus, breaking his promise.

From here, however, Paul and his entourage, according to Acts, travel straight to Cyprus and Phoenicia.[130] This does not allow for the scenario in Paul's Letter to Titus, where he leaves Titus in Crete.[131] In the Acts of the Apostles, Paul does land at Crete briefly,[132] but only after trial in Jerusalem and as a prisoner en route to Rome— still without mention of Titus.[133]

In his later letters, Paul is silent on his trip to Judea, apparently assuming that Timothy, the Ephesians, the Colossians and Laodiceans, and the Philippians know what has transpired, which they may have. The Acts of the Apostles has Paul going through Tyre, Ptolemais, Caesarea, and finally to Jerusalem.[134] Paul is arrested because of "the Jews from Asia," by which the author contrives to show that the Jews in Jerusalem had no complaint against him whatsoever and that Paul was therefore arrested unjustly.[135] Paul was at the Temple to pay the fees for four Nazarites, a symbolic act of Jewish piety designed to show that he was a devout Jew and innocent of the complaints against him. As soon as Paul was arrested, he was dragged out of the Temple precincts and the doors were immediately closed, an interesting detail which has the effect of preventing Paul from being blamed for causing

---

[130] Acts 21:2-3.

[131] Tit. 1:5.

[132] Acts 27:7-8.

[133] Eph. 3:1; 2 Tim. 1:8.

[134] Acts 21:7-15.

[135] Acts 21:27-36.

a disturbance in the Temple.[136] Clearly, any contrivance imaginable has been used to show that Paul was nothing but a devout, peace-loving, God-fearing, gentile-circumcising, Jew-appeasing, student of Gamaliel, wholly innocent of the accusations made.

After a few days in Jerusalem, according to the Acts of the Apostles, following more Jewish intrigue, Paul is taken to Caesarea to stand trial.[137] Paul then is supposed to have waited in Caesarea for more than two years.[138] This is pure fantasy since we know from Paul's letters that only a short time passed between the epistles 1 and 2 Timothy.[139] From Caesarea, Paul is carried as a prisoner to Rome through Sidon, Myra in Lycia, Cnidus, Crete at Fair Havens near Lasea, Cauda, Malta, Syracuse, Rhegium, and Puteoli.[140] None of this is mentioned nor disputed by Paul's epistles.

Finally, as we have already discussed, Paul was a prisoner at Rome. The Acts of the Apostles describes Paul as more of a guest than a prisoner for two years;[141] then, Acts mysteriously ends its narrative without further comment. Paul's letters, however, showed that he suffered and died a prisoner in Rome within a short time.

From this comparison, several things become clear: First, the author of the Acts of the Apostles did not follow Paul's letters in writing his account; the divergences are so great that it appears that he did not have access to them. He does, however, recount a very lengthy spoken

---

[136] Acts 21:30.

[137] Acts 23:33.

[138] Acts 24:27.

[139] 1 Tim. 1:3; 2 Tim. 1:17.

[140] Acts 27:3-23:13.

[141] Acts 28:30-31.

message to the Ephesians,[142] which suggests that, if he had the letters, he would have summarized them at the least.

Second, the author of the Acts of the Apostles was very knowledgeable about some of Paul's missionary activities. The author shows accurate and detailed information about most of locations that Paul visits and often in the correct order, agreeing with Paul's letters to a large degree. However, there are many notable exceptions: The author of Acts presents Paul as very active in Judea, although Paul insists that he was not. Acts does not mention Arabia, which Paul mentions in Galatians. Acts associates the collection for Jerusalem with the mission in Syria and Cilicia instead of the Aegean communities. Acts covers up the conflict between Peter and Paul at Antioch. Acts adds several extra trips to Jerusalem and has Paul revisiting communities that had rejected him— Antioch, Lystra, and Iconium. Acts postulates an additional visit to Galatia at precisely the moment that Paul wrote his scathing letter to them from Ephesus. Illyricum is not mentioned. Crete is placed out of order, after Jerusalem rather than before.

Although we have counted a great number of detectable inaccuracies, the author of the Acts of the Apostles still shows many points of agreement with what we can learn from Paul's letters. Paul did start out persecuting the Church. After his conversion, Damascus was the first place that he evangelized, escaping by being lowered in a basket. Next he did visit Jerusalem. Then he did go as a missionary into Syria and Cilicia, working with Barnabas. He did return to Jerusalem to establish an agreement about circumcision among the nations. He returned to Antioch and from there went overland through Galatia. From there Paul does end up in Macedonia, first Philippi and then Thessalonika. From there he does preach in Athens alone, and he is together with Silas (Silvanus) in Corinth. He does meet many from Italy at Corinth. He does appear in Ephesus after his first trip to Corinth, with Aquila and Prisca. From Ephesus, Paul does go to

---

[142] Acts 20:18-35.

Macedonia and then again to Greece. From Achaia Paul does leave for the East, although headed for Jerusalem rather than Syria. At Jerusalem, he is arrested and becomes a prisoner bound for Rome, where his story ends.

Before we continue to analyze the Pauline epistles, we need to know what we can depend upon— and what we cannot— from the traditions found in the Acts of the Apostles. We have already seen through only a cursory comparison with the narrative of Paul's letters that the author of Acts covered facts embarrassing to the Christian Church, both by adding details and by ignoring them. Some of this could have been inadvertent; but some could not have been accidental. It appears to have been the purpose of the work to rewrite the history of the Church into a more pleasant and ideal example, showing that the development of the Church had been guided by the Holy Spirit throughout. It also focuses much on Paul, praising him as a preacher and missionary but devaluing him as an authority and never calling him an apostle. The slant to this new "history" would tend to support the authority of the Jewish Christian leadership, without alienating the Greek churches loyal to Paul.

One of the most important traditions from Acts, that Paul was originally named Saul, has the effect of intensifying Paul's Jewish credentials. Although it is repeated many times among the Church fathers and among scholars until this day, this tradition is entirely derived from the Acts of the Apostles. Paul's letters do not even hint at the possibility of such a name change, and, consequently, it is very improbable that Paul changed his name. For had Paul been known as Saul before becoming a Christian, while he was persecuting the Church, then the churches of Judea could not have known that he was the same person since, as Paul says in Galatians, they did not know him by sight.[143] If they did not know him by sight and they did not know him by name, then they simply did not know him. If Paul had changed

---

[143] Gal. 1:22-24.

his name, he would have been obligated at this point in Galatians to explain the discrepancy, but he does not.

Paul seems to consider the fact that he had formerly persecuted the Church as contributing to his authority to speak about Judaism, and he mentions the fact again in Philippians 3:1-6. But he does not mention his former Jewish name, which would have added weight to his argument that he was just as Jewish as those demanding circumcision. Even the name change could have been used to advantage his argument, pointing out that God does not care about superficial, fleshly matters. Yet, notably he avoids attaching any significance to his name or anyone else's name. This correlates well with the fact that many apostles had Greek names, including some of the Twelve. Apparently, the Hellenization of a given name was not important. Even in the Acts of the Apostles itself, there is no real value attached to the ethnicity of given names, except in this one case, because Jewishness was an issue between Paul and his opponents. Therefore, the assertion that Paul was formerly named Saul could only be later propaganda to make Paul appear more Jewish.

We first meet "Saul" at the stoning of Stephen in Jerusalem. Of course, placing Paul at this event was a means of introducing him into the story of the Church. As he says, Paul was not known by sight to the churches of Judea;[144] therefore, if Stephen was stoned in Jerusalem, Paul was not present. Is it possible that this is the same Stephen (στεφανος) whom Paul had baptized and whose household were the first converts in Achaia (στεφανας), mentioned in 1 Corinthians?[145] Certainly not if events happened in this order, because στεφανας visited Paul at Ephesus;[146] whereas στεφανος was martyred much

---

[144] Gal. 1:22.

[145] 1 Cor. 1:16 and 16:15.

[146] 1 Cor. 16:17.

earlier than Paul's missionary work according to Acts. He was also named as a Hellenist and founding member of the Council of Seven.[147]

What was the purpose of the Council of Seven mentioned in Acts alone? It administrated a separate table fellowship, meaning separate finances, fellowship, and sacraments. Here, the Acts of the Apostles describes in the mildest possible terms what can only be a schism between the Greek churches and the Jewish churches.[148] The dissimulation that table fellowship was not important to the Church is pure distraction, disguising the worst possible failure within the early Church. Meals were sacred events— sacraments— in the original Church. Agape feasts and the remembrance of the Lord's Supper were symbolic of the Messianic age and of the Communion of the Saints. The primary function of the Church was and still is to make the sacraments available. Paul, Peter, and the Jews from James, in the confrontation at Antioch, epitomized the passion felt over table fellowship. Separation of fellowship was equivalent to separation within the congregation, a dividing of Christ. The result of this confrontation, of which the Acts of the Apostles treats lightly, was the formation of an independent government for the Greek church, the Council of Seven, constituting a complete separation from Jerusalem—a schism.

We have no reason to doubt that such a council was constituted— it certainly does not aid the rhetorical purpose of the Acts of the Apostles to imagine an authority other than the Jerusalem leadership. On the other hand, we do have every reason to doubt its timing and maybe also its location. If the Church had already instituted separate table fellowship, then what were Peter and Paul fighting about at Antioch? Paul was certainly not in favor of splitting the Church, so why did he not denounce the council in his letters? Or even mention it? Certainly, he would have if he knew of its existence early on; therefore,

---

[147] Acts 6:1-7

[148] ibid.

the Council of Seven must have been a later development than Paul himself. In this case, Stephen of the Council of Seven might have very well have been the same Stephen that Paul knew, but he would have been martyred later. In this case, we might speculate that the "seven" were bishops of churches rejecting the Jewish Christian authority, seven churches in opposition to Judaizers. We should note that another named member of the Council of Seven, Nicolaus, was probably the leader or namesake of the "Nicolaitans" condemned in Revelation 2:6.

This first schism of believers was well known throughout the early Church, and the author of the Acts of the Apostles could not ignore it completely. So, in order to hide the contentious nature of the separation, the author colored the event as a small matter, a minor event handled sensibly by all parties, under authority of the Twelve Apostles. In order to hide Paul's role in the controversy, the author of Acts moved the event to the time before Paul. This had the further advantage of giving the appearance of a reconciliation, because the Acts of the Apostles shows Paul working closely with Jerusalem after the separation of Greek from Jew.

Did the schism happen in Jerusalem? Nicolaus is associated with Antioch in the Acts of the Apostles.[149] The confrontation with Paul over table fellowship happened at Antioch. There would be little need for a separate gentile church at Jerusalem, because few gentiles, if any, were permanent residents. Therefore, this council must have originated at Antioch rather than at Jerusalem. The Acts of the Apostles appears to indicate that the Hellenists were displaced from Jerusalem to Phoenicia, Cyprus, and Antioch in the persecution by Jews resulting in Stephen's death.[150] This could be another manipulation to hide the tensions between gentile and Jewish Christians; because associating the Hellenist council with Jerusalem at

---

[149] Acts 6:5.

[150] Acts 11:19.

an early time gives the appearance of close cooperation, whereas two separate capitals of two separate fellowships is obviously a schism.

A similar dissimulation is found in the idea that Paul had to flee from Jerusalem because of the desire of the "Hellenists" to kill him.[151] This is very unlikely, knowing Paul from his letters, because Paul's gospel was precisely that Greeks and Jews were equal members in the Church. Consequently, it would be extraordinary beyond imagination for the Hellenists to find any fault with him, much less a reason for violence. The Acts of the Apostles implies that the Hellenists hated Paul because he argued with them— but about what? No topic is given. The impression left by this account is that the Hellenists were irrational and intolerant. It also assumes, of course, that Paul was against their views, which are conveniently unstated. The fact that the argument is not stated shows that the importance of this episode was not any argument over a theological difference; rather the only purpose of the story was to align Paul with the Jewish Christians against the Greeks. This serves to counter the very charge that the Jewish Christian sources level at Paul, as we shall see— that Paul was not a Jew.

Of course, as we have already seen, Paul denies that he ever preached in Jerusalem at all.[152] Therefore, this story in the Acts of the Apostles of a dispute between Paul and the Hellenists was purely a concoction, a smokescreen intended to falsely separate Paul, momentarily, from the Hellenists and to associate him more closely with the Jewish Christians, thereby hiding the real disagreements between Paul and the authorities of Jerusalem, between Greeks and Jews. In the re-telling, Paul becomes a Church-unifying figure at odds with some Hellenists and some Jews, but in these disputes always on the side of Jerusalem and the authorities there.

---

[151] Acts 9:28-30.

[152] Gal. 1:22.

This was probably not, however, the only purpose of this story, because it also serves to cloud another important fact. Paul claimed to be independent of Jerusalem in the Letter to the Galatians. But the apostles of Jerusalem believed that they, by their authority, had sent Paul out. Sending Paul out would of course imply that they were superior, but Paul does not accept the superior authority of these "super-apostles." In this story about a dispute between Paul and the Hellenists, the author of the Acts of the Apostles manages to explain Paul leaving Jerusalem and yet to skirt the issue of who sent whom by having the "brothers" save Paul from those raving Hellenists who were attempting to kill him. So, Paul is taken to Caesarea and "sent out" to Cilicia at the behest, although not necessarily the command, of the "brothers." Of course, if the brothers are not Hellenists, then they are necessarily Jewish Christians. They save Paul's life, indicating strong bonds of love and fellowship, and send him out. Although the author uses the Greek word for sending out an apostle, implying a command and an investment of authority, the context softens this to permit a non-religious interpretation without actually disavowing the Christian interpretation. This ambiguity allows the reader to choose their own interpretation: that Paul was under the authority of Jerusalem or that he was independent of Jerusalem. The ambiguous result, consequently, would be acceptable to both Jewish Christians and to Paul's Greek disciples.

The Acts of the Apostles leaves the reader to make assumptions about the relationship of Paul to the Hellenists. Of course, Paul had an excellent relationship with the Greeks, and it would be impossible to know much about Paul and not to know that he was the "apostle to the gentiles." So it would hardly be necessary to show a reconciliation between Paul and his spiritual children. But if any question should arise, the author of the Acts of the Apostles handles that as well through an innocuous contradiction. Paul argues with the Hellenists and is sent out to Cilicia,[153] but later in the text we find out

---

[153] Acts 9:29-30.

that the Hellenists had already been scattered to Phoenicia, Cyprus, and Antioch before Paul was even a Christian.[154] Having Paul retire from Jerusalem to the same place as the Hellenists due to persecution, together with the common knowledge that Paul was the apostle to the gentiles, implies that Paul had much in common with the Hellenists and that he reconciled with them. Thus, Paul becomes a unifying figure in the Acts of the Apostles, uniting Jew and Greek, Judaizer and Hellenizer, circumcised and uncircumcised.

What then of Peter's vision in the Acts of the Apostles?[155] We see here yet another dissimulation. If Peter had received a revelation early on that made all gentiles ritually clean, then his refusal to eat with gentiles at Antioch, as described by Paul, truly was hypocrisy.[156] Just as significant is that the entire scene of the council at Jerusalem in Acts 15 is moot, Peter's speech is nonsensical, and the ruling of the Jerusalem council is unnecessary;[157] because the Holy Spirit had already revealed that there was no difference between Jew and gentile.

After the account of the council in Jerusalem, we arrive at the split between Barnabas and Paul previously discussed, where Paul is obstinate against John Mark. At every point that we can compare the Acts of the Apostles to Paul's letters and other sources, we find the story badly skewed or simply falsified to show that relations between the Jewish church and the gentile church were peaceful and cooperative and that Paul was a unifying figure rather than a dividing force. As we further examine Paul's letters, the rest of the New Testament, and other sources, we learn a vastly different story.

From the epistles, we can come to some obvious conclusions about Paul's journeys. Paul's entire career as a Christian lasted about fifteen

---

[154] Acts 11:19-20.

[155] Acts 10:9-16.

[156] Gal. 2:11-14.

[157] Acts 15:7-11.

years, and he visited Jerusalem as a Christian only briefly on three occasions. From the time he left Antioch until the time he died at Rome, about two years had passed. In that short time, Paul visited a great many communities, making an extraordinary impression— so great an impression that we still have copies of his letters today.

Because the letters show a short period of time, Paul's opposition was not various groups over a long period of time. Therefore, we must recognize that Paul's opposition were the same group from Antioch to Rome. This group was authoritative and determined, pursuing Paul and even anticipating his actions. Paul had to write letters because his opposition had some success. They had success mostly due to their obvious authority. It is clear that Peter, Barnabas, and others from James were among those who actively undermined his efforts.

[Handwritten notes:] 'gentile' = diaspora Israelite?
— surely this is false!

Lefont doesn't clarify or prove the statement that "gentiles where also Israelites but were not pure occ. li Jewish law". This is pretty clearly false. They may might not be practicing Jews (musa...) but they

When is a Gentile a Jew?

Time and change have clouded the original meaning of some of the most important words in the New Testament. Jews adhered to Mosaic law. Gentiles were also Israelites but those who were not pure according to Mosaic law. Paul addressed the gentiles as potential Christians because they were Diaspora Israelites. Who was a Jew, and who was not, constituted the central conflict between Paul and the Jewish Christians (Christian Jews).

We are now going to examine a critical set of categories, important to understanding Paul's situation and his epistles. These categories have been traditionally misunderstood, conflated, and confused: Jews, gentiles, believer, Christian, circumcised, and uncircumcised. In order to understand the conversion of the gentiles, we need to rethink some common misinterpretations— some which have been retained for nearly nineteen centuries.

    One common difficulty that creates misunderstanding in historical study is *anachronism*, applying the circumstances of one time to another time where the circumstances were actually different. Similar to anachronism, in the endeavor of historical research, is *ethnocentrism*, applying the values or beliefs of one's own culture to evaluate another culture. Often in historical research these errors of judgment are not obvious, so they demand a fair amount of diligence on the part of the researcher wanting to avoid them. And we modern folk are not alone in making errors: ancient scholars and even writers of our text sources sometimes made these same kinds of errors, even though they were less distant in time and place from the actual circumstances.

    One example of such an error is that modern Christians often imagine that Jews today are the same as the Jews named in the New

Testament. Certainly there is a connection between those Jews of the New Testament and those of today, but the connection is not at all as straightforward as most people believe. Over the intervening two thousand years, the religions and the peoples of Jesus' time have evolved into new forms, and I would submit that even in ancient times the matter was complicated. Jews, like Christians, have changed, even as they have tried to remain the same. In fact, the Jewish religion that we know today did not really begin until the final destruction of Jerusalem in 135 CE, and it took nearly a millennium before the Babylonian Talmud had finally codified the norm of Jewish interpretation of what Christian's call the "Old Testament." Furthermore, the development of Jewish thought did not end even then, and Jewish study and reinterpretation of the Torah continues to the present day, among many groups with different views.

In Jesus' day, who was a Jew and who was not was already a significant issue of contention, and there were several sects of differing ideology and practice. Flavius Josephus recognizes at least three sects: the Sadducees, the Pharisees, and the Essenes, the last whom modern scholars connect to the Dead Sea Scrolls and John the Baptist. Josephus also names the Zealots, but it is not clear that they were a sect with a unique philosophy or theology; Josephus probably is referring to a political faction formed by the more zealous members of one or more of the other groups. Also, not accepted by other Jews, Samaritans refused and were denied participation in the Temple at Jerusalem, maintaining their own altar upon Mount Gerizim. Philo Judaeus adds the Therapeutae, whom he relates to the Essenes.[158] Epiphanius of Salamis suggests that the Essenes are a sect of Samaritans, along with the Gorothenes, the Sebuaeans, and the Dositheans.[159] The Gospels also mention the Herodians[160] and especially the Nazarenes (various

---

[158] Philo, On the Contemplative Life, I.1.

[159] Epiphanius, *Panarion*, 10.1.

[160] Matt. 22:16; Mark 3:6; Mark 12:13.

spellings) from whom Jesus came;[161] the earliest Christians were apparently called Nazoraeans or Nazarenes.[162] Epiphanius also describes the Nasareans[163] and the Hemerobaptists (daily bathers),[164] who may have been identical or related with one or more of the aforementioned. We also know of the Gnostic sect, Mandeans, who revered John the Baptist but not Jesus, suggesting that they originated even before Jesus. Later, there were many other Gnostics claiming Jesus as their founder. Therefore, we can see that the situation was already complex even at the birth of Christianity.

So when ancient writers refer to "the Jews," which group do they mean, or do they mean all of them at once? Or perhaps they are not referring to any particular sect but exclude some? There are surprisingly numerous possible meanings and usages for the word "Jew," and the meanings changed over time:

1. "Jew" is a shortened form of "Judah," which itself is a shortening of the Hebrew name "Yehudah," who was one of twelve sons of Jacob-called-Israel.[165] According to the Bible, this is the original use of the name.
2. It can refer to any other person of the same name. In English it is usually rendered as "Judah." From the Greek derivation Ἰούδας, it is also the names "Judas" and "Jude."[166]

---

[161] Matt. 2:23, 26:71; Mark 1:24, 10:47, 14:67, 16:6; Luke 4:34, 18:37, 24:19; John 18:5, 18:7, 19:19; Acts 2:22, 3:6, 4:10, 6:14, 22:22, 26:9.

[162] Acts 24:5, 24:24.

[163] Epiphanius, *Panarion*, 18.1.

[164] Epiphanius, *Panarion*, 17.1.

[165] Gen. 29:35.

[166] Acts 1:16; Jude 1:1.

3. It can refer to all the descendents of Yehudah as a collective.[167]
4. It can refer to the existing tribe of the descendents of Yehudah at any particular time as a collective.[168]
5. It can refer to the household of David and his descendents.[169]
6. It can refer to the conglomerate of all political factions supporting David, including the tribe of Benjamin.[170]
7. It can refer to the rulers and officials of the United Kingdom of Israel.[171]
8. It can refer to the ruling caste at any time after David became king.[172]
9. It can refer to the land originally granted to Yehudah.[173]
10. It can refer to the land occupied mostly by the descendants of Yehudah.[174]
11. It can refer to the entire southern kingdom during the divided monarchy after the death of Solomon.[175]

---

[167] Gen. 49:10; Num. 33:7.

[168] Ex. 31:2; Num. 1:2; Josh. 11:21.

[169] 2 Kings 8:19.

[170] 2 Sam. 19:16.

[171] 2 Sam. 19:42.

[172] 2 Sam. 2:4.

[173] Num. 34:2; Deut. 34:2; Josh. 15:12; Judg. 1:16.

[174] Josh. 15:63.

[175] 1 Kings 1:35.

12. It can refer to the land controlled by the southern kingdom during the period of the divided monarchy.[176]
13. It can refer to the whole nation of Israel still remaining, including the priests, before the exile.[177]
14. It can refer to all those in Babylon during the Babylonian Exile.[178]
15. It can refer to all those returning after the Babylonian Exile.[179]
16. It can refer to the entire land of Israel excluding Samaria after the Babylonian Exile.[180]
17. It is equated with all of Israel after the Babylonian Exile.[181]
18. The region came to be called by the Greeks and Romans "Judea," Ἰουδαία. Therefore, a person from Judea could possibly be called a Jew by the Hellenes, regardless of culture, race, or religion.
19. Many Jews of the Diaspora assimilated to the societies in which they lived, and so would become indistinguishable from other Semitic or oriental non-Romans, who also assimilated. The Romans, and perhaps others, might have

---

[176] 1 Kings 12:23.

[177] Jer. 7:30.

[178] 2 Kings 25:21, Jer. 13:19.

[179] Jer. 7:2.

[180] Jer. 7:17, 9:11.

[181] Jer. 31:31.

23. A person who did not want to conform to Roman religious practice might call himself a Jew to escape legal action.
24. The Romans had difficulty early on distinguishing Christians from Jews, naming the former as the latter and, originally, there was little or no distinction.

This list of the possible shades of meaning is probably not complete, but it is sufficient to alert us to the difficulties inherent with language, especially with certain politically important words such as "Jew." We can never take for granted that we know what is meant, and we always must consider alternative possibilities, because the context may alter the understanding of the word. Furthermore, the misunderstanding can be used deliberately to achieve some political and rhetorical advantages. For example, as the story is told to us by Jewish sources, especially Flavius Josephus, the Samaritans first attempted to hinder the rebuilding of the temple after the Babylonian Exile, then later under Alexander they claimed to be Jews, trying receive the same dispensations and privileges that Jews received. So, as Flavius Josephus describes, sometimes Samaritans were Jews and sometimes not, depending upon political needs. Therefore, in addition to staying on guard against our own misinterpretation, we will also have to be on the lookout for political purpose on the part of the ancients as well.

In the earliest meaning of the word, from Genesis, Judah was one of the twelve patriarchs of Israel, whose descendants formed one of the twelve tribes. In the original use of the word, a Judahite or "Jew" was any of those descendants of that legendary patriarch. This means that, strictly speaking, the Levites and Benjaminites were not Jews, because they descended from Levi and Benjamin and not Judah. This also means that the priests could not be Jews, because they were supposed to be Levites, descended from Levi.

Nonetheless, the doctrine of hereditary castes underwent a transformation due to historical events and, beginning with the Assyrian deportation of the Northern Kingdom, Judah began to be identified with and to become synonymous with all the remnants of Israel. The process of identification seems to have been completed by the time of the return from the Babylonian Exile, perhaps by default, because the other tribes had been lost or incorporated into a people calling itself "Judah." It is clear from the book of Ezra, where the priestly circuits were filled by drawing lots, if the genealogical records ever existed outside of myth, those records had disappeared in the destruction of the Temple and the subsequent Babylonian Exile.

The story in Ezra created a precedent whereby any or even all the Israelite tribes could have been repopulated by drawing lots, with the faith that God would ensure that the result was good. The procedure is echoed in the Acts of the Apostles when the remaining eleven of the inner circle of apostles draw lots to replace Judas Iscariot, with the subsequent confirmation of the result by the Holy Spirit. By this procedure, following the precedent in Ezra, conversion to the Israelite religion, or rather readmittance into the people of Israel, thereby became possible, because anyone could be identified, by lots and prophecy, as a lost descendant of Abraham, Isaac, and Jacob. Thus, all the hereditary covenants would remain theoretically intact, at least as a matter of faith. There is even a possible Gospel reference to this, when Jesus says that God can raise up children of Abraham from "stones," stones being a common form of lots.[182]

Another example of the redefinition of a genealogical category through faith is found in the Dead Sea Scrolls, within the text known variously as the Zadokite Document, the Cairo (Geniza) Document, the Damascus Document, or the Damascus Rule. Even though the

---

[182] Matt. 3:9.

priesthood described in the Torah was an hereditary office granted to the Levites in perpetuity, this text redefines the priesthood:

> As God ordained for them by the hand of the Prophet Ezekiel, saying, *The Priests, the Levites, and the sons of Zadok who kept the charge of my sanctuary when the children of Israel strayed from me, they shall offer me fat and blood* (Ezek. xliv, 15). The *Priests* are the converts of Israel who departed from the land of Judah, and (the *Levites* are) those who joined them. The *sons of Zadok* are the elect of Israel, the men called by name who shall stand at the end of days.[183] (italics in Vermes.)

This kind of reinterpretation of a Biblical text through commentary is called a *midrash* or, among the authors of the Dead Sea Scrolls, a *pesher*. As the reader can see, besides moving the Biblical context forward in time, using it as a prophetic statement, the reinterpretation sometimes completely upends the traditional understanding of the text and of the meaning of a word. In this case, the priests and Levites are redefined as converts rather than genealogical descendants of priests and Levites.

If those most holy to God, the sons of Aaron, the sons of Levi, and the sons of Zadok can be arbitrarily redefined by faith, could not the same procedure change the understanding of "Judah"? Certainly, the Jewish historian Flavius Josephus uses "Jew" freely as a substitute for "Israelite." We might argue that Josephus tailored his writing for a Hellenist audience, who did not really know the difference; however, Josephus follows the traditional Biblical usage based upon tribal divisions until the Babylonian conquest of the lands of Judah and Benjamin. Thereafter, all Israelites, even the priests, he calls Jews without regard of tribal affiliation. Indeed, although Josephus provides

---

[183] Vermes. *The Dead Sea Scrolls in English.* Third Edition. 1990.

in his autobiography his own claim to priestly family of the very highest rank, he noticeably fails to claim Levitical descent. Instead, he states that the priestly office was a function of family honor. His avoidance of genealogy suggests strongly that he, and probably no priests, were able to prove a genealogical claim to the priesthood in the time of Jesus. And if the priests could not determine precisely their lineage, it is certain that neither could any other Israelite.

Yet, Saint Paul confidently claims to be of the tribe of Benjamin. I cannot explain with any certainty this discrepancy, but it is clear from the texts that Josephus could not assert his lineage and Paul did. I can suggest some possibilities. Perhaps, Josephus knew that his lineage did not correspond with the Biblical law for priests, that is, he knew he was not a Levite and so he avoided discussing his own genealogy in those terms. Assuming, however, for argument sake, that genealogical records existed, Josephus position as a "non-Levitical" priest would suggest that a large number of powerful priests had a similar problem, permitting them to override the law by the weight of their power. This might account for Josephus' forwardness in claiming priestly office without genealogical proof. Since Josephus was a Pharisee, it might be that many of the Pharisees were "non-Levitical" priests sustaining their office by the power of their faction, which by all accounts was the most powerful faction. This, however, seems to be an incomplete answer, because it would be difficult to explain why such a powerful faction would permit the continued existence of proof against their claim to power. Logic demands that if genealogical records had existed, a powerful "non-Levitical" priesthood would have destroyed them. So, it is really not reasonable to believe that useful genealogical records still existed and it is far more likely that, if such records ever existed, they were lost during the utter destruction of the Temple and Jerusalem by the Babylonians.

Therefore, if the existence of genealogical records is illogical, how else could Paul have claimed tribal membership? He could have learned from his parents, as they learned from their own parents, the information passing from generation to generation. This answer, at first, seems very plausible, but some historical facts argue against it.

After the Babylonian Exile, the position of the tribe of Benjamin was very lowly in relation to the tribe of Judah. Benjamin had been degraded enough before the Exile, despite that the first king of Israel was Saul, a Benjaminite. Benjamin had always been the smallest tribe, but Judges 20 and 21 describe how it was further cut down by the other Israelite tribes in a battle of retribution and how the Benjaminites were forced to take Jebusite wives. Of course, by comparison Judah was large and rich, having been the tribe of the dynastic king. Consequently, with the Exile and loss of their land, Benjaminites had little reason to insist on a distinction among their more numerous, rich, and powerful brethren, and we see that from the Bible that very little distinction is made between the tribes of Benjamin and Judah in scriptures written after the fall of Jerusalem. Only the Book of Nehemiah makes a point of distinguishing the Benjaminites, by means of a single list, referring to volunteers for repopulating the ruin of Jerusalem. For, although Ezra does use the formulaic "Judah and Benjamin," no division is made in the lists of the non-Levites. In fact none of the prophets, have much to say about the people of Benjamin. Even Jeremiah does not mention the sons of Benjamin, except for a single reference to their doom.

This also follows well with the evidence of Flavius Josephus, as discussed above, where "Jew" becomes synonymous with "Israelite." Josephus repeats a quote from Aristotle in his *Against Apion*, suggesting that Israelites are called "Jews," because they come from the land of Judea— a very reasonable explanation. We can easily see how the Babylonians, conquering the kingdom of Judah, would call all their captives "Judahites," that is, "Jews," without concern for tribal distinctions— a practice apparently adopted by the Jews themselves, probably because, away from the tribal lands, any difference between the tribes was irrelevant.

Ultimately, the question of tribal affiliation was dropped altogether; so, for example, we find in the Dead Sea Scrolls that the priesthood and the Levites are offices initially populated exclusively through faith. In the writings of Philo of Alexandria, the word "Jew" refers to the whole race of the Israelites from Abraham forward. Philo lived from about 20 BCE to 50 CE, which includes the time of Jesus Christ, and we find that his use of the Bible is almost wholly allegorical.

Therefore, it would be very unlikely for Paul's ancestors to maintain a tribal identity for so many generations, when the distinction was no longer relevant and offered only lower status than their Judahite brethren. What then is the best explanation of Paul's explicit affiliation with the tribe of Benjamin? It is almost certain that Paul or his family had acquired membership in the tribe of Benjamin through prophetic revelation of some kind. The restoration of the people of Israel was a theological concept of both Jewish and Christian eschatology. Jews were anticipating the arrival of the Messiah, and Christians were announcing the arrival. Probably, the identification of tribal membership was included as a secret part of the baptismal conversion ceremony, at which point the convert was welcomed into the elect people of God reconstituted— raising up children of Abraham from stones.

By the time of Paul, the demarcation of who was or was not a Judahite was no longer defined by heredity. Thus, Paul claims to be descended from Benjamin and yet to have left a life in "Judaism," ignoring the genealogical meaning of the word. He also did not define Judaism by culture, because Paul emphasizes his share in the same culture— having been circumcised, a zealot, and rising to high position. He spoke the same languages (Aramaic, Greek, and Hebrew) as educated Jews. Furthermore, as will become apparent from his letters, like Paul, some Jews believed in Christ but remained Jews, like those from James. Thus, even the belief in Christ was not the distinguishing feature between Paul and "the Jews."

The only difference between Paul the Christian and other Jews, and the Jewish Christians as well, was practice. Jews and Jewish-

Christians required circumcision and adherence to purity laws and a traditional interpretation of certain scriptures. Paul held that Christ had superseded all of the practices of Judaism, and he then reinterpreted scripture in order to justify the new practices instituted by Christ. It was the adherents to Judaism, both Christian and non-Christian, that Paul called "Jews."

At this moment, however, it seems prudent to briefly address an important point. A strange thing has been suggested by some writers, and the idea is intriguing. Did Paul create Christ in his own image? Did he define Christ by his own reinterpretation of scripture? The idea is preposterous. Every bit of evidence suggests that Paul fully expected Jewish Christians (or Christian Jews?) to agree with his theology— an expectation that would have been mad folly unless his theology came from Jesus Christ. Paul's letters reveal that he was shocked and pained that his gospel did not please his Jewish Christian brethren, indicating that he sincerely expected agreement. Therefore, he must have believed his gospel to be identical or at least compatible with the gospel of the Jewish Christians.

"Jew" is one of the most contentious words in history largely because of the Gospel of John, the Acts of the Apostles, and the name "Judas." The enemies of Jesus in the Gospel of John are categorically called "Jews," which is in contrast with the other three gospels of Matthew, Mark, and Luke (called *Synoptic Gospels* because they are so similar that they seem to represent a single point of view). In these gospels, Jesus' enemies are the scribes, the Pharisees, the Sadducees, the crowd, etc. but never the simple epithet, "the Jews." Quite simply, "the Jews" as an all-inclusive category meaning Israelites could not be the enemy of Christ to the authors of the Synoptic Gospels, because the believers that produced those gospels were themselves Jews.

"The Jews" in the Gospel of John and in the Acts of the Apostles are never defined. Both texts appear to refer to the groups emphasizing Mosaic purity, especially zealous adherents to "Judaism," who were the ruling elite and who opposed the teachings of Jesus and his claim to be the Messiah. The Acts of the Apostles, however, distinguishes them from the Jewish Christians and the Hellenists.

There were many people who identified themselves as "Jews," that is to say, "of Yehudah." Some were the priests and Pharisees ruling Israel and some of sectarian Judaism who wanted to be the ruling caste. For the most part, these factions opposed Jesus, because of his rejection of Pharisaic casuistry and their heaping burdens on the faithful. Later, as various kinds of Jews adopted Jesus Christ as their Messiah, each brought their own vision of Messianic Israel with them, so that the divisions and dissensions within Judaism soon became the divisions and dissensions within Christianity.

After seeing how problematic the word "Jew" is, it really should be no surprise to us that its complement, "gentile," is not an easy word either. The expression "gentile" is generally taken in modern language to mean the opposite of "Jew" or "Israelite." This is certainly accurate now, but the word rarely was used this way in the New Testament. The New Testament word is a translation of expressions in Greek, Hebrew, and Aramaic that mean "of the nations." In the Greek, the expressions are derived from ἔθνος, literally meaning "people," "multitude," or "nation." It does not literally mean "non-Jew," but it has acquired that connotation over the centuries through an habitual pattern of usage.

Since most of the Bible is written from the perspective of the nation of Israel, the plural of "the nations" came to signify "the *other* nations." As Jews spread far and wide, however, the expression came to refer metonymously to Jewish peoples living or "sojourning" *among the nations*, those *of the nations*, or those *from the nations*. This usage is found in the Old Testament, the New Testament, and the Talmudic writings. An example of this is *zab* (wolf, an unclean beast) in the Mishnah, used as a slur referring to a "gentile," who could become ritually clean given the proper procedures. No true alien or non-Israelite, however, could ever be ritually clean, a favored person of

God, anymore than a real wolf could be made into kosher lamb,[184] so the "gentile" must clearly refer to a non-resident Israelite who has been polluted by failure to maintain ritual purity or by contact with non-Jews. Note also that an Israelite is explicitly referred to by the Hebrew word for gentile, *goy*, in Isaiah 1:4 and Genesis 12:2. However, generally the references are obscured in the plural.

After the destruction of the Temple in 70 CE, it no longer was advantageous to emphasize that the covenants did not apply to ritually impure Israelites, because ritual purity through the Temple was no longer achievable and complete separation from the nations was not possible. It was no longer useful to recognize that "gentiles" had previously referred to Jews who lived among the aliens rather than to the aliens themselves. So, through habitual usage, the meaning shifted to signify quite specifically a non-Israelite person— the modern sense as we understand it today.

In his letters, Paul often said that he was the apostle *to the nations*, but he was not talking about evangelizing the heathens, as is the modern misunderstanding. In using the word for gentile, he was usually, but not always, talking about the Israelites of the Diaspora who lived *amidst the nations*. That is why all his arguments and proofs quote the Old Testament, assuming that his audience knew the text. And his arguments were convincing enough that his letters are still available to us today— because the Jewish scriptures were indeed known and venerated by the communities to whom he wrote. The people to whom Paul wrote may have been converts to Judaism or dispersed Israelites, but by faith they were the lost sheep of Israel living or sojourning among the foreign nations. This is especially clear in the Letter to the Romans, where Paul is preaching to a community that he had not yet even visited, much less evangelized. He does not use pagan myths or sophistry to make his case, but he tells the stories from the Old Testament. And this is effective! Later, I will show you further

---

[184]This is one probable meaning of the proverbial wolf in sheep's clothing, cautioning against gentile, uncircumcised Israelites wearing the garments of religious Jews.

When is a Gentile a Jew? 85

evidence that the congregation whom he names as the "Romans" were not only Jews but that they were already Christians.

Confusingly, Paul did (on three occasions) use the expressions that we render "gentiles" to refer to the foreign peoples directly, *contrasting* them with the Israelites of his communities.[185] This use of gentile to draw a contrast demonstrates positively that his followers were not pagans. He ordinarily used "gentile" to refer to Jewish sojourners when discussing his vocation as an apostle, referring to all the Israelites outside of the Holy Land, i.e. the Diaspora. Speaking directly of Jewish believers who are not ritually pure and not circumcised, he preferred the word "Hellene," translated as "Greek" or "the uncircumcision" as complementary opposites to "Jew" or "the circumcision."

Of course, Paul called himself a Jew and he taught his communities in the same manner that he would teach any Jew. Nonetheless, in quoting key scriptures and in talking about his communities in the aggregate, he did use "gentile" to denote his communities in the same manner that Jews understood the word. His followers were Israelites not practicing Judaism according to kosher standards, and they lived among alien nations; and kosher Jews in Judea saw them as different from themselves. The Gospel of John also shows a similar usage in John 7:35:

> Where is he about to go that we will not find him? He is not about to go to the Greek Diaspora and teach the Greeks?

Because of the repetition, it is easy to see that the question uses the word Greek to signify Jews who speak Greek, and it is not intended to suggest that Jesus would teach Jewish religion to aliens.

The Israelites *of the nations* did not practice ritual purity for the most part, because it was impractical when it was not outright

---

[185] 1 Thes. 4:5; 1 Cor. 5:1; 2 Cor. 11:26.

impossible. Even if they practiced as much as they could, the Israelites *of the nations* could never achieve sufficient ritual purity to be equal to their Judean brethren, because they did not have ready access to the Temple and because daily contact with heathens rendered them impure. They were effectively cut off from full status in their own religion; and, when they did attempt to practice, they faced prejudice and ostracism from Romans and Greeks. Many of the Diaspora were merchants and their most important business would be conducted in bath houses and gymnasia, where circumcision would be a constant reminder that they were different. Even if that were not the problem it certainly was, the proscriptions against idolatry would have effectively forced them to become vegetarians. Ritual purity would demand that they could not entertain foreigners, and they could not accept invitations either. They would have been cut off from business associates and their very livelihood.

Furthermore, when they did manage a pilgrimage to Jerusalem, in matters of purity they were not treated with much more respect than a true foreigner, because they were uncircumcised and contaminated. Without circumcision and purification rituals that required a week, strict Jews made little distinction between a Diaspora Israelite and a foreigner; for purposes of ritual purity and religious practice, they were all "gentiles." If they did achieve ritual purity, however, the gentile Jews were legally allowed the same rights as any Israelite; but that did not guarantee them full acceptance and social parity in reality. They were strangers in their own homeland:

> Wherefore recall that when you, the nations in flesh, those being called the uncircumcision by those being called circumcision in flesh hand-made [by human artifice], that you were at that time without Christ, having been alienated from the commonwealth of

Israel and strangers from the covenants of the promise,
hope not having and godless in the world.[186]

While most translations simplify this pericope calling the Gentiles just "aliens," the Greek here is more complex, and the translation above "having been alienated" is a literal phrasing of the word that Paul chose deliberately. Looking closely at the literal translation, we should note that Paul considers the Ephesians as those who had been alienated, which of course implies that they had once been participants in the commonwealth of Israel. His description also implies that they had been cut off through the rite of circumcision artificially, which also implies improperly, by those preaching the Jewish gospel.

On the other hand, the separation between Greek and Jew was not always unilateral. Greek Israelites enjoyed Hellenistic literature, philosophy, and culture. While they also appreciated the humanist tendencies of their own monotheist tradition, many were embarrassed by the barbaric practices of Mosaic law, which Justin Martyr called Jewish superstition.

Moreover, even among the adherents to the Torah and other writings, there was no consensus. Rabbis squabbled and disputed without end over every minuscule nuance of the law. Therefore, as long as Mosaic law continued to obtain, there would be division among Jews, even if all those Jews were Christian. The Messiah was expected to reunify Israel into one nation victorious over its enemies, but this could never happen while ritual purity and variances distinguished between good and bad Israelites. Jesus Christ, according to Paul's gospel, however, had instituted a new creation and a new freedom from the law of the Mosaic tradition, the law which was dividing Israel. Jesus Christ made Mosaic law obsolete.

Paul preached this version of the gospel of Jesus Christ without reservation. Having been a zealous Jew, he was well aware of the law

---

[186] Eph. 2:11-12..

and its demands. Having been a Greek, he knew that fulfilling the law was as impossible as it was unnecessary. He knew that never would men, not even the best men, be able to resolve the paradox of ancient law and modern people. Only God could resolve the paradox, through the freedom granted in Jesus Christ.

Sadducees, Pharisees, and Essenes

The main sects of Judaism were the Sadducees, Pharisees, and Essenes. Jesus and John the Baptist belonged to a sub-group of Essenes, the Nazoreans, the name of the believers in the early Church.

Continuing with the theme of identification, let us look at the divisions within Israel proper, that is to say, the divisions within the first century Jewish tradition. Calling them sects, Flavius Josephus names three major divisions of Judaism: Pharisees, Sadducees, and Essenes. He also mentions the militant Zealots, who agree in belief and practice with the Pharisees. Josephus estimated that the Essenes in monasteries were about four thousand in the late decade of the first century. The Sadducee and Pharisee priests might have been of comparable numbers but could not have been too many more. However, these were the elite religious professionals; the vast majority of Jews were "men of the land," living in country and city, about whom we can say very little with confidence.

Josephus did not mention those Essenes who did not live in communal monasteries, at least not clearly, but we know of their existence from Philo of Alexandria. It is likely that the Pharisees and Sadducees also had lay supporters, providing maintenance through tithes and sacrifices. As a Pharisee, Josephus does not count the Samaritans as a sect of Judaism.

All the sects shared reverence for the Torah, the first five books of the scriptures, believed to have been written by Moses. The Samaritans and the Sadducees limited their scriptures to the Torah only, but the Pharisees and Essenes also valued the prophets, the histories, and the literary books, with some valuing even other writings according to their personal predilections.

The Gospels of the New Testament also name other groups not discussed specifically by Josephus: the Nazareans, the Herodians, and the scribes. Epiphanius lists numerous Jewish and Samaritan sects, some of them virtually identical to one another in many ways with only minor differences— suggesting that Epiphanius chose to err on the side of creating distinctions rather than risk omitting some small variant. Because the scribes are often paired with the Pharisees in the Gospels, it seems prudent to see them as closely connected and in agreement with each other. Josephus states that Herod favored the Essenes, which probably indicates that the Herodians were a subgroup of the Essenes.

The Nazareans (or Nazoraeans) are a special and important case, because Jesus was himself called a Nazarean, and we know that Jewish Christians were called Nazareans and this is still reflected in the common Arabic word for Christians. Was John the Baptist also a Nazarean? John the Baptist also clearly stood in opposition to the Pharisees and Sadducees; therefore, with the evidence of the Dead Sea Scrolls, we can safely conclude that John the Baptist belonged to the Essene branch of Judaism. Because John baptized Jesus in the beginning of his ministry, we would expect that they belonged to the same sect. Therefore, logically Nazareans must have been a subgroup of the Essenes. Moreover, the Essenes may have been constituted from many or most of those lesser known Jewish sects named by Epiphanius, who appears to have made as many distinctions as possible in his work, *Panarion*.

It is both notable and significant that the whole New Testament does not mention the Essenes at all, in spite of their importance as one of the three major sects of Judaism. The reason is simple: the Essenes did not have to name themselves within their own writings, addressed to and written for themselves. In other words, the Essenes were the original Church and wrote the New Testament. The other sects and subgroups within the Gospels needed to be named precisely because those sects rejected and stood in opposition to Jesus, the Essenes, and the Church. Indeed, the Dead Sea Scrolls themselves do not name the Essenes, although these texts are nearly universally recognized now as Essene writings. Moreover, we might notice a pattern where labels are often coined by outsiders as a way of identifying other groups, emphasizing their differences.

The exact relationship between the Essenes as the major sect and the Nazareans as a subgroup is not clear, but perhaps the names provide us a clue. The most likely derivation of "Essene" is from "Jessean," from the scriptural allusion to the "root of Jesse." Jesse was the father of David and thus the ancestor of the dynasty and, of course, of the Messianic Son of David. Therefore, very likely, the Essenes were a sect of Messianic adventists. The derivation of "Nazarean" is also not clear, but Matthew 2:23 seems to quote Judges 13:5 referring to Samson as a Nazirite, one made holy to God through a special vow and ascetic practice.

The Mishnah, which became the basis of Talmudic scholarship, discusses the Nazirites in their holiness as equal in stature to priests; and this seems to be further borne out in the Mishnah by restricting Nazirites to a limited term, which was not originally the case with Samson, for example. Recognizing that the Mishnah was written later than Jesus, we might see this as a reaction to the Nazarean sect, especially Jesus and James, claiming priestly authority outside of the usual genealogical proofs. If so, then the Nazareans could have been the priestly caste within the Essene sect, which explains how Jesus could be both the Son of David of the tribe of Judah, yet with the authority of a priest as a Nazirite. We should remember that the Gospels make much of John the Baptist as an ascetic, and Flavius Josephus agrees; so, it seems plain that the baptizer of Jesus the Nazarean was himself a Nazirite.

If Nazarean, as the Gospel hints, derived from Nazirite, then it is more likely that the town Nazareth received its name from its inhabitants than vice versa. Also, the current location of Nazareth cannot be correct for two reasons: First of all, the archaeology does not support any settlement from the first century by the name of Nazareth in Galilee. Second, if John the Baptist was a Nazarean, then he likely lived in Nazareth also; but all of our sources say that he conducted his activities on the eastern bank of the Jordan River. Therefore, the location of ancient Nazareth was probably located in Transjordan with John the Baptist, in the same place that the Nazareans later retreated from Jerusalem, near Gerasa in Perea. Ironically, this could still have been described as "Galilee," because Transjordan was part of the tetrarchy of Herod Antipas.

The reason that we cannot pinpoint the location of Nazareth more precisely probably lies in the need for secrecy, since the Messianic movement was by its nature political and revolutionary, a threat to the established priesthoods of the Sadducees and the Pharisees and, of course, to the Romans. Later Christians, disavowing asceticism, preferred to see Jesus and his followers as named after the town, rather than seeing the town as named after their ascetic practices.

In addition to the Nazareans, Epiphanius also describes a group called the Nasareans. The difference in the pronunciation is probably not significant; but it is useful for us to distinguish between the two groups, because the Nasareans did not accept Jesus as the Messiah, or even as a good teacher. Instead, they revered John the Baptist, although not as the Messiah. This group has survived to the present day and call themselves "Mandeans," after the hut that they build for religious rituals. Their priests also call themselves "Nazoreans." Today, the surviving remnant lives in southern marshes and some cities of southern Iraq and Iran, where they are also called the Marsh Arabs. They are the last remaining ancient Gnostic sect, and their word for gnosis is *naṣirutha*, which is startling close to the sound of "Nazareth." The fact that they esteem John the Baptist to be a great teacher, earns them yet another name, "St. John Christians." Their traditions and texts are ancient and much of their tradition appears to derive from the time of John the Baptist and Jesus. If so, we can confirm that gnosticism dates at least from his time, although this idea is controversial still.

The texts revered by these Mandeans, Nazoreans, are not suspicious in the least. For the most part, the Nazoreans have kept their beliefs and texts to themselves, even secretively, and the texts were studied in the twentieth century only through the extraordinary anthropological work of Lady E.S. Drower. The translations and descriptions of Lady Drower do not emphasize any serious implications to Christianity, although she recognized some elements that she believed were adopted from Christians. Thankfully, she was apparently oblivious to the magnitude of her discoveries, because otherwise we could not trust them so well. Now, forty years after her death, we can plumb the wealth of her scholarship with confidence.

What we find are surprising facts that contribute to a new understanding of both Christianity and Judaism. First of all, the Mandeans seem to have revered the Old Testament enough to appropriate many names as demi-gods into their own scriptures. They show a tremendous influence of Judaism, and they had strong opinions about Jesus. They claimed that Jesus deceived people and "betrayed secret doctrines."[187] This suggests that Mandeans believed that Jesus' teachings were authentic but not meant for general distribution. Even more significantly, in their view, Jesus relaxed and ignored purification rules, which coincides well with the accounts about Jesus in the Gospels and in Paul's teachings. While there is much in their literature to distract us from the probable Christian and Jewish connections, we have to recognize that the Mandeans gained no advantage among their Persian and Arab rulers by being critical of Jesus nor by embracing John the Baptist. From this I would conclude that the Mandeans did migrate to the delta of the Tigris and Euphrates, as Lady Drower reports their tradition, from Israel near the Jordan River. Consequently, we should see their tradition as an important tributary of the Nazarean heritage.

While the Nazarean contributions to Judaism and Christianity deserve a book of their own, a couple of factors may have greatly influenced the dialectic between Saint Paul and the Jews: First, the

---

[187] E.S. Drower. The Mandaeans of Iraq and Iran: Their Cults, Customs, Magic, Legend, and Folklore. Oxford: Clarendon Press, 1937. Page 3.

modern Mandeans do not circumcise. In fact, they believe that a priest must be physically whole and physically perfect— an idea echoed at least theoretically in Jewish rabbinical traditions. If this was true in ancient times, and likely it was because such practices do not change easily, the sect of the Nazareans might not have been completely Jewish, according to the usual definitions of Judaism. In fact, their own traditions recall that their origin was in ancient Media, and their religion reflects more the Zoroastrian tradition than Judaism or Christianity. The purpose of the Nazareans in disguising themselves as Jews is understandable, although not respectable; they would have appeared as priests, and they would have enjoyed the same status. Matthew 2:1 speaks of magi, sometimes translated in English as "wise men," but the Greek word μαγοι is the word for Persian Zoroastrian priests.

This does not mean that Jesus and John the Baptist were not fully Jewish and circumcised. The Mandeans, like the ancient Essenes, have a strict taboo against nudity and baptize fully clothed. There would have been little opportunity for anyone to have verified whether they were circumcised or not, except in the secret ceremony for entering the priesthood where nudity is mandatory. To all outward appearances, the Nazareans would have been Jewish priests and monks, although Jesus and John would have certainly known their disguise.

Consequently, Saint Paul may have known that some highly placed within the Nazarean leadership were not circumcised, and this may have strengthened his resolve against the Jewish insistence on the purity laws. He might well have known, without disclosing the secret, that the demand was arbitrary and hypocritical.

We might speculate that if the Nazareans were foreign, then John the Baptist and Jesus would have known. This to me suggests that the Gospel may have been intended for all peoples from the very beginning, although at the early stages it was directed only to Israel. In this case, Paul and the Jewish Christians might well have been following a larger plan in their mission to the nations.

We should emphasize that outside of the Gospels, the label "Nazorean" is not used in the New Testament, and "Essene" is never used. The goal of Christians at that early point was not to found a separate new religion but to unify the Israelites under the Messiah, Jesus Christ. In that situation, distinguishing labels worked against unity rather than for it.

The Early Days of the Gospel

Reconstructing the narrative of Paul and the nature of his mission from his letters and other sources. Paul converts communities who were already prepared to receive the Gospel, from Damascus to Thessalonika. Paul faces opposition who are apostles and connected to earlier persecutions at Antioch and in Judea.

As a Jew, Paul zealously persecuted Christians. As a Christian, Paul was zealously persecuted. This is very curious, since in 2 Corinthians 10:10 Paul acknowledges that some find him unimpressive in appearance and demeanor. Yet, he often found himself at the center of controversy. If these troubles were not due to his demeanor, then they must have been due to his message.

From his letters, we know that Paul was very highly schooled and had achieved rank beyond his years in Judaism, as he himself stated. He was eloquent and often brilliant. He had many followers and notable compatriots. This could account for some of his confidence, but he indicates that his apostleship and his gospel were entirely based upon a personal revelation of Jesus Christ.

In 1 Corinthians 14, Paul discusses spiritual gifts, and his position is quite moderate and sober. He is not at all in favor of excesses in behavior nor in overemphasizing the importance of ecstasy. Yet, his own revelation has led him into many persecutions, even endangering his life.

Paul's faith in himself is as unquestionable as his faith in Jesus Christ, but it is difficult to understand how someone so sober can be so carried away by a single vision of any kind for fifteen years. I suspect that there is a great deal more to the strength of his faith than a brief revelation. From Paul's letters, we can account for about five years of his time as a Christian, and not much more. Even if we generously postulate an equal amount of time in the Aegean and in the regions of Syria and Cilicia and Cyprus, this still leaves about eight years unaccounted for. All of that time was spent in Arabia.

Perhaps even more significant than the great length of time that Paul spent in Arabia is the fact that his going there was a response to his revelation of Jesus Christ. He did not go to Jerusalem to confer with Jesus' apostles. He did not go to confer with Jewish authorities, presumably his superiors, in Jerusalem. Perhaps, he went to authorities in Damascus? That was the likely location of his revelation, since he says he later returned there. No, he says that he immediately went to Arabia— whatever he means by that. Because of the close relationship of the Jesus movement to John the Baptist, whose own followers supplied most of Jesus' disciples, a place connected to John the Baptist would be the most likely place to find an authority on Jesus Christ that was equal or even superior to the Twelve. That Paul did find such an authority is the only reasonable explanation for the fact that he returned so many years later, absolutely confident in his own gospel of Jesus Christ and in his qualifications to preach it, equal even to the Twelve.

Paul returned to Damascus to begin his missionary activity. After three years, he barely escaped with his life, being lowered in a basket from a window.[188] Why he returned to Damascus is not stated. Certainly, as this is the first place that we know that Paul preached, it seems likely that this was Paul's home base. He received a revelation and went off into Arabia, and then he returns to evangelize where he was already known as a good Jew of high rank. Paul probably enjoyed some authority there.

If Damascus was the origin of the Essenes, it might still have been the capital of the sect at the time of Paul, in which case Paul was highly placed in one of the three major Jewish sects, the Essenes. Paul is quite clear about calling himself a Pharisee, though. Yet, he also had nothing to do with Jerusalem. This dilemma can only be resolved if the

---

[188] Paul was at Damascus twice in his telling, but he does not state which time he had to escape by means of the basket. Tradition from Acts 9:25 puts this escape just before Jerusalem, and this seems the most logical.

Essenes considered themselves Pharisees, too. However, in the Dead Sea Scrolls, they also seem to have claimed to be Zadokites, "Sadducees" in English through Greek derivation.

Paul escapes and immediately goes to Jerusalem and he meets with Peter and James, the brother of the Lord— and no other apostles— for fifteen days. Why fifteen days? It is likely that Peter and James used the time to check on Paul's credentials as an apostle and to decide what to do with him. After all, this was apparently their first meeting and without introduction. With whom, though, did they check? Could it be that they simply evaluated Paul's behavior and understanding of the gospel? Probably, Peter did both, speaking with others who knew Paul for background on this stranger and evaluating the man directly. Paul would have spent a minimum of two Sabbaths in Jerusalem, and probably celebrated the Sabbaths with James and Peter. Clearly, Paul's credentials as an apostle were initially accepted, and he was sent out into the regions of Syria and Cilicia.

Or, rather, Paul agreed to begin his mission in those regions. Does it matter how we describe this moment, when Paul goes to Antioch? Whether Paul was sent, or whether he decided his own course, the fact is that he went to Syria and Cilicia and probably Cyprus and Pamphylia and Pisidia, etc. It did, however, matter to Peter, John, and James, saying, as we are about to see, that Paul was initially sent by them. And it mattered also to Paul, saying that he was not under Jerusalem's authority in his Letter to the Galatians.

Who was right? Probably both. Paul would have done whatever the Spirit moved him to do, regardless of the opinions of those in Jerusalem. On the other hand, he did tolerate, and he certainly knew, that they evaluated him and his credentials as a Nazarean. He did agree that Syria and Cilicia needed evangelizing. And, apparently, he did partner with Barnabas, who was already an apostle subordinate to them, which somewhat implies by association that Paul was subordinate as well. Perhaps, Peter and James thought Paul needed watching, but there is no outward indication of that. It was an early tradition to send out apostles in pairs, as the Gospels attest. So, Paul may have believed himself independent, but others could be forgiven for seeing him as subordinate.

So Paul and Barnabas went out into Syria and Cilicia to preach the gospel. They apparently had some initial success, but quickly they began to face strong opposition. Jews objected to the abrogation of Mosaic law. The equality and freedom of the gospel was intolerable for them, because following the purity prescriptions and proscriptions of the Torah, "the covenant," made the Jews uniquely special among the peoples of the Earth and concretized their favored position with God.

Judaism preached a development of covenants with God based upon the story told within the Bible. They saw each subsequent contact with God, from Adam until the current time, as resulting in new obligations and corresponding benefits in a series of contractual agreements, binding both upon the Jewish people and upon God. Almost always they saw these contractual agreements as cumulative, so that the covenant made with Abraham added to, rather than replaced, the covenant made with Noah and the covenants made with Adam. One could see in this a progression that increased the purity of the Jewish people, until the arrival of the Messiah, who arrived presumably because the necessary level of purity had been achieved.

Seen in this way, the Bible acting as a legal contract with God, one of the most basic obligations of the Jewish people, separating them from the rest of humanity as special to God, was circumcision. This was the first act that Abraham performed to dedicate himself and his descendants to the service of the One God. It was so fundamental to being a Jew that it was performed upon male infants on the eighth day of life. Ritually, it was the consecration of a male individual's membership into the people of Israel.

Paul and Barnabas were preaching that circumcision was unnecessary, and they were preaching this to those who believed themselves, and who wished to identify themselves as children of Abraham. Soon, according to the Acts of the Apostles, some persons arrived who identified themselves as coming from those in Jerusalem, who demanded that everyone be circumcised, becoming Jews, in order to comply with the law that Jesus Christ had superseded. The arrival of some claiming to be from Jerusalem in Acts corresponds well with Paul's comments in Galatians. Then Paul had another revelation, and he responded by visiting Peter, John, and James in Jerusalem.

What was the nature of this revelation? We must remember that Paul always considered himself equal to those in Jerusalem. In fact, he did not see their responsibility or his own as any different than any other apostle of Jesus Christ, and he believed that Peter, John, and James thought the same. On the other hand, he certainly noticed that there were different concerns and issues among the nations that did not apply to Judea. He saw that preaching uncircumcision in Judea would not promote the gospel, while preaching circumcision to the nations would also disadvantage the Gospel. His revelation seems to have been that it was not necessary to create an artificial obstacle to the Gospel by fighting over circumcision and uncircumcision; Jewish apostles could serve the needs of Judea, and Hellene apostles could serve those among the Greeks. He did not see this as dividing the Church but simply as dividing the labor of preaching the gospel. Eventually, as the Gospel of Jesus Christ took hold, the division between circumcision and uncircumcision would cease to matter, because all would be united in Christ. This may appear naive, but Paul was a man of faith. Furthermore, I suspect that he was right and things might have proceeded as Paul thought, if those leading in Jerusalem had been in agreement. But that did not happen.

According to Galatians, Paul, Barnabas, and Titus went to Jerusalem to speak to the leadership. Paul points out emphatically that Titus was not required to be circumcised. Some Jews, however, were present at the meeting, apparently monitoring the actions of the Jerusalem leadership. Paul says that they were spying, but there is no indication that Peter, James, and John objected to their presence. The order of Paul's statements in Galatians 2 suggests that Titus was forced by the Jews to leave, and this is supported by the fact that, when the leaders extend the hand of fellowship to Paul and Barnabas, Titus is not mentioned.

Paul's tone is bitterly sardonic over the exclusion of Titus. He chides those reputing to be pillars— Peter, John, and James— for accommodating the Jews. Remember that appeasement could easily be interpreted as a lack of faith in God or a lack of vocation from God. Yet, even so, he shakes hands believing that the meeting has ended successfully, and he was pleased by the agreement.

They did not actually have an agreement, however, although all parties thought they did at the time. Paul used the words "circumcised" and "uncircumcised" metaphorically to refer to ritually pure "Judeans" versus "those of the nations," who were not pure according to Mosaic law. Paul thought that the stipulation that he would remember the poor meant agreement that he had full and exclusive authority among the nations, which is exactly what he sought. Peter, John, and James did not understand the agreement in the same way. They understood the words "circumcised" and "uncircumcised" literally, and they fully intended to continue to proselytize *to the nations*, i.e. the gentiles, in the same way that they had before, circumcising them on conversion. They were pleased that, as they understood the agreement, Paul would not interfere with their converts. They would circumcise all that they could and leave the uncircumcised to Paul as lesser, impure believers.

This misunderstanding over the division of apostolic authority was itself a product of a more fundamental misunderstanding between Paul and the authorities in Jerusalem. The gospel of Peter, James, and John was different than that of Paul. Paul saw the gospel of Jesus Christ as a new covenant overturning the old completely. Consequently, the issues regarding ritual purity were no longer his concern. This is why he used the word "circumcision" in a metaphorical manner. The Jerusalem authorities, on the other hand, following Jewish tradition, saw the gospel of Jesus Christ, the New Covenant, as another addition to the list of covenants already listed in the Jewish scriptures, the final installment completing the Old Covenant. One way to express this is to say that, for the Jerusalem authorities, Christians were Jews first. They did not even consider the possibility that a person could be a Christian without being a Jew and without following the requisite purity practices of Mosaic law. This is why they understood Paul literally, and why they did not imagine that Paul expected them to refrain from circumcising those Jews among the nations.

Paul was no longer concerned with Mosaic purity and Peter was. Paul mistakenly believed that Peter agreed with his own understanding of the gospel. Peter, equally mistaken, thought that Paul was a good Jew, concerned with purity and the law. So, when Peter visited Antioch, he naturally accepted Paul's invitation to table with Christians, who claimed and appeared to be Jews. But Peter did not know that these Hellenist Jews were not ritually pure and not even circumcised. When Jewish Christians arrived from James, they found out, or they may have already known from previous visits, that those at table with Peter were not circumcised, ritually pure Jews. On being informed, Peter immediately cut off fellowship with the uncircumcised, because contact with them would be ritually polluting. This prompted Paul to openly accuse him of hypocrisy.

Peter must have felt confused and shocked by the turn of events, and he surely felt betrayed by Paul, having been tricked, from his point of view, into ritual uncleanness. We know certainly, however, that Paul felt betrayed, because we have his comments in Galatians. Paul wrongly believed that Peter was accommodating the Judaizers out of hypocrisy, because he thought that Peter shared with him the same understanding of the gospel. He also thought that Peter was reneging on their agreement by imposing Jewish purity customs. Peter, on the other hand, had not understood in their agreement that uncircumcised Christians, under Paul's tutelage, would remain permanently uncircumcised and thus permanently outside of the direct control of the Jerusalem authorities. Had Peter apprehended exactly what Paul's position was, he probably would have denounced Paul even more strongly than Paul was denouncing him.

What happened next is unclear. It seems unlikely that Peter openly condemned Paul personally, else Paul could not have hoped for reconciliation, but there can be no doubt that the community at Antioch drove him out with even greater vigor than Paul had felt at Damascus. Paul never again returns to Antioch, nor does he write to Antioch, much less express a desire to return. He shakes the dust from his feet. Yet, some who were at Antioch sided with Paul. Eusebius, the great Church father and historian, says that Luke came from Antioch. Timothy and Titus were with Paul at Antioch, and probably Silvanus too. Barnabas sided against Paul at Antioch. And some time later, Ignatius called Theophorus, bishop at Antioch, who faced persecution and like Paul traveled to Rome to be martyred, showed Pauline tendencies in his letters, suggesting that Paul did not fail completely at Antioch.

Did Paul know at this point that his gospel differed from that of Peter and James? The evidence in his letters about a doctrinal dispute is extraordinarily circumspect. His letters do show that he continued to hope and to actively work for reconciliation up until his final condemnation at Jerusalem. This explains the importance of the collection for the saints, because through it he could demonstrate his value and loyalty to the Church. It does not mean that Paul was naive about his chances, however.

After Paul suffered at Antioch, he headed across land towards Macedonia, intending to preach the gospel. What an amazing faith this man had! He is beaten by his fellows and driven out of the community that he had nurtured, and he immediately sets out by any means to preach elsewhere. His body failed en route, probably weakened by the castigation, and he laid up for a time in Galatia.[189] Since he was there anyway, he taught the gospel.

Paul stresses that he did not intend to preach the gospel there. Why not? This is peculiar and inexplicable and probably important. The fact that Paul avoids some towns indicates that there was something different in them from the towns in which he did preach. It may be that he did not wish to preach among circumcised Jews,

---

[189]Gal. 4:13-14.

thinking the agreement with Jerusalem still obtained. The Letter to the Galatians, however, indicates there was a fight over circumcision in this community, which implies that there were at least some who were uncircumcised and, therefore, under Paul's charge by any understanding. In any case, Paul did preach to the Galatians and he did well there; so well that he later expected them to contribute to his collection for the poor.[190]

Paul then continued on to Macedonia, skipping other vast areas and many towns, as though he were in a hurry. He entirely ignores Byzantium, though it was on his way. There is only one reasonable explanation for skipping all of these towns even including Byzantium: Paul did not believe that he had business there, which means that these towns and cities did not need evangelizing. Therefore, the people of those cities did not qualify for the gospel. Recognizing now that Paul did not preach to non-Israelites, he may have been unaware of Jewish communities in the towns that he skipped.

This is a very controversial conclusion, but it is inevitable. Modern Christian theology demands a view that Jesus Christ always intended to save the gentiles, meaning the non-Jews. This is understandable since nearly all Christians today are gentiles. Paul's language is often quoted to support this theology, but Paul's language assumes many things which for him were obvious facts, but which have long been forgotten. One of those facts was that Jesus Christ was the King of the Jews— not the Romans and not the Greeks nor any other gentile. When Paul refers to Greeks, he means Hellenist Jews. When he refers to Romans, he means Jews of Rome. And when he says gentile, he usually (but not always), means gentile Hebrew, i.e. a Hebrew living among the nations. Paul did not need to make this clear, because it was already clear to all of his followers and compatriots. They were Hebrews too, and they shared the same assumptions.

The theology that brings all peoples into a universal Church of Jesus Christ had not yet been invented. This is reflected in Matt. 10:5:

---

[190] 1 Cor. 16:1.

These twelve Jesus sent out with the following instructions: *"Go nowhere among the gentiles, and enter no town of the Samaritans, but go rather to the lost sheep of the house of Israel."*

If Jesus had always intended to open the gospel up to all peoples (and he may have), he certainly did not indicate it here; otherwise, he would not have excluded the Samaritans, who as followers of Moses had some claim upon the gospel already. The Samaritans were excluded here, because they were not considered Jews, although they worshiped according to the Torah. They were impure by race and heterodox practice. Of course, had Jesus said differently, the revelation to Peter found in Acts 10 would have been meaningless as well as unnecessary.

Paul was in the midst of a battle over circumcision and Jewish purity laws. This context is nonsensical if the mission had already been extended to the gentiles. Of what use would Jewish purity be to pagans, whose very ancestors made them impure? This is not to say that pagans could not be converted to Judaism. Jews could be "found" among all the nations of the Earth; but that is the point, they were unknown Israelites who were found, by means of the Holy Spirit, among the nations, the "lost sheep of Israel." Whether they had been pagans or not, at their conversion, they were Hebrews, descendants of Abraham, and subject to Israelite law— until Paul's revelation of Jesus Christ.

Paul was skipping towns without Jewish communities in them, but still that is not specific enough to explain his travel plans. Certainly, he knew that there was a Jewish community in Galatia. Certainly, there was a Jewish community in Byzantium? Yet, Paul purposefully intends to travel right by. It is clear that Paul has a definite itinerary; he knows where he wants to go. How? It could be that he had friends in those specific communities, but this could not explain his disregard for the great numbers of other Jewish communities in preaching the gospel. Paul has an itinerary, but it is not his own; it is God's. Paul shows not the slightest doubt in his next move, because he is not the driver. It cannot be proven, but it appears that Paul was visiting specific Jewish communities that were already prepared to accept his apostleship and the announcement of the Messiah. Paul was following a list of potential believers. This would also explain his staggering success in spreading the gospel.

In Macedonia, Paul, Timothy, and Silvanus had some opposition but won over the Philippians, who then supported them in Thessalonika. In Thessalonika, again there was opposition and success. From Corinth, Paul wrote his first letters to reassure the Thessalonians. Paul's style is the epitome of tact— so much so that it is often easy to overlook that he is writing in response to some trouble that requires his immediate attention. In 1 Thessalonians 1:6, he remembers to the Thessalonians the persecutions that they have already suffered. Then in 1:7-9 he tells them the good that came of their perseverance, and in 1:10 he mentions the reward to come. Clearly, Paul desires to reassure them that their suffering has not been for naught.

Paul immediately continues saying that his own work among them was not in vain. Then Paul reminds the Thessalonians that he and his companions have suffered along with them in the face of great opposition. Paul does not say who opposed them, although presumably the Thessalonians knew. We can guess, however, that Paul was not speaking of the Romans, who had no interest in Jewish theology. Paul was visiting very specific Jewish communities, synagogues. Roman officials might have been involved in the persecutions, but only at the request of those who cared, Jews who opposed the gospel, in the same way that Jesus was tried before Pilate at the behest of Jewish leaders.

This brings up an important question: To whom did Paul write his letters? To the synagogues or to the churches? When Paul shakes the dust off his feet, he leaves the whole community forever. He does not return for those few who might become believers. He did not even write them letters by our current knowledge. If some individuals believe strongly enough, those few leave their community to travel with him. As an example, after Paul left Syria and Cilicia, he did not return nor did he write to Antioch in spite of the fact that there continued to be some there who believed in his apostleship. On the other hand,

Timothy, Titus, Silvanus, and others left with Paul. The fact that Paul does not write to communities who have rejected him, with the notable exception of Galatians, shows that he does not expect a church to be there, needing his guidance.

On the other hand, the exception of Galatians shows that Paul saw the Jewish community there as a single entity. When Paul asks, "Who has bewitched you?" the failure there is a total failure: it is not that some are remaining Jews and some are not. The community is not split into Jews and Christians. To Paul, the community has fallen entirely.

Consequently, it seems that the Jewish community and the Christian church were one and the same congregation. This is why Paul talks about elders as established personages: because they were. And he speaks of bishops and deacons as institutional offices. This was not difficult to explain under the theory that Paul's missions took years and that his career spanned two decades; however, as we now know, Paul's missionary activity took only weeks in each location. The high level of organization is only explainable if the church was fundamentally formed already, *before Paul*.

Logically, it would seem that Paul was addressing synagogues. We should not, however, imagine synagogues as we know them today nor even from the Medieval period. At the time of Paul, rabbinical Judaism still would not exist for centuries to come. It is often assumed that Paul is using the word ἐκκλησία, church, to contrast with συναγωγή, synagogue— both words mean assemblage, gathering, congregation; however, it is just as likely, if not more so, that Paul is following the earlier usage and that "synagogue" supplanted "church." In any case, regardless of nomenclature, these communities did not have the fully-formed rites, practices, and liturgies of the modern synagogue. When Paul speaks of Judaism, he is referring to an institution that is a pre-Talmudic Judaism.

Had Paul only been addressing those whom he had converted, we could not expect him to face much opposition. Yet, his letters are full of references to opposition precisely because the groups he addressed were not homogenous. Paul addressed the synagogues as Christians because Christ has come and claimed all Israel as his own. Paul, as the messenger of Christ, does not ask the Jews and other children of Abraham to become Christian, because the king does not ask his subjects to obey. The king must be confident so that the subjects will have confidence in him— especially if the king is God, because God is never hesitant. In Paul's mind, which seems to have been in agreement with the other apostles and believers, Israelites are already Christians by virtue of being Israelites. The choice of the gospel is the decision to be loyal or to be disloyal to the king.

Therefore, when Paul converts a community, he converts the whole community as a unit. This often leaves some individual dissenters, but their choices are limited to finding a place in the new dynamic or to leave the community. If the dissenters can sway the majority, however, they can drive Paul out of their presence. If a single or a few individuals continue to disrupt the community, those few can be driven out or turned over to Satan, i.e. the Romans. The Romans, because of their love for order, seem to have made a practice of accommodating the ethnic leadership.

Most Jewish communities were small enough to meet in the houses of prominent persons. Later, Christians could also meet for training, support, and fellowship away from the synagogue. But in these early days the focus was still upon the unity of the Israelite people; the Christian religion as an entity separate from Israel had not even entered the minds of believers at this point.

However, need we say that the synagogue that Paul addressed was the entire Hebrew community? We do not need to assume so. There may even have been different kinds of synagogues, reflecting different kinds of communities. Paul is going to communities of a particular kind that obviously have some experience with apostles. In 1 Thessalonians 2, Paul explains why he did not claim his full rights as an apostle. How could the Thessalonians know how an apostle should behave beyond Paul's own example? Paul and his fellows, therefore, were not the only apostles to visit the Thessalonians.

One of the most important historical pericopes within the New Testament is 1 Thessalonians 1:14-16, because it says so much. First, Paul says that the brothers in Thessalonika became imitators of the churches of God in Judea in Christ Jesus. If we analyze this simple statement carefully, we can see the outline of extraordinary possibilities. Paul emphasizes that the churches are of God, but he specifies that they are also in Christ Jesus. This suggests the possibility that there are churches of God in Judea that are not in Christ Jesus. Notice that Paul does not speak about the suffering of individual Christians in Judea but about the suffering of the assemblies.

Paul says that the Thessalonians suffered in the same manner as the churches in Christ Jesus suffered from the Jews, who both killed Jesus and the prophets and chased out Paul. This statement is interesting for its rhetorical power, simultaneously associating Jesus with the known prophets and associating both with Paul. It also equates the sinful enemies of the prophets with the enemies of Jesus and the enemies of Paul.

Who were the enemies that attacked Paul at Thessalonika? Although Paul does not tell us of any great opposition or persecution at Athens, we know he was unsuccessful because he says that Satan blocked his returning to Thessalonika and because amidst his later activity he is silent about Athens. If his tribulations had been great, however, he would have said so, as he did in 1 Corinthians about Ephesus. How could he be blocked from returning to Thessalonika? I suggest, without more information, that he avoided returning to Thessalonika to avoid further confrontation with his enemies who were still there. Most likely, the enemies of Paul were the same group that had persecuted him at Antioch.

Paul goes on to say that his enemies do not please God and are contrary to all men by hindering Paul and his companions from speaking to the nations in order to save them. He says that they do this to always fill up their sins. Clearly, these are Paul's enemies, but they are also Christians because they do not speak against Christ. Paul then makes a very enigmatic and curious statement that God's wrath overtook them in the end. Most likely, some of Paul's enemies fell into great misfortune near Thessalonika. Paul's vituperation here reveals the depth of his passion against his enemies.

In 1 Thessalonians 3, Paul is revealing some weakness. He had concern and even doubts about the Thessalonians, suggesting that he had news or suspicion about trouble there. Verse 3:3 leaves open the possibility that Paul's difficulties in Athens may be connected to those facing the Thessalonians. From 3:4 it is clear that Paul knew what was coming against his mission and himself, so that he had prophesied about these persecutions when he was with the Thessalonians. Finally, in 3:5, Paul reveals his worry. This display of normal human emotion is surprising only because Paul so often shows a superhuman faith and confidence in his mission and its success. Any sign of doubt, no matter how trivial, seems out of character for him and for an apostle; although his frank vulnerability is endearing. Consequently, we must say that at this point he was surprised, not by the persecution which he had even prophesied, but by the vigor of his opposition.

Chapter 4:1-8 shows that, although Paul preached freedom in Christ, freedom did not mean immorality. Paul's enemies, as we will see, made accusations of immorality against him, but from his letters we know that Paul's rejection of the old purity laws did not signify an embracing of concupiscence. The mere fact that Paul had to address this means one or both of two things: Firstly, apparently some Thessalonians had misinterpreted Paul's message of freedom *from the law* as freedom *to sin*. Secondly, Paul's enemies were already blasting him for preaching sinfulness.

First Thessalonians 4:5 is the earliest example of Paul contrasting the community of believers with the "nations not knowing God," meaning the pagan non-Israelites. This contrast could not work if the Thessalonians considered themselves gentiles. Next, Paul reassures the Thessalonians that dying is not the end. Is there a more fundamental doctrine of Christianity? The fact that Paul must explain to the community that death is not the end shows that his initial evangelizing was extremely minimal.

On the other hand, Paul's description of the *Rapture*, in 1 Thesssalonians 4:13-18 is rich with detail and doctrine. Is Paul creating this doctrine right here out of whole cloth? This is extremely unlikely, because Paul's description is a complete vision that is still compatible with Christian doctrine today. Had Paul made up such a scene in the moment, we would expect that refinements would be needed. Paul, already under fire by authoritative persons, would not have given his opposition the chance to call him a false prophet by creating esoteric doctrines that were previously unknown, unvetted, and untested by time.

Therefore, we can be very sure that Paul is repeating here doctrine that was already known and accepted, at least by informed Messianic Jews. It was probably a secret doctrine, reserved for those proven faithful, but a doctrine well developed and tested nonetheless. We can see here, in this first of Christian writings, the advanced development of Christian theology even at this early date. It shows that "high" Christology already existed, possibly even predating Jesus Christ; for, the arrival of the Messiah would not be of much use if no one knew enough to recognize the event. The very purpose of the apocalyptic literature and preaching was to develop the expectation of salvation, and the purpose of the gospel of Jesus Christ was to fulfill those expectations.

In Chapter 5, Paul continues by reminding the Thessalonians of some of the things that he did preach to them. He taught them that "the day of the Lord will come like a thief in the night," a saying also found in the Gospels. The motif of a woman in labor in 5:3 is equivalent to Revelation 12:2. The theme of the children of light in 5:4-5 shows the influence of the Essenes as described in the Dead Sea Scrolls. The motifs of staying awake, being sober, and being drunk are found in other apocryphal Gnostic texts, and they also receive some mention in the Gospels, albeit in disguised fashion. Paul then gives the militant imagery a metaphorical treatment in 5:8. He ends, however, by repeating the assurance that the dead will live and the exhortation to support each other.

In conclusion, we can see that the purpose of the apocalyptic imagery is to reassure the hearer of the power and complete sovereignty of God in order to renew faith and hope in salvation. The imagery excites the mind to extremes where anything is possible and miracles are ordinary. We will see another level in the use of the apocalyptic genre in discussing the Revelation of John, where the apocalyptic imagery excites the mind to extremes of zealotry.

Next, Paul exhorts the Thessalonians to good Jewish behavior: Respect and love elders and each other. Care for, exhort, and support brethren. Do not repay evil for evil. Rejoice and pray and give thanks always. Do not quench the Spirit, by blaspheming and despising prophecies. Test everything and hold to the good while eschewing evil.

In this brief passage, Paul gives a remarkable summary of Jesus' commands to his followers and he underlines the Jewishness of Jesus Christ. Considering the letter as a whole, we must conclude that Paul has received a full education as a Jew and has proven competent as an apostle. Because Paul's authority comes to him through a revelation, Paul's opponents are limited in their attacks upon his claim to apostleship; because the one absolute commandment of Jesus Christ, the uniquely Christian commandment, was to not blaspheme the Spirit— he said that all other sins could be forgiven save this one.[191] Consequently, Paul's opponents could not simply deny his revelation outright, because they would risk their souls and their lives. They needed to prove that his revelation was a lie indirectly by discrediting Paul himself. They needed to show that Paul was flawed as an apostle, which means that he could not have been sent by Christ. Paul, on the other hand, showed through his knowledge, his behavior, and his preaching that his revelation, and therefore his apostleship, was truly

---

[191] Matt. 12:31-32; Mark 3:28-29.

valid. But, in spite of exhortations, he could not always control his converts, and he could not force a peace upon his enemies.

The Man of Lawlessness

With hindsight we can identify the Man of Lawlessness as James, the brother of the Lord, also known as James the Righteous or the Just. Paul states that the Day of the Lord has not come. James claimed to be the Messiah and was killed for it, but nonetheless created a dynastic succession among the Nazoreans. James' gospel of works countered Paul's gospel of faith.

The enemies of Paul hit Thessalonika with a hard and sustained persecution, and it was necessary for Paul to follow up with a second letter. He begins 2 Thessalonians by praising the church for steadfastness and faith under persecution. Paul says that the Thessalonians have proven that God's judgment of them was righteous. He then comforts them that their affliction will be counted against the persecutors at the revelation of Jesus, employing apocalyptic imagery to intensify the condemnation.

Paul's words here are very inflammatory, matching the crime, calling his enemies "the ones not knowing God" and "the ones not obeying the gospel of our Lord Jesus." These phrases are paired equally, intensifying his condemnation by repeating it poetically. This would mean that Paul views the two phrases as exactly equivalent, such that one who does not obey the gospel of Lord Jesus does not know God. He also is here applying the same language that he used to refer to pagans, equating his enemies with Roman and Greek aliens, inherently polluted. This corresponds well with his actions, treating communities who reject the gospel as anathema.

Paul's choice of the word "obeying" is also very telling, because he expects these Jews to obey.[192] Consequently, his phrasing likely indicates that he was speaking of Jewish Christians, who should know better. This explains the nature of his vehement passion, because it is an internal conflict, a family argument. Paul does not say who his enemies are, and in fact he never will say directly. Apparently, this was part of a code of behavior. Paul only names a couple of his enemies, after they were turned over to Satan, in 2 Timothy, which was a private letter and not meant for public consumption. Ancient Christians and Jews did use symbolic language to attack one another namelessly, as we will see not only in Paul's letters but in the rest of the New Testament and beyond.

Such is the case in 2 Thessalonians 2, where Paul talks upon the Man of Lawlessness. The Man of Lawlessness is an apocalyptic symbol similar to the "Spouter of Lies" or the "Wicked Priest" found in the Dead Sea Scrolls. While such symbols, which are called *eschatological*, purport to be prophetic revelations of the end times, we should not lose sight of the fact that for ancient Jews and Christians the end times were already present. Consequently, although the language is prophetic and phrased in future tense, it always refers to someone or something in the current time. And the reference was almost never complimentary; rather, an eschatological symbol was nearly always an invective of the very strongest ilk, used to associate someone or something with Satan. Such symbolic epithets were rhetorically more effective than cursing someone directly, not only for their poetry and their claimed prophetic authority, but because the hearer made the connection to the person or event in their own mind, giving the argument maximum credibility.

Understanding the rhetorical purposes of apocalyptic language, we should expect that the Man of Lawlessness is not an imaginary person but an existing person whom Paul is cursing. Moreover, he is

---

[192] Compare to 2 Peter 2:8, where Peter calls Israelites who reject the gospel of Jesus Christ disobedient.

not just being drawn off topic in an unrelated digression. His purposes here directly follow from his encouragement of the Thessalonians in the preceding section to withstand the persecution by Jewish Christians and from his heart-felt lament over their mistreatment. Paul is moved to anger over the injustice and the wickedness of his enemies, and the apocalyptic epithet "Man of Lawlessness" reflects that anger. We need to remember that the versification and the division of Paul's letters into chapters is a modern convenience for our study, and these conveniences do not reflect the original form of the letter. There was no change of topic. Paul is connecting the persecution of the Thessalonians to the eschatological symbol of the Man of Lawlessness, who represents the unnamed person Paul believes to be responsible.

Who was the Man of Lawlessness? We actually have enough information here to make an educated guess. Paul says that he is the one "setting himself against and raising himself up above every thing called 'god' or object of worship, so as to sit himself in the Temple of God, declaring himself to be God." There is one person, known to us from other sources, who matches this description— James, the brother of Jesus, also called James the Just.

Eusebius quotes Hegesippus, a church father who knew some disciples of the original apostles:

> James, the brother of the Lord, succeeded to the government of the Church in conjunction with the apostles. He has been called the Just by all from the time of our Savior to the present day; for there were many that bore the name of James. He was holy from his mother's womb; and he drank no wine nor strong drink, nor did he eat flesh. No razor came upon his head; he did not anoint himself with oil, and he did not use the bath. He alone was permitted to enter into the holy place; for he wore not woolen but linen garments. And he was in the habit of entering alone into the temple, and was frequently found upon his knees

begging forgiveness for the people, so that his knees became hard like those of a camel, in consequence of his constantly bending them in his worship of God, and asking forgiveness for the people.[193]

We know that only the high priest was permitted in the Holy of Holies and only once per year, wearing only linen garments. Consequently, Hegesippus appears to be describing that James arrogated the office of High Priest in a way that broke many associated traditions.

According to Flavius Josephus, James was stoned illegally by the Sanhedrin under the Roman-appointed High Priest Ananus.[194] Hegesippus blamed the Jews, scribes, and Pharisees in a more general statement. Such an open move was risky even for the high priest, remembering that the Romans retained the authority of capital punishment for themselves alone. This Ananus, son of the Ananus (Annias?), had only been high priest for a couple of months, and he could easily be deposed. Yet, he took unilateral action that he knew would anger the new prefect, Albinus, usurping his Roman authority. The risk only makes sense if the high priest saw James as a serious threat, i.e., a potential Messianic high priest, which would make his own position questionable at best. Of course, this is speculative, but it also makes a great deal of sense considering the evidence that we have.

The Mandean Gnostic literature says that Jesus and his brother set themselves upon Mount Sinai. The reference to Mount Sinai is probably a confusion of Mount Zion, Mount Horeb or Sinai, and Mount Moriah as one mountain. Mount Zion was the hilltop in Jerusalem of David's palace, and so it represents the kingship. Mount Moriah was the location of the Temple. And Mount Sinai was the mountain in the desert where the Israelites received the Law of God. Therefore, the

---

[193] Eusebius. *Ecclesiastical History*. Book II, Chapter 23.

[194] Flavius Josephus. *Antiquities of the Jews*. Book XX, Chapter 9.

confusion of these various symbols and the pairing of James with Jesus is highly suggestive that James did make Messianic claims.

Some apocryphal Jewish Christian texts also support the idea that James claimed authority over the entire Church. He was sometimes called "lord" and "bishop of bishops." The *Didache* was a very early collection of doctrine attributed to the "lord," which most likely refers to James. The Acts of the Apostles also reveals the prominence of James and his authority within the early Church. Furthermore, as we have discussed, Paul refers in Galatians to those coming from James in a negative light. The fact that James is sending anyone implies a high level of authority, and that these persons were so influential to impress even Peter probably indicates that James' authority was even superior to his own.

In Galatians, the real enemies of Paul at Antioch were those sent by James. Although Paul did confront Peter at Antioch, his complaint in Galatians was only that Peter had succumbed to the persons from James, thereby falling into hypocrisy. Paul does not place the blame for his persecution upon Peter, but he appears to consider Peter to be almost as much a victim of the false believers as himself. It is clear that he viewed those from James as the instigators, and, of course, naming them the way he does implicates James himself.

Paul is careful in Gal 1:19 not to call James an apostle directly, but he does not close off that possibility either. Paul's ambivalence suggests that James' role and authority at that time was not well defined to Paul at that point. Probably, James and Peter did not reveal their plans to him, since at that point Paul was an unknown entity himself. Had Paul known their intentions of seating James in authority as a Messiah, it is unlikely that he would have continued working with them, because Paul did not recognize any authority but Christ. On the other hand, his prophecies about James seem to suggest that he did find out about James' intentions, and his ambivalence could have been a strategic choice to delay confrontation.

In 1 Thessalonians 2:1-2, Paul is concerned that the Thessalonians will be fooled into believing that the Day of the Lord has already come. According to Jewish and Christian understanding, the "Day of the Lord" is Judgment Day—a violent period when the sinners will receive their deserved punishment and the elect will receive their reward. The Day of the Lord was to be the setting right of the world—the establishment of true and ultimate justice. It would not necessarily be a single day, although the violence surrounding the idea suggests great change occurring over a short period of time. Also, it was always depicted as coming suddenly, "like a thief in the night," and swiftness was definitely part of the understanding.

But the Day of the Lord was more than just final judgment, it is the establishment of the Kingdom of God in the literal sense—God's personal rule over the Earth and His people. For Jews, this meant that Yahweh would reside on Earth in his Holy of Holies and the Son of David would be king of Israel. For both Christians and Jews, this day would be the first day of an eternal age of peace and perfection, under God's infinite justice.

To Paul, the Day of the Lord had not come and would not come until Jesus Christ descended from Heaven riding upon the clouds.[195] Paul's vision, however, was one of many, and other visions of the Day of the Lord permitted other possible conclusions that could upend the gospel of Jesus. Suppose that Jesus Christ, although he was of the line of David, was not *the* Son of David. Perhaps, he was the Branch of Jesse who was prophesied to be the Messiah? In that case, Jesus himself was not the last and final king of Israel, but the precursor of an eternal Messianic dynasty. This would mean that the kingship would have been restored to the line of David, the Vine, rather than simply the embodiment of a single man. Of course, a dynasty means succession, and succession means family, and James was the brother of Jesus.

Now this would be pure speculation, except that we do have some evidence that this is exactly what was intended by James, Peter, and John. First of all, there is the fact that many sources show James

---

[195] 1 Thessalonians 4:16-17

as having been very prominent in the Church and in Judaism. He has been called in extra-Biblical texts bishop of Jerusalem, bishop of bishops, and lord of the Church. Furthermore, he was succeeded as bishop of Jerusalem by Simeon son of Clopas, who appears to have been a cousin of Jesus. Eusebius, in his Ecclesiastical History, also reported the words of Hegesippus saying that:

> But there still survived of the family of the Lord the grandsons of Jude, His brother after the flesh, as he was called. These they informed against, as being of the family of David; …[196]

Of course, the mere fact that people maintained knowledge of the lineage of Jesus' family hints that his family was considered royalty. Eusebius further attributes to Hegesippus the statement:

> And that when released they ruled the churches, inasmuch as they were both martyrs and of the Lord's family; and, when peace was established, remained alive until Trajan.[197]

Consequently, we have evidence that the family of Jesus was treated as a line of royal heirs. Of course, this means that the idea of inheriting the lordship of the Church by someone related to Jesus had some currency, a royal dynasty founded upon his name.

Paul, having discovered the ambition, anticipated that James would claim that the Day of the Lord had come. Paul prophesied that the Man of Lawlessness will claim to be above every so called God or object of worship because he knows that, in order to be the heir of

---

[196] Eusebius, *Ecclesiastical History*. Book III, Chapter 32.

[197] Eusebius, *Ecclesiastical History*. Book XXI, Chapter 20

Jesus, James would have to claim to be the Davidic king, i.e. the Messiah; he would have to claim to be Christ.

Although Paul was apparently concerned in 1 and 2 Thessalonians that his own name would become entangled in a "deception by Satan," James would not have purposely lied. Christians shared in God through Christ, and God never lies. Therefore, Christians could not lie and maintain any credibility. Even to unintentionally misstate the facts could invalidate one's authority as an apostle, because God is never wrong. To misstate the truth would show that God was not working in you; this is why Paul was so defensive about the accuracy of his own statements. Although James would not have deliberately lied, he may not have understood the degree to which he and Paul disagreed, however. Certainly, those he sent out would not necessarily know Paul's mind, and they could easily have mistaken Paul's mild manners for concurrence. But in 2 Thessalonians 2, Paul makes himself clear without having to make an open accusation against James, the advantage of couching his words in apocalyptic symbolism.

James, on the other hand, must have considered the situation differently, perhaps because of a revelation of his own. We do have indirect evidence that he claimed to be the Son of David, found in the one of the earliest Jewish Christian writings, the *Didache* (Teaching), so named because it purports to be the "teaching of the Lord through the twelve apostles to the nations." This text is reminiscent of some Dead Sea Scrolls in its uncompromising dualism. In the *Didache*, "the Lord" refers to James, and the statement that the teaching was "to the nations" or "to the gentiles" makes this certain. We should also note similarities between the Letter of James and the *Didache* in the concern with fulfilling the law, doing good works, and with an antagonism against wealth.

The *Didache* reads in its ninth paragraph:

> Now, about the Thanksgiving, thus you should give thanks— First about the cup: "We give thanks to you, our Father, for the Holy Vine of David, your servant,

which you made known to us through Jesus, your servant. To you the glory forever."[198]

The Greek word παῖς is best translated here twice as "servant" but it could also mean "child" and so, when referring to a male child, "son," especially in a religious context. However, the use of this word does not indicate a descendant heir. The Greek word that is closest to the English "son," υἱός, used throughout the Gospels in referring to Jesus and emphasizing a male child as an heir, is here not used and not intended. Notice the emphasis on the absolute equivalence of David and Jesus. Also, "Christ" is not attached to Jesus' name, as it is in most of the New Testament, excepting the Gospels.

Jesus is not himself described as the Holy Vine, but as the one through whom the Vine is revealed. The statement is ambiguous about whether Jesus or someone else is meant. The Vine, similar to the metaphorical "branch," would be a metaphor for the lineage of David. The only possible reason for removing the symbolic designation "Holy Vine" from Jesus, as he calls himself in the Gospel of John, would be to apply it to someone else— James and his successors.

In the above pericope, the *Didache* parallels and explains an otherwise incomprehensible statement found in the Gospels that the Messiah is *not* the Son of David:

> "How then does David in spirit call him 'Lord' saying: 'Said Lord to my Lord, "Sit on my right until I put your enemies underneath your feet"?' If then David calls him "Lord," how can he be his son?"[199]

The gospels of Matthew, Mark, and Luke are emphatic that Jesus is the Son of David, so the inclusion of Jesus' refuting that the Messiah is the

---

[198] *Didache* IX.1-2

[199] Matt. 22:44-45.

Son of David in the same texts is strange and contradictory. If we understand, however, that the gospels are formed from a collection of early traditions, then we can see that this refutation was from a separate tradition that aimed to open a path for the claim of James to be revealed as the Messianic king.[200]

The Acts of the Apostles 2:29-35 quotes Psalms 110:1 putting into Peter's mouth the argument that Jesus *was* the Son of David, attempting to use this psalm to support his statement. The argument, however, is nonsensical, because the conclusion does not follow from the psalm in the way it is used. It is very curious that the author of the Acts of the Apostles, who obviously knew the Gospel of Luke, chose to give this scripture a meaning opposing Luke. In any case, the contradiction suggests that the author of the Acts of the Apostles either did not know or opposed the gospel of James, which distanced Jesus from the exclusive claim to the kingship role of the Davidic Messiah. Acts 2:36 completes the repudiation of this doctrine by emphatically attributing both roles to Jesus, apocalyptic Messiah and king.

This dancing around the issue of who is the Messiah was obviously important politically. It was necessary for John the Baptist to declare that Jesus was the Messiah, and the Gospels are unanimous that he did so; even though, the Gospel of John is not so straightforward about it as the Synoptic Gospels. The followers of John the Baptist were numerous, they were the main body of believers at the start, and perhaps they had to be won over. From then on, however, the doctrine gets a bit muddled. Most of the outright declarations of Jesus as the Son of David come out of the voice of a demon, or a sick person—which implied someone possessed by a demon in Jesus' time. Or from Pilate, a Roman and by definition possessed of Satan. Or from Samaritans and prostitutes, by definition ritually unclean and

---

[200]The Gospel of John does not explicitly state that Jesus was the son of David. Jesus claims the titles Son of God and Son of Man. John labels him Lamb of God and later implies that Jesus is the Messiah. Nathaniel calls him the "Son of God, King of Israel," and this would imply Davidic descent to ancient Jews. John 7:40-43 shows the crowd debating the possibility, and the author seems to be having fun with the question, mocking the unbelief of the Jews. Jesus does say, however, that he is the Vine, and that makes the view of the evangelist absolutely certain. Or does it?

possessed. Such people, under the influence of demons, would be expected to lie, so the attestation that Jesus was the Son of David from them should be strongly suspected as false. This was apparently the point. The artifice of demon-witnesses left a lot of room for speculations, which certainly was the intention.

The canonical Gospels have something to say about succession as well, although nothing obvious about James. James, the brother of Jesus, did not figure prominently in a positive fashion in any of the canonical Gospels, although Simeon Cleopas, (or Clopas),[201] the successor to James, or possibly the father of this Simeon, does appear prominently in Luke 24, which probably supported the acceptance of Simeon Clopas as lord and bishop of Jerusalem. His traveling companion, potentially any of the disciples, is unnamed, which may be simply to keep Cleopas the focus of the event, but also permitting speculation about a further successor.

In a passage that is suspect because it contradicts Paul's treatment of all apostles as equals within the same letter, 1 Corinthians 15:3-11 states that Christ appeared first to Cephas (Peter), then to the "Twelve," then to more than 500 brothers and sisters at one time, then to James, and then to all the apostles, and last, "as to an abortion," to Paul. Even if the passage is inserted by an editor, it is an early and valuable witness that James was special. The fact that James appears on the list individually indicates that he was as important as Peter, although that James is named much later also suggests that Peter did have primacy for a while before James. The inclusion of James in the special appearances of the resurrected Jesus and the shift in doctrine shown by the *Didache* support that James did claim the kingship of Israel, forming a royal bloodline from the family of Jesus.

According to Hegesippus as quoted by Eusebius in his *Ecclesiastical History*, this bloodline was still important into the time of the Roman emperor Trajan:

---

[201] Perhaps, Simeon Cleopas is being directly referred to here, being referenced by only his family name.

> But there still survived of the family of the Lord the grandsons of Jude, His brother after the flesh, as he was called. These they informed against, as being of the family of David; and the "evocatus" brought them before Domitian Caesar. For he feared the coming of the Christ, as did also Herod. (Book III, Chapter 20)

Eusebius later paraphrased Hegesippus:

> And [he says] that after this Domitian in no way condemned them, but despised them as men of no account, let them go free, and by an injunction caused the persecution against the Church to cease. And that when released they ruled the churches, inasmuch as they were both martyrs and of the Lord's family; and when peace was established, remained alive until [the time of] Trajan. (Book III, Chapter 20)

The fact that they ruled the churches by virtue of being family of the Lord argues strongly that they formed a royal lineage. (The word "martyr" here does not necessarily refer to their deaths but to the original meaning of the Greek word, "witness.")

When Hegesippus said "they ruled the churches," he did not say that they ruled the whole Church, which would give a most desirable impression of complete unity. But, nor did he say that they ruled only the church in Jerusalem. He implies that their authority was widespread; but it could not have been universal or he would certainly have stated the fact, because it would have greatly supported his contention that the early Church was "virgin." Hegesippus also did not say "some" or "many" or "a number of," which he also easily could have done, to indicate that they individually ruled various churches. Therefore, it appears that the rule of the Lord's family was a general authority extending to many churches but not universally accepted by all churches.

Eusebius enumerated the first fifteen bishops of Jerusalem, all said to be of Hebrew origin:

> It will be right, then, since the bishops of the circumcision came to an end at that time, to give here a list of them from the first. The first, therefore, was James, the Lord's brother, as he was called; after him the second, Symeon; the third, Justus; Zacchaeus, the fourth; the fifth, Tobias; the sixth, Benjamin; John, the seventh; the eighth, Matthias; the ninth, Philip; the tenth, Seneca; the eleventh, Justus; Levi, the twelfth; Ephres, the thirteenth; the fourteenth, Joseph; last of all, the fifteenth, Judas. Such is the number of the bishops in the city of Jerusalem, from the apostles to the time of which we are now speaking. All of them were of the circumcision. (Book IV, Chapter 5)

Let us call to our attention that all of these were circumcised Hebrews; not a single uncircumcised person was bishop of Jerusalem until after the Second Jewish War of Bar Cochba in 138 CE. No uncircumcised Christians, nor even circumcised Greeks, qualified for this responsibility for over eighty years, in spite of the heavy turnover during the last forty years. Could it be that circumcision and Hebrew were prerequisites? It appears so. Notice also that neither Peter nor any of the Twelve held the honor of Bishop of Jerusalem.

We are, therefore, left with a nagging question: If James was the first Bishop of Jerusalem, the Bishop of Bishops, and ruler of the Church; then, why did Paul not submit to his authority? Or, why did the author of Acts not write it so? It may be a matter of timing. Paul's mission was mostly during the reign of Claudius 41-54 CE and Nero in 54-55 CE, as we shall see, but James was not killed at the Temple until 62 CE. So it appears that Paul understood what James was planning, but James did not actually become ruler of the Church until sometime later than Paul's mission.

Paul simply did not accept the spiritual validity of James' new gospel of the dynastic Messiah. By the time the Acts of the Apostles was written, the political and religious situation had changed, and the primacy of James was moot. Also, the timing of James ascension to power may have been known as later than Paul. I can only speculate that the enormous internal conflicts within the Church, generated by the installation of James, were a source of the embarrassment to the author of Acts.

From Epiphanius we can glean that many who were formerly Christians were later considered heretics:

> Now at that time all Christians alike were called Nazoraeans, although for a short time they were also called Jessaeans before the disciples began to be called Christians at Antioch.[202]

> In this alone do they differ from the Jews and the Christians: from the Jews in believing in Christ, and from the Christians in being bound still to the law, to circumcision and the Sabbath and the rest.[203]

> The Nazoraean sect exists in Beroea near Coele Syria, in the Decapolis near the region of Pella, . . . That is where the sect began, when all the disciples were living in Pella after they moved from Jerusalem, since Christ told them to leave Jerusalem and withdraw because it was about to be besieged. For this reason

---

[202] Epiphanius, Saint, Bishop of Constantia in Cyprus. [Panarion. English. Selections] *The Panarion of St. Epiphanius, Bishop of Salamis.* Trans. by Philip R. Amidon. New York: Oxford University Press, 1990. Page 90.

[203] Ibid. Page 93.

they settled in Peraea and there, as I said, they lived. This is where the Nazoraean sect began.[204]

"Nazoraeans" clearly equates to Nazarenes or Nazareans, the earliest name for believers in Jesus Christ. While Epiphanius does not state that they were the disciples themselves, it would stretch the imagination to propose that they could be anyone else. Look at their beliefs as Epiphanius describes them; they were Jewish Christians professing the same as James.

For Epiphanius in his time, it was enough that they followed Jewish law to be considered heretical. Those distinctions, however, were new to Paul and the earliest Church; Paul did not think that James was heretical for following Jewish law. Paul objected to the arrogation of Messiah-ship by James and his attempt to change the gospel of Jesus Christ.

One more point from Epiphanius, speaking of the Nazoraeans:

> But concerning Christ, I cannot say if they too, . . . regard him as a mere human being, or if they affirm what is true: that he was born of Mary through the Holy Spirit.[205]

Viewing Jesus as human would be natural for James, as the brother of Jesus; whereas Jesus Christ, on the other hand, had already been fused into a deity in Paul's theology; Christ could not be human. Jesus was human; Jesus Christ, definitely not.

At nearly the same moment that Paul was prophesying that James was the Man of Lawlessness, James was earning his famous eponym, the Righteous or Just One. This was not simply a courtesy title in ancient

---

[204] Ibid. Page 93.

[205] Ibid. Page 93.

Israel; there was only one righteous man in the whole of the world, who was the high priest of Israel. By his virtue, he was permitted into the very presence of God, the Holy of Holies of the Temple, once per year, to ask forgiveness for the sins of Israel. A few high priests earned the appellation for eternity, like Simeon the Righteous; but at any one time there was only one high priest, one known to all Jews as the Righteous One.

From Hegesippus' description, James had achieved sufficient status that many influential rabbis and priests believed that he was, or at least he could be, a priestly Messiah. He had gained access to the most sacred space, the Holy of Holies, which was empty, since the Ark had long been lost. He prayed regularly for the sins of the people in a manner that not only supplanted but superseded the high priest.

James was doing what Jesus had not achieved; he was taking political power. Flavius Josephus did not make the connection in his Wars of the Jews, perhaps because James was so peaceful a figure, but he described a time of anarchy leading up to the Jewish Revolt. False prophets were rising up, and Romans were putting down rebellions of up to thirty thousand fanatics. The Sicarii were assassinating enemies in the streets. James was praying in the Temple and behaving as the high priest. Nazareans with James backing were announcing that the Messiah has already come in Jesus Christ. There was violence in the churches and synagogues, and gentile Christians were persecuted. James was himself killed at the Temple by the highest Jewish authorities in 62 CE. Rome burned and Christians were blamed in 64 CE. The first Jewish revolt began in 66 CE.

Now add in what Paul has told us so far: James was setting himself above all other authority. People from James were instigating persecutions within the churches outside Judea. Many churches inside Judea had already suffered in similar fashion. Apostles were being beaten and persecuted, and the persecutors insisted on adherence to Jewish law.

James

In reading the Epistle of James addressed to the twelve tribes in the Diaspora, we see only the most pious and reasonable of Jews and the most devout of Christians. On only three points of this letter can we see a difference with Paul: James showed open hostility towards the rich, he insisted that faith alone will not save, and required the strictest adherence to the law. As we will see, the latter points were very much opposed to Paul's gospel of salvation through faith. Although Paul was not opposed to good works and he did preach right conduct, he viewed them as the result and measure of faith and not as the means of salvation. It was also a key point to the conflict because, good works could also be interpreted as adherence to tradition, law, and ritual practice in addition to kindness and charity. If faith alone were sufficient, adherence to the Jewish law would not have importance; this was Paul's view. On the other hand, if good works were necessary to validate faith, then the Law of God as a guide for what was good was of paramount importance, and neglect for the precepts of Jewish law would negate salvation and invalidate faith; this was James' view.

James was an ascetic, an Ebionite, which was a sectarian group whose name means "poor ones." He led this movement that promoted asceticism in the Church, and the movement was widespread and influential in the beginning. The later orthodox Church, however, rejected asceticism as a potentially heretical movement, possibly because of its coincidence with some heresies related to Ebionism.

The Epistle of James almost was not included in the New Testament because of opposition from some later Church fathers to its Jewishness. We should notice, however, that unlike most of the letters of the New Testament, the Epistle of James has no goodbye salutations and benedictions. The letter may have been truncated and we can never know what was cut out. One pericope of the letter, James 2:10, sums up the extremely radical nature of his gospel and his opposition to Paul:

> For whoever may keep all the law but stumble in one [thing], he has become a transgressor of everything.

The theology of James was doomed from the start. The prohibitions of Jewish law forced everyone outside the land of Israel itself to be vegetarian. Remember that the Talmudic scholarship was still in its infancy: it would be over one hundred years before the Mishnah would be complete. Rabbinical interpretations to Jewish law had not yet made kosher existence without the Temple a practical reality in the first century of our era. Circumcision and purity laws would have set apart Jewish Christians from other citizens, limiting business opportunity. Pragmatically, we must realize that a large number of Jews would never convert under these conditions, and many did not. Many would not accept a second Messiah and a Messianic rule that did not include the perfection of the world.

Yet, with the obvious political impossibilities of the Jewish Christian gospel, we must know that without the evangelizing, organizing, and regulating provided by the Jewish Christians, the teachings of Jesus and of Paul would have been lost and the Church could never have existed. It was James and the super-apostles who established norms and enforced them, creating a strong orthodoxy. They built a hierarchy subject to Jerusalem that could maintain order across national boundaries. While the proto-orthodox gentiles maintained their separation, the desire for eventual reunification meant a continuing influence from the Jewish Christians. They sustained a focus, which was a goal of apocalyptic world domination that has served the Church well for millennia. Orthodox Christianity came to emphasize both faith and works equally.

Fighting with Beasts

Success in Corinth became troubled, prompting a letter from Ephesus, where Paul battled with wild beasts. The Corinthians had issues over idolatry, fornication, circumcision, and forming factions. Paul's opposition are other apostles and the brothers of the Lord and Cephas (Peter). Other New Testament letters from Peter, Jude, John, and a Revelation of John. The heresy of the nonhuman Christ, Doceticism. The number of the beast identified the risen Jesus and the Antichrist, and Paul was the second beast.

Because the apostle Paul did not refer to difficulties in his original visit, as he discusses in the two letters to the Thessalonians, Paul had apparently converted the Corinthians and the other Achaians without serious opposition or conflict. He may have been as successful in Nicopolis of Epirus, where he planned to meet Titus after Jerusalem.[206]

The peace, however, did not last, because the Corinthians out of their own weakness continued or fell into human vices. They quarreled, forming factions. More seriously, they took Paul's teaching of freedom in Christ literally and to its logical immoral end, shocking Paul, who had not foreseen this outcome. His rhetorical eloquence was amazing, however, as he deftly argued for both freedom and for moral restraint. The elegance of his arguments was a product of his sobriety and his absolute faith in the Gospel of Jesus Christ.

Paul also had to address basic questions of practice including marriage, sex, chastity, idolatrous meats, and especially circumcision. His policy on circumcision was that it does not matter; it was not a matter of shame nor of pride.

---

[206] Tit. 3:12.

Paul also addressed behavior in spiritual meetings: head coverings for women and comportment towards the Eucharist and spiritual gifts. Then he gave a homily refuting an unusual doctrine. Paul said that some had claimed there is no general resurrection of the dead— a belief peculiar to the Sadducees— and he employed their faith in Jesus Christ to refute this idea.

Surprisingly, in 1 Corinthians 9, Paul defended his apostleship. He argued for his rights to claim support and a sister-wife. Here Paul mentioned "other apostles and the brothers of the Lord and Cephas" in order to make the point that he was their equals. The fact that Paul was making the argument indicated there was some question, although not necessarily from James or Cephas themselves. The argument depended upon an assumption that the Corinthians did recognize general parity between Paul and these others.

Barnabas was mentioned as being treated similarly to Paul at Corinth. Yet, nowhere in the letter is there an indication that Paul and Barnabas were working together. Paul never sent greetings to or from Barnabas. When Paul wrote the Thessalonians from Achaia, he never mentioned Barnabas. In his descriptions of his missionary activity, he refers only to Silvanus, Timothy, and Titus. This suggests that Barnabas was visiting Corinth in opposition to Paul and that he was part of the reason that the Corinthians were stirred up, although Paul does not make any specific complaint against the apostle. Rather, Paul argued that the Corinthians should treat Barnabas in a manner befitting any apostle; however, this does not mean that Barnabas was not in opposition to Paul. Other evidence also suggests opposition by Barnabas. The Acts of the Apostles indicates that Barnabas was not working with Paul, because it has Barnabas separating permanently from him in Antioch.[207] This agrees with Paul's epistles, because he too discontinued his association with Barnabas after Antioch. Barnabas was notably not included in the greetings of 1 Corinthians. Therefore, the generous attitude of Paul was simply an example of Christian love

---

[207] Acts 15:39.

of one's enemies, an example which was all the more impressive because of the severity of the differences.

Paul also mentioned Barnabas later in the Colossians 4:10, where he appears to have told something that he did not wish to state outright. He started out as warning the congregation against Barnabas, but then there was an adjustment. We cannot know if this was Paul adjusting his own words, because what he just stated sounded harsh and he wanted to avoid a misunderstanding; or possibly, it was a later scribe who added the correction to avoid the evidence of conflict. Either way, the passage still rings negative about the relationship of Paul and Barnabas, and this is intensified when we remember that Paul was in prison and dying, after a trial in Jerusalem where Barnabas would have figured prominently against him.

We have an existing letter from Barnabas. Some of the fathers of the Church had no doubt about its author being Barnabas, even if critical of the letter, and it received honor in some of the earliest collections of the New Testament. Because of a mention of the destruction of the Temple, it is generally dated as sometime between 70 CE and 137 CE; but it is more likely that the letter was referring to the first destruction of the Temple by the Babylonians over 600 years prior in 587 BCE. In this case, the letter probably dated before the second destruction in 70 BCE but after Paul's death in late 55 CE.

This letter includes a preaching of the Two Ways similar to the *Didache*, without mention of the other ideas in that text, and so was probably written after James' death. It is interesting that the version in the *Epistle of Barnabas* is not exactly the duplicate of the exposition of the Two Ways found in the *Didache*. This part of the letter appears to be an addition after the main body of the letter was completed suggesting the possibility that this part was as an afterthought or that a later scribe added this part to salvage the doctrine of the Two Ways for gentile Christians.

All things considered, the letter as a whole probably is authentically from the apostle Barnabas. This creates another problem, however, because from Paul's letters we would believe that Barnabas is supporting the literal imposition of Mosaic law. Yet, the Epistle of Barnabas takes an entirely different approach, insisting on the allegorical interpretation of key requirements of Mosaic law. In fact, this position is somewhat closer to Paul's own preaching, especially in the matter of circumcision being metaphorical rather than literal. I think that this letter shows a transformation of doctrine later than the events in Paul's letters, adjusting Paul's position.

Paul's teaching obviously had tremendous effect for the short time that he proselytized. Greek Christians were naturally inclined to insist on the validity of his revelation. It appears from the transformation of doctrine shown in the Epistle of Barnabas that this quick and wide acceptance of Paul's teaching tipped the scales against the Judaizers, and Paul's doctrine won out among gentiles soon after his death. But not entirely. The doctrine of the Epistle of Barnabas has much in common with the writings of Philo Judaeus of Alexandria, with his extremely allegorical interpretations of tradition. It accepts the whole of the Old Testament and law, but as a prophetic writing that must be interpreted symbolically. This contrasts with Paul's position that Mosaic law was categorically dead, having been replaced by Christ; so we can see the transformation of Barnabas' position as a compromise revelation, aimed at re-unifying the Greek and Jewish churches into one. However, the compromise does not appear to have been successful.

Peter

First Peter was addressed to Galatia and surrounding areas of Asia Minor. Peter is with the church in "Babylon," which is a symbolic reference to the city of Rome. Silvanus is mentioned, indicating that it was written sometime after 1 and 2 Thessalonians, when Sylvanus was at Corinth with Paul. The fact that none of Paul's letters mentions Silvanus working with Paul after Corinth makes clear that he joined Paul's opponents shortly after that time.

These facts may permit some speculation that Silvanus went with Paul to Illyricum after Corinth but split with Paul there to join

Peter. Paul, discovering that Peter was in Rome, doubled back toward Corinth to avoid a premature confrontation. It is unknown, of course, but seems likely, that Paul sent Silvanus to Peter with some message or as a representative, perhaps hoping to gain more information about Peter's activities. Silvanus, however, was apparently swayed by Peter and sided with him; thus, Peter makes a point of saying that Silvanus is a faithful brother, indicating to the churches that Silvanus is no longer with Paul. The fact that Silvanus could so easily switch sides indicates that there were not great differences between Peter and Paul in faith or practice.

A reference to gentiles is not completely clear but probably is referring to non-Israelites, because it is closely followed by an exhortation to obey the emperor and other non-Israelite authorities. There is no obvious reference to Paul, although the mention of suffering and of the devil prowling as a roaring lion is suggestive.

First Letter of Peter is a letter of general exhortations and of no specific issues, yet it targets some very specific communities. Probably its main purpose was to prove the authority of its bearers. The stone and rock scriptural references prod the hearer's memory that Peter means "rock" from the Greek translated from the Aramaic *Kepha*, thus reminding them of whence he gained his authority. It may be that Paul's Letter to the Galatians was in response to the upheaval caused by emissaries carrying 1 Peter.

In 2 Corinthians 3:1, Paul mentions letters of recommendation carried by his opponents, who included Barnabas. This may well have been the Epistle of James and 1 Peter. Clearly, 2 Peter expected his hearers to know his first letter, suggesting a short interim.[208]

Second Peter is not addressed to any one congregation. It is exhortatory, but it also includes some pointed references to false prophets. Peter mentions his opponents' "cleverly devised myths" and counters that "we" were eyewitnesses of the Lord Jesus Christ. In

---

[208] 2 Peter 3:1.

chapter two, he discusses the false prophets.[209] The contrasting of eyewitnesses to the false prophets is a clear and strong condemnation of Paul and his followers. Second Peter 2:18 shows that he is addressing new churches. The emphasis on licentiousness is reminiscent of what Paul describes in 1 Corinthians, so it seems likely that Peter had Corinth in mind when he wrote this letter. Peter's reference to scoffers in 3:3 is an exciting connection to the apocalyptic "Scoffer" known from the Dead Sea Scrolls.

In the conclusion of 2 Peter 3:15-16, there is a direct mention of Paul; however, this is, obvious to us now, a scribal attempt to disguise the animosity between the two great saints. It would not have been possible for Peter to call Paul's letters equal to other scriptures at that time. Rather, a pious scribe was embarrassed that Peter failed to mention Paul and his letters to communities that Paul had famously evangelized; the insertion appears to be a deliberate attempt to diminish the appearance of conflict between Peter and Paul.

There is no obvious difference from the letters of Peter and Paul distinguishing the faith and practice of Paul from the faith and practice of Peter. At least in his letters, Peter is not demanding anything that Paul did not. However, Peter's reference to "myths" and "nonsense" suggests there were some differences. Was this a reference to the "Man of Lawlessness" motif from 2 Thessalonians? Or could this be an allusion to the description of Jesus Christ coming from heaven in 1 Thessalonians? Recall that Silvanus was Paul's scribe for both letters to the Thessalonians, and he was Peter's scribe, at least in 1 Peter, and probably for 2 Peter as well.

It is also interesting that no direct mention is made of circumcision, although we know from Paul that this was the main issue between him and Peter. Still, we need to recognize that circumcision was thought to have an effect on sexual morality, so the railings against licentiousness do support the argument for circumcision, albeit indirectly.

---

[209] 2 Peter 1:16.

More problematic is that Peter barely mentions the law or commandments, which presumably would accompany adherence to the previous covenants. Perhaps, it was not necessary to mention the importance of the law to Jews. In any case, adherence to the commandments is exactly what was meant by Jews living in "godliness" and "holiness" and avoiding "the error of the lawless."

Returning to the claim of being an eyewitness, it is strange and startling that this is the only basis for Peter's superior authority. It is interesting because of what is missing. There is no claim of secret knowledge nor even superior understanding gained through private teaching, only a claim of having witnessed some miraculous events. There is no claim of the bestowal of authority, although probably Peter's name itself might evoke the story of its gifting. So, perhaps the lack of boasting is itself evidence of his indisputable authority. This, however, leads back to the puzzlement of his mentioning that he was an eyewitness. It does not appear that Peter had any greater claim to the blessings of the Holy Spirit than any other apostle, because, if he was set apart by a revelation, this would have been the moment to remind his hearers. The emphasis on being a material eyewitness is certainly a counterpoint against Paul, whose revelation was spiritual and not physical.

Jude

Closely related to the Second Epistle of Peter was the little letter from Jude. Jude (Judas) says that he is the brother of James. Because he does not need to elaborate on which James, Jude almost certainly is the brother of Jesus also, but we should notice that he does not state the fact.

Jude speaks in the same manner as Peter, referring to his opponents' licentiousness and sexual immorality and evoking the allusion to Balaam who was a false prophet. It is clear from the inherent similarities that he is attacking the same false teachers as Peter; he also is attacking Paul and his followers.

Jude 1:23 seems to suggest violence but appears to be poorly covered by the addition of the word "pity." There is also noticeable violence in 2 Peter 2:12, even suggesting that the opponents deserve death. These harsh words agree with Paul's statements that he had suffered violence from his opponents.

Paul Embattled in the Aegean
The letters of 2 Peter and Jude may have caused the foment in Asia Minor. Such harsh condemnations from obvious authorities would tend to rally those opposed to Paul's teaching.

Paul was probably at Ephesus when Timothy caught up to him with the bad news from Galatia. He described to him a deteriorating situation, where the Christians were adopting Jewish practices and circumcision. So, Paul made a second attempt by letter to lay out for the Galatians in clear terms the nature of his gospel. It seems likely that he sent Timothy back with this letter to counter the heresy.

Paul's gospel is simple: Faith in Christ has saved us from the law of death that condemns us. The law is fleshly and mean; the spirit is uplifting. The law is for sin; the spirit is for the freedom of Christ.

We have already discussed that Paul was adamant that he was not sent by Jerusalem and that he did not consider himself inferior to any authorities there, not even Peter, whom he seems to hold in some reverence. From the rest of Galatians we see that he was opposed to the whole of Jewish law, and to those pushing it, even suggesting vehemently that those promoting circumcision might cut from themselves more than just the prepuce!

Paul's Second Letter to the Corinthians is a masterpiece of inspired rhetoric. Paul has just left Ephesus where he faced persecution nearly to death, even fighting wild animals, and he writes the Corinthians from Macedonia to console them in their affliction. For the Corinthians are being torn apart in a conflict between those who oppose Paul, questioning his authority as an apostle, and those who support him. Paul responds not denying but embracing the troubles.

He begins by acknowledging what the Corinthians already know. He suffered at Ephesus, and his authority has been attacked at Corinth. Yet, he has survived and he points to this as proof of God's favor. Next he answers a criticism which alleged that his change in travel plans shows that he is not guided by God; he was accused of being double-minded, and therefore not completely faithful and inspired. Paul says he altered his plans to save them pain and to avoid conflict, so his change in plans was out of love. In 2:5-11, Paul calls in strong terms for the Corinthians to forgive the perpetrators, presumably Barnabas and other Jewish Christians.

Paul also mentions that he did not find rest in Troas, which he blames on missing Titus. Troas (Troy) was a port north of Ephesus and on the way to Macedonia. From 2 Timothy, however, we know that he failed to gather his cloak, scrolls, and notebooks on leaving. This suggests that he left in a hurry, a fact that he is apparently hiding from the Corinthians.

In 3:1, Paul asks if "we begin to commend ourselves again" to the Corinthians. This clearly suggests that the Corinthians had in some measure disrespected Paul and his co-workers. Yet, Paul passes off the disrespect as nothing and uses the contrast of recommendation letters, a tool of human authority, to the spirit, which is God's authority. In 3:12-18, Paul contrasts himself with those who depend on the words of Moses, and he blames the old covenant for deceiving men by hiding the Spirit. This is a strong condemnation not only of the law, but of the Jews and therefore of the Jewish Christians. Paul goes on to say that it is the "god of the [current] aeon," i.e. Satan, who has blinded these unbelievers.

Paul's own troubles are God's gift to the Corinthians, creating life in them through his continually being delivered up for death. It is the example of his faith in Jesus Christ that is a blessing to them.

It is not possible to summarize the miraculous agility of Paul's thought and match also his sincerity. He is fighting for his very life out of love for his fellow Christians. His eloquence is supreme; and he never strays beyond what his audience knows is true yet leads them to the opposite of their previous conclusion. What appeared to be shameful to Paul becomes his crown, and no one who is good can deny his Godly inspiration. Even Paul's opponents recognized his power of oratory, as we shall see, describing Paul as even bringing fire down from heaven.

In Chapter 8, Paul talks about the collection for the saints. He praises Titus in strong terms and sends with him another brother "of whom the praise in the gospel [is] throughout all the churches." In other words, this person is famous as a Christian, either from promoting the gospel or from being mentioned in the gospel. It is not clear to us which is meant, but probably his fame came from missionary activity. This other brother is not named, although Titus is named twice; so this omission is clearly not accidental. Perhaps, it is the apostle Barnabas, known for preaching the gospel with Paul, who was just at Corinth, and it may be that Paul does not name him for the reason that his presence is not friendly. For it appears that the purpose of this other brother traveling with Titus was to ensure that Paul committed no malfeasance in administering the collection; therefore, his presence was not a vote of confidence.

From Chapter 10, Paul defends his ministry. We can see from his defense the nature of his opposition. Paul, in person, is considered to be meek, unlike a true apostle who would be bold. However, Paul argues brilliantly that his meekness shows the power of God, and that he will punish disobedience when he has the Corinthians obedience. He promises them that he will do what he has written, showing apostolic authority.

Paul says that he is not boasting beyond God's assignment to him, beyond his own works, contrasting with his critics who are taking credit for his evangelizing the Corinthians. Of course, the Corinthians saw the obvious truth of this. And Paul concludes this statement powerfully:

> The one boasting, let him boast in the Lord. For not the one commending himself is the one approved, but [the one] whom the Lord commends.

From here, Paul moves on to chastise the Corinthians for accepting a different gospel and a different Jesus. Then, Paul tells us precisely who his opposition is by stating that he is not inferior to the "super-apostles." There were few who could claim higher authority with the Corinthians than Paul, and it could only be those who claimed authority before Paul, who were already known by fame to the Corinthians. The few would include the Twelve, the family of Jesus, and some well-known apostles like Barnabas. In 11:15, Paul takes off the gloves and calls them false apostles and ministers of Satan.

Then Paul gives an impressive accounting of his ministry in his own "boasting." He also speaks of his mystical revelation "fourteen years ago." He claims that an unnamed physical affliction is of divine origin and for the service of Christ. I fancy that the affliction was epilepsy, which could have easily been interpreted as a spiritual gift by the ancients. Finally, Paul ends with a polite threat of apostolic violence, although the nature of the consequences were vague.

It is evident that Paul's Second Letter to the Corinthians had its intended effect— such was the power of his argument. For he returned to Corinth in success, completed the collection, wrote letters from there to the Romans and the Hebrews, and we have his letters still to this day.

However, we should not believe that his return to Corinth was peaceful or easy. It is telling that after his trial at Jerusalem, he did not send further letters (that we know of) to Corinth from his captivity in Rome. He did not mention the Corinthians to the other congregations in the letters that he did write— Ephesus, Collossae, Laodicea, and Philippi.

As with his previous letters, Paul tells us about his opponents' positions through his defense. In Chapter 15, he argues against some who say that there is no resurrection of the dead! This position was held only by the Sadducees, so it appears that at least some of the Jewish Christians opposing Paul were Sadducees in their philosophy.

In 2 Corinthians 15:42-49, Paul reveals that Jesus Christ came from heaven. Notice how easily this could be taken as a statement of high Christology, deifying Christ, except that he explicitly calls Jesus Christ a man. He then goes on to reveal a further mystery, explaining for us by chance still more reasoning behind the doctrine, by stating categorically that flesh cannot inherit the kingdom of God. Here it sounds like he is referring to heaven, but we cannot be sure. We should see in this explanation of the spiritual body, the nature of Jesus Christ as a heavenly human, the transformed flesh of Jesus.

1, 2, and 3 John
Let us turn now momentarily to the letters of John. None of these letters have any connection with the author of Revelation, who was John of the Twelve. These letters were written by John the Elder, who might be identical with John the Divine.

The writer of 1 John appears to be the same as the author of the Gospel of John, because the letter has a similar manner of expression and pattern of thought. This letter is written in opposition to the heresy that Jesus Christ was not a creature of flesh but only spirit, a heresy known as Docetism. It is interesting that the author says the heretics went out from "us." This suggests that the heretics were themselves apostles, similar to Paul's situation and the subtle manipulations about whom was sent out by whom found in the Acts of the Apostles. However, opposed to Docetism, Paul is always clear that Jesus Christ came in the flesh and was resurrected in the flesh, which agrees with the views of the author of 1 John. So this letter is accusing other apostles, who do not agree with Paul's witness, whom we may identify as Paul's opponents. We can also see this argument in aspects of the Gospel of John, especially in narrating the resolution of the doubts of Thomas who needed to physically touch Jesus Christ.

Is it possible that there was yet a third group, apart from Paul and from Peter, promoting this new doctrine? This seems really unlikely and an unnecessary complication, which is not substantiated by any text. There is nothing in the letters of Peter, James, and Jude that denounces the new heresy, which would have been appropriate to the situation. Also, there is little in those letters to support orthodox Christian doctrines other than moral teaching, obedience to the law, and doing good works. Missing is any substantial reference to the importance of Jesus Christ, except possibly in his coming return. Therefore, we lack evidence that there was a third gospel at this point. Consequently, we can be confident that 1 John is criticizing the Twelve and the family of Jesus, who were claiming that only the heavenly spirit of Jesus Christ was holy and not the person of flesh, Jesus.

At first glance, Docetism seems to be opposed to both Paul and the Jewish Christians, because Paul emphasized that Jesus was a real human being of the seed of David and the Jewish Christians were followers of adoptionist doctrine. Adoptionist doctrine holds that Jesus received the Holy Spirit at baptism, becoming Christ with the infusing of God's spirit, "descending like a dove." Docetism insisted that Jesus Christ was not substantial, not a fleshly person, an apparition. However, it is not a great distance from an apparition to a spirit or from spirit to apparition; they are really equivalent descriptions differing only in emphasis on the method of perceiving. Docetic descriptions emphasized the heavenly spirit of Jesus Christ as an entity separate from Jesus, the fleshly son of Mary. Consequently, we can see Docetism as an expansion and development of the adoptionist doctrine to an extreme position that in some texts separates the heavenly Christ from the crucifixion completely.

Second John and 3 John both explicitly claim John the Elder as their author. Second John is addressed to an "elect lady and her children." The main purpose of this letter is to oppose the Docetic heresy. The letter is condemning some false apostles, Jewish Christians denying the flesh of Jesus Christ. By itself, this makes it likely that the

1 John and 2 John were written by the same person, but also there are many parallels in language and thought.

It is not possible to identify the elect lady from the letter alone; however, the title which is translated "elect lady" in English, is the feminine equivalent (κυρία) in Greek to the masculine κύριος, "lord," "ruler," or "master." The reference to "her children" almost certainly refers to spiritual children and shows that she has authority within a congregation. Suggestions that this letter went to a church named metaphorically as "elect lady" are unlikely, because such a use would have forced the naming of the church as well, otherwise the praise of the children would be meaningless pomposity and not in keeping with the serious subject.

The style of address towards the woman ensures that the recipient was of the highest stature, certainly an apostle or family member of Jesus. In fact, within the New Testament, no one other than Jesus Christ and God received the title "Lord," so that this was an extraordinary woman to be recognized in this manner by a Christian. This suggests her status was higher than any apostle, and she was so unique that the title alone served to identify her. Only Mary, the mother of Jesus, or Mary Magdalene, if she was married to Jesus, really fit as possibilities. Mary Magdalene seems most likely, and recent discoveries at the Talpiot tombs strongly support that Jesus and Mary Magdalene were married.[210] As wife to Jesus, Mary Magdalene would have been the queen of the Jews and deserving of the title "ruler."

On the other hand, in spite of her title, the letter of 2 John does not have a deferential tone to the elect lady as in addressing an authority, let alone a ruler of the Church. Far from it, John the Elder, takes a superior position and talks of commanding her, quite confident of his own authority. Indeed, the letter is almost entirely a list of

---

[210] *The Jesus Family Tomb: The Discovery, the Investigation, and the Evidence that Could Change History* by Simcha Jacobovici and Charles Pellegrino. *The Jesus Discovery: The New Archaeological Find that Reveals the Birth of Christianity* by James D. Tabor and Simcha Jacobovici. These books document beyond reasonable doubt the discovery of the final tomb of Jesus; however, I do not think this was the tomb of the Resurrection. For the location of the Resurrection tomb, I prefer the site of the Church of the Holy Sepulcher.

imperatives; so after recognizing her high status John immediately disregards it. The only possibility is that John considered his own authority as clearly higher than hers, which is confusing to us if she was Mary Magdalene and a ruler of the Church.

While the position of women was lower in ancient cultures, the earliest Christians did have many women in significant authority, even the apostle Junia mentioned by Paul. It is difficult to see how this John the Elder could be higher than the elect mistress of the Church whose sister he also calls elect. The resolution of this contradiction might be possible if and only if John, as a priest, was higher in stature than rulers within the Church. This is quite natural if the Church came from the Essenes, because we see from the Dead Sea Scrolls that the Essenes had both priests and laity, with priests entirely superior. One of the writings, describing an assembly of the entire congregation in the Messianic age, states explicitly the order of the hierarchy such that the Messiah, although first among the laity, followed in rank the lowest Levite. Perhaps, this John the Elder even considered his position higher than Jesus Christ? This would correspond with the Essene writings about the structure of the Messianic congregation, but we cannot easily reconcile this view with 1 John, in which the author emphasizes the sovereignty of Jesus Christ and his authority to forgive sins. It is in 1 John 1:7 that we find the most explicit statement of what became orthodox doctrine: "the blood of Jesus, His son, cleanses us from all sin." This clearly exalts the importance of Jesus Christ above any mortal, even a priest.

I am making a leap here that presbyter, which we translate usually as elder, meant a priest. There is not very much evidence for this beyond the hints of authority in John the Elder's writings. The Gospels do not indicate any priesthood except for Jesus. In Acts 6:12, presbyter is used for some of the authorities arresting Stephen, and there is no indication that these are priests. In 1 Corinthians 12:27-31, where Paul talks about those appointed by God, presbyters are notably absent. Paul does mention male and female elders in 1 Timothy 5, but we cannot say definitively whether he is referring to priests or to older brothers and sisters. However, earlier in 1 Timothy 4:14, we can be quite certain that "elders" indicates authorities in the Church, very likely meaning priests. The laying on of hands in prophecy is an example of spiritual power that would fit a priestly role. Furthermore, if we go back to Paul's other letters, he was constantly referring to a group called "the saints" or "holy ones" separately from the brothers and sisters. These saints could well have been priests, as I believe, also called presbyters, because Jewish priests were holy to God, so the title of saint would be fitting.

An example from a different direction, 1 Peter 5:1 does use the word "presbyter" as a title of authority quite clearly, because Peter claims that he is also an elder. It is interesting that he felt the need to assert this claim also as well as underscoring his being a witness to the Crucifixion. Clearly, he was not stating just his age or high position, but he was asserting spiritual authority beyond what his readers knew of him already. Therefore, we must believe that a presbyter was a title of high authority, and logically we should suspect that it meant priest, conforming well to the attitude of high authority assumed by John the Elder. We can only speculate on why priests were not simply called priests, but it is not hard to imagine the violence that would follow in Judea with the Sadducees and Pharisee priests over use of that title and the lucre it awarded.

Third John is addressed to a man named Gaius and mentions also Diotrephes and Demetrius. Diotrephes appears to be a high-ranking person and is spreading false charges, refusing some visitors, and expelling some. Demetrius appears to be one of those accused and John the Elder is vouching for him; this appears to be the purpose of the letter. John the Elder calls Gaius his child in the Truth, suggesting that Gaius is of lower rank.

Paul mentions a Gaius twice prominently in Achaia in his letters 1 Corinthians and Romans. In 1 Corinthians 1:14, Paul says that he baptized Gaius. In Romans 16:23, he names Gaius as his host. Acts mentions Gaius from Derbe traveling with Paul from Corinth into Asia en route to Jerusalem, and this is probably meant to be the same person.

If so, the letter is probably going to Corinth or Cenchreae from Ephesus; however, the letter from John the Elder then contradicts Acts, as we shall see, because 3 John seems to have been sent as Paul left Ephesus. Also, we should note that Paul did not send along greetings to the Corinthians from Gaius, which argues strongly that Acts is inaccurate and that Gaius was not at Ephesus with Paul.

The Third Letter of John was clearly a reply to a letter from Gaius, and the primary purpose of the letter is to vouch for some brothers and guests who are not named, but whom we should identify as Paul and his cohorts. John the Elder exhorts Gaius to support them. They have already praised Gaius to him, which shows that they already knew Gaius previously at Corinth. They are worthy for support because they journey for Christ, accepting no help from the nations. This sounds precisely equivalent to what Paul says about Timothy and his apostleship in 1 Corinthians 9:12-15 and to what Paul said in 2 Thessalonians 3:7-9 about not burdening them and setting an example against idleness while he was with them. Moreover, John the Elder exhorts Gaius to welcome and support the guests, and in Romans 16:23 Paul calls Gaius his host. Therefore, barring some amazing coincidence, we can identify the guests and the timing— Paul and his coworkers returning to Corinth after Ephesus and a second pass through Macedonia.

We know that Paul faced wild animals in Ephesus, whether real or metaphorical. We also know that John of Patmos, the author of Revelation, whom I also identify as John of the Twelve and pillar of Jerusalem, wrote Revelation after a significant conflict in western Asia Minor, including Ephesus, with those who say they are Jews and are not. From 3 John, we must see that John the Elder, traditionally located in Ephesus, supported Paul in Asia Minor against the Jewish Christians. With his other letters, which denounce Docetists as false apostles, we can connect the dots to a conclusion that the two conflicts between Paul and the Jewish Christians were fundamental disagreements about Christology, whether Jesus the human being continued to be Jesus Christ after the Crucifixion, and about the need to adhere to the law. Could there have been a connection between these two arguments? Did Jesus preach a new Judaism after the Resurrection, setting aside some of the Torah?

Both John the Elder and Paul opposed Docetism. The Docetic heresy is by scholars often explicated as opposed to adoptionist doctrine. The Jewish Christians, such as the Ebionites, were adoptionist, because they insisted that Jesus was a righteous man, born of human parents, who became the beloved son by God's choosing and anointing with the Holy Spirit. This contrasts with the idea that Jesus was God born as a man, which is the ultimate position of orthodox Christianity. The Docetists, however, held that Christ was never human but only took on human form or appearance. Thus, Docetists held that Christ did not really suffer and die, but only appeared to do so.

There appears to be clear opposition between adoptionist Christology and Docetism, since one insists on a human existence of Jesus and the other a purely spiritual existence of Christ. However, they may actually have been two sides of the same coin. Jesus was a flesh and blood human, but Christ was angelic spirit. In anointing Jesus with the Spirit, one could imagine Jesus as blessed (or possessed) by the Christ spirit from the time of his anointing to the moment that the Christ spirit left his body. This separation of Christ-spirit and Jesus-flesh was not necessarily at the moment of death, but it could also have occurred before, which is the most extreme view of Docetism based upon the idea that the heavenly Christ could not suffer fleshly pain. I see a range of emphasis in the Jewish Christian and Docetic Christological doctrines based upon the degree that the human Jesus was permitted to be identified with Christ.

The distinction of the Christ-spirit from the human Jesus also yielded a third possible view, or a degree of Jewish Christian Christology, that was known as Arianism or the doctrine of the two hypostases (substances), which is that Jesus Christ was a composite being of human and Christ, flesh and spirit. Notice that this is not necessarily in opposition to Docetism. This doctrine is maintained even today by the ancient Nestorian (Assyrian) Church. There is even scriptural support for this view retained in the Gospels of Mark and Matthew, when Jesus says, "My God, my God, why have you forsaken me," and the image of the dove descending upon Jesus at baptism, also included in the Gospel of Luke.

The strict Docetic view is simply a discounting of the importance of the human Jesus, emphasizing the exalted nature of the Christ. Some Docetists might also be adoptionists emphasizing that the Christ-spirit remained separate from the flesh of Jesus, while some adoptionists are to some degree Docetists emphasizing that Jesus was the Son of God because he expressed the Christ spirit, but without declaring his flesh to be sublime. Yet, both adoptionists and Docetists are emphasizing that Christ is not flesh even while Jesus was Christ. The view that became orthodox claimed that Jesus Christ was God made flesh— flesh and spirit completely united in one substance. Was Paul adoptionist, Docetist, orthodox, or all three?

The Docetists were a faction theologically opposed to the perceived degradation of Christ by contact with flesh, a doctrine which hints at rather extreme asceticism. Their resistance to Christ suffering held some sway and created heretical but authoritative traditions where another person was actually crucified and engendered visions of Christ laughing while Jesus is crucified. Perhaps, these ideas are maintained as vestiges in the traditions of Simon the Cyrene carrying the cross in the Synoptic Gospels of Matthew, Mark, and Luke, hinting at the substitution for Jesus that finally became explicit in part of the Qur'an.

One important extra-canonical text seems to suggest that the Nazareans were of Docetic orientation. It is the *Gospel of Peter*, an apocryphal gospel generally thought to be written only a little later than the canonical gospels. However, the fact that the author does not appear to know the story of the suicide of Judas and differs in its presentation of Pilate may mean that it is even earlier.

In the *Gospel of Peter*, one element that suggests a separation of Jesus' flesh from the Christ spirit, supporting a Docetic reading, is when Jesus quotes the Psalm, which is reinterpreted in this gospel as:

My power, my power, why have you forsaken me?

This re-working of the psalm emphasizes more clearly that Jesus is lamenting the loss of his Christ-spirit rather than despairing from doubt. This version actually is more compatible with an exalted Jesus Christ than the traditional version seeming to show Jesus humanly questioning God's intention, which has been troublesome to the image of the perfect God-man; so it could well be that this was the original significance in the use of this psalm in the passion narrative. Another element in the fragmentary Gospel of Peter that suggests Docetism is that the risen Christ was described as gigantic, taller than the sky, obviously a spiritual apparition, while no mention is made of his human body.

    The Docetic interpretation separates Christ from death and suffering, but it also creates a theological problem in that the human Jesus is no longer the Christ when he dies and is raised from the dead. One way to get around this complication is to conclude that the Christ rising directly to heaven was the real Resurrection and the physical raising of Jesus was a parody of that event.

What was the relationship between John the Elder and Paul? John the Elder was associated with Ephesus. It is plain that John the Elder agreed with Paul that Jesus Christ was a real person, who had been crucified, died, and resurrected. Both Paul and John the Elder exalted Jesus Christ but opposed Docetists, in other words, the Jewish Christians. John the Elder calls them antichrists. Both Paul and John the Elder describe Jesus Christ as a sacrifice for atonement, which is a doctrine not found in the letters from Peter, James, and Jude nor in the Revelation of John. This doctrine was never supported by Jewish Christianity or it was at some point discarded, according to the Jewish Christian sources known to us.

    In Galatians, Paul scathed ironically against those reputed to be pillars, referring to Peter, James, and John. In 2 Corinthians, he called them sarcastically super-apostles, and he mentioned that some apostles are carrying letters of recommendation— almost certainly the letters of James, Peter, and Jude. After Antioch, however, he had managed to avoid direct confrontation with the Jewish Christian apostles, but at Ephesus he faced deadly opposition. Acts claims Paul's opposition was pagans or idol manufacturers, but we have another source that is more trustworthy and impressive. The Revelation of John is a work which has been long thought to be from a much later author than the famed apostle; but, in examining its content, we can place it precisely to this moment when Paul was at Ephesus.

A Revelation of John

In Revelation, the first three verses and also the last four verses are the additions of a scribe introducing and concluding the text. Starting with 1:4, it is a letter from John, most likely the Son of Thunder, one of the Twelve, to the seven churches of Asia, referring to the western regions of Asia Minor. John is himself located just off the coast of Ephesus on the island of Patmos, and he is writing to exhort and to chastise the churches, who have accepted false teachings. In writing this letter, however, he is claiming that it is not his own judgment but a dictation from Jesus Christ himself through a revelation. Imagine the situation that would demand such a letter— dire circumstances must have required a direct revelation of the Christ, and the power of such a claim among believers from such an authority as John would have been awesome.

First, Jesus Christ addresses the church at Ephesus, saying that they have forsaken their previous loyalty and fallen, and he says that they should repent. He does praise them for avoiding the works of the Nicolaitans, probably referring to those who followed Nicolaus, who was an important member of the Council of Seven. This is the council which Acts describes as being set up by James to govern the Hellenist believers. It was probably located at Antioch, where Nicolaus has been traditionally located. This means that this letter was written after Paul had been driven out from Antioch, because the Council of Seven had not yet been formed at that time. It may be that the schism and the subsequent financial separation from the Jewish Christians is what is meant by their works; in which case, Jesus Christ is praising the Ephesians for not separating from Jerusalem's authority.

To Smyrna, Jesus Christ says that he knows their affliction and poverty, although they are rich, and he knows the blaspheming of those who claim to be Jews and are not, but who are a synagogue of Satan. Notice that the author was a Christian who cared if some were claiming to be Jews falsely. Falsely claiming to be a Jew could be a crime only to another Jew, or to a Jewish Christian. Who would claim to be a Jew falsely? Only a gentile or the apostle to the gentiles, by "gentile" meaning a Hellenist believer. Why were they not Jews? Because they were not circumcised adherents of Mosaic law.

To Pergamum, Jesus Christ says, like the letters of Peter and Jude, once again evoking the evil example of Balaam, the false prophet, that some were teaching the people of Israel to eat food sacrificed to idols and to fornicate. These are the same charges that Paul must answer in his letters. Jesus Christ also says that they do have some who have accepted the teaching of the Nicolaitans, meaning presumably that they have separated themselves financially from the Jewish Christians.

To Thyatira, Jesus Christ upbraids them for tolerating "Jezebel," who was maybe Prisca (Priscilla) or Thecla, two famous women apostles associated with Paul, or perhaps even Mary Magdalene. Again the crimes are eating sacrificial meats and fornication.

To Sardis, Jesus Christ only exhorts them to repent and remain strong. To Philadelphia, Christ again mentions the false Jews, the synagogue of Satan. To Laodicea, he exhorts them to repent.

From the nature of the concerns in this long apocalyptic letter, John could only be addressing the "heresy" of Paul and those who followed him. And yet, this is only the introduction of an apocalyptic vision of struggle between the Church and Satan. In Chapter 12, we might see in the great red dragon the symbol of the Roman empire as Satan, which is paralleled and so explained in chapter 17, with the seven crowns being seven emperors including five fallen, one living, and one yet to come: Julius, Augustus, Tiberias, Gaius, Claudius, Nero, and a future emperor. So we are clearly in the reign of Nero.

From this reference, we can approximate a date for these events. Since Nero was emperor, we know that this letter was written 54-66 CE. Nero ascended in the fall of 54 CE and this is too early for Revelation, because there is no mention of the emperor Nero just having ascended to power. We can further narrow the date, because James has not yet claimed power as Lord of the Church; if he had, John could not have ignored James' importance in his writing. Since James was killed in 62 CE, this is the latest possible date for the Revelation of John. Because James was well-attested and recognized as the first bishop of Jerusalem, we must believe that he ruled the Church for a few years at least— although he may not yet have publicly claimed the high priesthood of the Temple. Time was needed to spread the new gospel and to establish his authority among the churches, so the time period must be some years earlier than 62 CE.

This dating also seems convenient, because somehow Christianity had not yet made much progress since the Resurrection, still requiring those among the nations to be evangelized; consequently, an earlier dating seems more likely. Moreover, the description of the situation is the same conflict and persecution faced by Paul in Ephesus but seen from the opposing view. Traditions including the Acts of the Apostles place Paul's missionary activity during the reign of Claudius rather than Nero, so we should not expect that Paul was at Ephesus much later than 55 CE. This is Paul's fourteenth year as a Christian, as he tells the Corinthians and the Galatians; therefore, if the year was 55 CE, then Paul became a Christian around 40–41 CE.

John prophesies that there would be another emperor after Nero, who would not reign long. This sets up a limited time until the arrival of the next age and the final battle, the coming in power of the Son of Man— the death of Nero and installation of the seventh emperor.

In Revelation, John implies Jesus Christ to be the Son of God only with the inclusion of three Greek words in 1:6: *"and Father of him."* Such a paucity of expression creates some doubt that John subscribed to the same Son of God doctrine that Paul did. Jesus Christ is also called the "faithful witness," "the firstborn of the dead," and "the ruler of kings of the earth."[211] It is noticeable and important, however, that the visions of the Revelation of John are devoid of any significant reference to the divine son-ship. Moreover, Jesus, the Lamb, is not even himself seated on a throne in the vision, although the twenty-four elders of the Old Testament are.[212]

Jesus is called "one like the Son of Man," "the Lion of the tribe of Judah," "the Root of David," and "the Lamb." Certainly, he is exalted and shares in the glory of God. He is symbolically described as the son of the Church, but not as the Son of God. We should also notice that there is no hint of a fleshly resurrection; rather, although "the Lamb" implies clearly that Jesus Christ was slaughtered, he was "snatched up to God and to his throne." This leaves open possibilities other than the orthodox doctrine of reanimation by God.

In the concluding vision, Jesus identifies himself as "the root and descendant of David, the bright morning star." Notice also that no one worships Jesus Christ even in heaven. While he is exalted, he is not deified. Moreover, there is no indication of equality or unity with the Father.

Perhaps even more significant, Jesus Christ is never identified as the Messianic Son of David. He is a descendent and the root, but not specifically the Messiah. Obviously, describing Jesus Christ as the "root" recalls the phrasing of the "Branch of Jesse" and of the "Holy Vine," leaving the possibility open for James to claim the Davidic Messiahship.

---

[211] Rev 1:5.

[212] Rev. 4:4; Rev 5:5-6.

The plainest statement of the Christology, of the meaning of Jesus Christ, of the Revelation of John is found in the first sentence:

> A revelation of Jesus Christ, which God gave to him to show his servants things due to happen in a hurry; and he [God] made known sending through his angel to his slave John, who reported the word of God and the testimony of Jesus Christ, everything he saw.[213]

On reading closely, we can see that the angel which God sent is Jesus Christ himself, and the role of Jesus Christ is to give testimony as an angel rather than to initiate any action. Thus, in addressing the churches, Jesus Christ is voicing the judgment of God and not his own. In Revelation 1:8, it is God and not Jesus Christ who says, "I am the Alpha and the Omega."

There is some paradox in how Jesus Christ is portrayed. At times, he is passive, a mouthpiece for God. At other times, Jesus Christ is shown as a commander, an authority who holds the other angels in his hand, represented by the stars. Notice that in Revelation 1:20, the seven stars representing the angels are separate and distinct from the seven lamp stands representing the churches, emphasizing that the angels are not the churches. In the same way, we find that the angel Jesus Christ is not the human Jesus.

In the first beast of Revelation 13:1-9, we can see a remarkable likeness to Jesus in that the beast was wounded mortally but survived. The beast blasphemes and boasts against God, heaven, and the saints. It conquered the saints? Yes, the beast gained authority over them. Who could have achieved such a thing except Jesus? It converted all the earth, being tremendously successful in its authority, subjecting all who were not true believers of the Lamb.

---

[213] Rev. 1:1-2.

The identity of the first beast only becomes clearly Jesus with the description of the second beast, who is Paul. It appears like a lamb but speaks as a dragon. It exercises all the authority of the first beast, and most significantly it makes the earth worship the first beast. It performs great signs, and by the signs it deceives those dwelling on the earth. It told them to make an image of the resurrected beast, and he gave the image life.

What is meant by the "image" is unclear. Perhaps, it is metaphorically referring to the worship of Christ equal to God as a kind of idolatry. The bishop of Antioch, Ignatius, had the appellation, "Theophorus," which means "God-bearer," which implies from pagan practice bearing some kind of iconography, idol, or physical manifestation of God. However, we are not privileged to know what the form of the image was. Could it have been a crucifix?

The second beast caused all who would not worship the image of the beast to be killed. And he causes all who worship to be marked on the right hand or forehead with a number identifying the first beast. Now, our modern translations generally have the number of the beast to be 666, and this number is attested from ancient tradition. However, there were equally ancient traditions mentioned by the church father Irenaeus for another number, 616. Textual criticism has not been able to conclusively determine the correct version, although orthodox traditions, including Irenaeus, preferred 666. However, some coincidences do support the alternative, 616, given our better understanding of the conflict within the earliest Church. In some of the ancient versions that contain this number, the number is written as a Greek number would be abbreviated rather than spelled out as words, as found in the orthodox versions. It is more realistic that the number originally was written as an abbreviation rather than the lengthy Greek words, because it was a mark for the forehead or the hand.

The number 616 is either very controversial or very significant in its abbreviation. The number 616 in Greek would be written with the letters "XIϚ"— an obvious abbreviation for "Christ Jesus." (It equates to X for Christ and JS for Jesus.) Of course, orthodox Christians would not be comfortable that their Messiah's name equaled the same number as the beast, so there would be strong impetus among Christian scribes to make an adjustment. Moreover, in hand written uncials, 616 differs from 666 in only a single stroke, because 666 written in uncials was "ΧΞϚ"— where the vertical stroke of the iota is made the horizontal stroke of xi. This might seem like it could be a careless error by a scribe, but actually that is highly improbable. Certainly, no scribe could be so careless in such an important and unusual part of the text. The change had to be purposeful, which leaves us the question: which version was original? Because it is far more likely that a Christian scribe would change 616 to 666 than vice versa, therefore, the former must have been the original. In other words, the number of the beast was the abbreviation for Christ Jesus.

Revelation 13:16 says that the second beast caused all to be marked with this "number." Is there any support for this elsewhere? The answer is yes, although limited, for in Galatians 6:17, Paul says that he carries the pricking or branding marks (στιγματα, stigmata) of Jesus Christ on his body. This has usually been interpreted metaphorically, referring to his scars of suffering; and this is a quite reasonable interpretation, since we know from his own testimony that he had been whipped and beaten many times. However, in the context of the Galatians, which was an apostate congregation, perhaps already believing Paul to have been properly castigated for heresy, the branding that he was boasting about probably was something less ambiguous in meaning and more clearly positive.

One of the most common ways to name oneself as a Christian, at least among the apostles, was to call oneself a "slave of Christ." Paul so calls himself in four letters; James and Peter also name themselves in this way. Stigmata were a common method of identifying slaves in the ancient Roman world. Therefore, the more likely meaning of Galatians 6:17 was that Paul had himself branded as a slave of Christ, like all slaves, with the name of his master, thereby demonstrating his faith in a tangible fashion. We do not, however, see him advocating such marks in others, so there is no real evidence for a general practice.

However, in the time of persecutions, such marks would be a bold manner of professing faith in Christ.

Recent scholars have proposed another identity for the name of the beast, an interpretation more widely accepted and in some ways seeming more plausible: that is, that of "Caesar Nero," which in Hebrew would also add up to the 666 or even 616, depending on the form of the name used. There are some very good arguments supporting this view, including that: Nero appears symbolically elsewhere in the text. He was the ruler of Rome at the time of writing. Unfortunately, there are some other factors which argue more strongly against "Caesar Nero." The initials do not add up to 666 or 616, so the second beast would have been marking persons with the entire name, "Caesar Nero," which is not likely, and we have no evidence that anyone was worshiping the emperor in this way. Certainly, persons claiming to be Jews or Christians— remembering the context of the situation— would not have gained anything by worshiping Nero. The "mortally wounded" detail is very descriptive of Jesus and not at all of Nero.

It is difficult to accept and also baffling that John, one of the Twelve, could exalt Jesus as the redeeming Lamb in his revelation and also call him the Antichrist in another part of the same text. I would point out, however, that in reviewing the imagery of the woman in labor, the woman seems symbolic of the Church and the child of Jesus; and the child is taken to heaven *before* the dragon could devour him. Also, notice that although the Lamb is described as slain and as the redeemer, he is never described as resurrected! This is an amazing omission in a religion that was founded, according to Paul, solely on the Resurrection. Obviously, the Revelation shows the Lamb as alive in Heaven, even exalted as a powerful Heavenly being, but the Resurrection is not even mentioned.

Not all of the hearers of this letter to the seven churches of Asia would have understood that the beast was Jesus. The symbolic imagery is not so plain that uneducated persons would have considered the words in such a light, but we must assume that the literate and theologically knowledgeable persons probably did grasp the import— else there would be little point to including this passage.

What could this passage mean to John in the context of the situation? Jesus, before and through the Crucifixion, was a special messenger of God— he was the righteous servant, the Lamb, whose innocent death condemned the world and was an example to the saints. Jesus suffered mortally and his spirit, the Lamb, was raised to heaven. Jesus survived or revived, John appears to hedge about the actual death of Jesus further distancing himself from the doctrine of the Resurrection. Jesus then began to preach with a different spirit, which John symbolizes as a beast. Jesus did miraculous signs while he "preached blasphemies for 42 months," suggesting that the teaching of Jesus after the Resurrection was significantly different from before and objectionable to Jews. John claims that the whole world followed him, obviously referring to all the churches. This implies that the Twelve were themselves deceived temporarily.

The wide acceptance of Jesus as the Christ had proven to his followers that he was the Christ— that Jesus was the Messiah sent by God. Beyond this simple statement, we must remember, however, that all the apostles and all the Jews were on new and uncertain ground. No one had anticipated that the Messiah would die, not even the apostles, and the meaning of all of this was definitely unclear. Certainly, the expected victory of God over the foreign powers had not yet happened. Jesus' death and Resurrection was something new and momentous in the Messianic narrative, but also unknown and fearful. How this would play out politically and historically was not following the apocalyptic patterns expected. John is now nearly twenty years after the Resurrection and nothing had been fulfilled as expected. After many violent confrontations, the Jewish leaders were still sitting on the fence: unwilling to reject Jesus out of hand but also unwilling to commit to the Gospel. So, while Jesus Christ received wide acceptance as a prophet, the Gospel acquired little Messianic authority.

In Revelation, John gingerly rejects the parts of the Gospel that assert Jesus as the prophesied Son of David and heavenly Son of God.

Likely, if we can take Paul's comments and other Jewish evidence into account, John does so because he supports a new candidate for the Davidic Messiah— James, the brother of Jesus. This is the reason that the Jewish Christian apostles needed to reassign Jesus as a new Messianic symbol, the Lamb of God.

However, this new Nazarean revelation of the fleshly Jesus as both vessel of the Christ and the Antichrist did not eliminate his importance to the Jewish Christians. While the human Jesus could be denigrated as a blasphemer after the Resurrection, prior to the Crucifixion he was the angelic being, Jesus Christ. As such, Jesus Christ continued to be exalted by Jewish Christians, almost but not quite as a deity.

The Gospel of Peter, which was used by the Nazareans, shows that Jesus Christ was an angel, but it also describes Jesus Christ as larger than the other angels depicting symbolically his greater rank. We should notice that the Gospel of Peter says absolutely nothing about the fleshly Jesus: the tomb is empty and only spirits are described, including the spirit cross. The flesh of Jesus is entirely absent and ignored. It is in the Gospel of Peter that we see the significance of the 101st Psalm on Jesus lips, also quoted in Mark, with the words redefined to suggest that Jesus lost his power, the Christ-spirit, before his death— an important element of the Docetic heresy. Also, while Jesus is an exalted angel, he is not portrayed as qualitatively different from any other angel. Jesus Christ is the Redeemer, the Lamb of God, but this makes him a very special angel and not the Messianic Son of God.

Contrast this new doctrine with that of Paul. Paul is clear that Jesus Christ is the Messiah. He was also of the seed of David, implying strongly that he was the Messianic Son of David. Notice that he feels the need to insist on this, which is a hint that he is countering other opinions.[214] More than that, Jesus Christ is the Son of God and the Savior, whose righteous death redeemed humankind. Paul holds Christ

---

[214] Rom. 1:3-4; 2 Tim. 2:8-9.

as divine, a co-deity with the Father, potentially suggesting even the doctrine of the Trinity.[215]

Yet, reinforced by the Jewish Christian hostility, the linking of the first and second beasts in the Revelation of John forces the conclusion that Paul's teaching was consistent with that of the risen Jesus. John could have claimed that Paul had maligned Jesus, but he does not. Rather, he maligns the risen Jesus as himself a blasphemer, no longer of God but of Satan. This division of Jesus from the angel Jesus Christ at the Crucifixion demanded new doctrines (or heresies) to explain the apparent contradictions. We can see the opening to the Docetic position in the separation of the spirit Christ from the human Jesus. The symbol of the Lamb was such a doctrine, explaining the role of Jesus Christ as an exalted precursor of the Messianic Son of David, and it received wide acceptance, even entering the Gospel of John. It is probably significant, however, that Paul does not mention the Lamb of God, suggesting that it was a wholly new Jewish Christian invention separate from his own gospel. (Although it is mentioned in 1 Peter 1:19.)

Ultimately, the Jewish attack on the deification of Jesus Christ failed to sway the gentile churches, and the teachings of Paul eventually prevailed. Yet, it appears that for a period, Jewish Christian doctrines managed to dominate and to influence what would become orthodox doctrine.

Indirectly, from its openly hostile position both to Jesus and Paul, we get a valuable opposing and objective witness in the Revelation of John to certain specific facts about the gospel of Jesus. First, John stated that Jesus was mortally wounded and recovers, thus verifying both the Crucifixion and the Resurrection. Second, Jesus spread blasphemies and corrupted the whole Church for 42 months after the Resurrection,

---

[215] The doctrine of the Trinity was a necessary foundation for the assertion that Christ was God, because all Jews, including Christians recognized only One God; however, this kind of extra-personification was not unknown to Judaism, and Rabbinical sources assert the existence of a Shekinah and a Metatron associated with Yahweh, the Most High God.

meaning that he continued to teach for three and one-half years after the Resurrection and his teaching was then substantially different, so as to be unacceptable to Jews— at least it was convenient for the Jewish Christians to make such a clear division. Paul exalted Jesus to an extent that was offensive to Jews, spreading accurately the gospel of Jesus, and resisting the Jewish heresy.

However, we cannot say really that the Paul's gospel was materially different from that of the apostle John. The difference is mostly in emphasis and very subtle. When Paul talks about Christ as the Son of God, he is talking about the spirit of Jesus Christ and not the flesh of the human Jesus. Paul seems to assert a theology where the spirit that later inhabits Jesus is the pre-existent Christ. When the spirit descends upon Jesus, he becomes one and the same with the Son of God *in power*, that is to say, Jesus the human being was not God; he became the embodiment of Christ through the power of God.[216]

Likewise, John too believed that Jesus became the Lamb at the moment of the anointing, the descent of Christ into the person of Jesus. Paul believed that Christ was begotten of the Father in Heaven,[217] therefore literally the spiritual progeny, the divine spirit Son of God, who later descended into the human Jesus. Paul never states whether this was at birth or at baptism, but his doctrine is not necessarily opposed to adoptionist dogma nor to the orthodox God-at-birth dogma. John, the author of Revelation, on the other hand, is purely adoptionist, meaning Jesus became king of Israel at the anointing, following the text "this day I have begotten you" in the metaphorical-mystical sense— but not in the fleshly sense, which he, like most Jews, would view as a horrendous blasphemy.

Consequently, for John, God never had a literal son, not even in Heaven. This suggestion was blasphemous to many Jews, not only because it suggested that God was sexual, but because it created, in

---

[216] Rom. 1:4.

[217] Heb. 1:5, 5:5.

effect, a second God. Nonetheless, Jesus Christ remained to John an exalted being, the Lamb of God.

By contrast, for Paul the Resurrection, or the raising-up (ascension?), Jesus Christ was unified miraculously into Heavenly flesh inseparable from the Spirit, which ascended to Heaven. Paul describes his doctrine of the perfected and exalted spirit-body in 2 Corinthians, and presumably Jesus Christ would in his view have experienced that same transformation at his ascension to Heaven.

Therefore, we can see in John's theology the Docetic vision of Christ, because Christ was more or less separate from the flesh of Jesus. Paul emphasized the union of Christ with the fleshly Jesus, while John emphasized the distinction of Christ from Jesus the fleshly human. Separating the Christ from Jesus permits the Docetic theological position found in some ancient texts that Christ only appeared to suffer, because real suffering and death was impossible for the Heavenly spirit. Jesus could suffer, but Christ could not. The major difference at this point between John and the later Docetists is that John does appear to accept the suffering of Christ for the sins of the Jewish people, thus the doctrine of the heavenly Lamb of God. Notice how close this idea is to the perfect sacrifice described in the Letter to the Hebrews; this demonstrates the point that Paul's theology was not much different from John and the Twelve, although their minor disagreements became bitterly important.

We should note that, while the Revelation of John, in the visionary letters from Jesus, sees the Nicolaitans of Antioch as connected to Paul, almost conflating them as the same heresy, Paul never mentions Nicolaus or the Nicolaitans. Paul was attempting to maintain the unity of the Church, inspired by his faith in Jesus Christ to seek a compromise between the Hellenists and the Judaizers, and he opposed schisms. So, if he knew about Nicolaus, which is likely, Paul deliberately avoided associating his position with the new council at Antioch. The purpose of the collection for Jerusalem was to demonstrate Paul's faith, loyalty, and goodwill to the Church as a whole, thereby winning respect for his revelation and peace with the Jews. As Paul states in Romans, he never stopped believing in the salvation of the Jews. It is only after his trial and condemnation at Jerusalem, that Paul advocates separate finances and leadership.[218] So, although Paul was part of the initial upheaval at Antioch that lead to separation from the Jewish leadership, he was not actually involved nor supportive in the schism. He had already been driven out of Antioch before the establishment of the Council of Seven.

---

[218] 2 Tim. 2:4. Paul, using coded language, requests or commands Timothy to be loyal to him and to keep the collected donations and finances separate from his enemies, the Jewish Christians.

Trial at Jerusalem

The Letter to the Romans and the nature of Paul's argument to the gentiles. The Romans were already Christians. Paul used scriptures from Judaism to prove that his gospel was correct and from God. Only descendants of Isaac and Jacob are qualified to be called by Jesus Christ. Paul argues that the law is the cause of sin, but he hopes for the Jewish Christians still. Letter to the Hebrews, Titus, and 1 Timothy. Many questions about doctrines and practices. 2 Timothy. Many desert Paul.

Paul had not yet been to Rome when he wrote his great treatise, his gospel for the gentiles. He said that he would come to them soon, and he did— as a prisoner. If we had questions before about the nature of his gospel and the manner of his teaching, we should have even more when considering that he can actually evangelize through a letter. Certainly, we are learning something important about the nature of the early Church— that it was far more advanced in some ways than we have believed until now.

Paul's elaborate greeting shows many things. He expects the Romans to know who Jesus Christ is, and he expects them to accept Jesus as the Lord. He names them as "ones called by Jesus Christ," "ones beloved of God," and "ones called holy." How would this be possible, if he has not yet evangelized them?

First of all, we have already made the point that Paul was not starting with blank slates. He was evangelizing Hellenist Israelites, who already knew something of the biblical traditions and writings. Moreover, these people were not entirely cut off from Jerusalem. Many were merchants and still more made pilgrimages to the Temple. They were organized in congregations, called synagogues or churches, where they would presumably study their ancestral traditions and texts, and they had the benefit of cultural exchange with other people similar to themselves. So they were not necessarily ignorant of apocalyptic Judaism and Messianic speculations, which became the basis for Christianity.

Secondly, we have already mentioned that Peter had been in Rome. From Rome, Peter's letters were among those carried by Barnabas and other Jewish Christian apostles to Corinth, Ephesus, and elsewhere. Paul says that he had wanted to come to Rome before but was prevented, although he does not say what prevented him. We know that he made it as far as Illyricum, on the west coast of the Grecian peninsula, probably after his first trip to Corinth; so it appears that maybe he had already been on his way to Rome but was turned back. Of course, Paul would not want to admit that it was Peter's presence and a repeat of the conflict at Antioch that he had been avoiding. We should notice that Silvanus, who traveled west with Paul, was Peter's scribe at Rome. Paul never mentions Silvanus again after reminding the Achaians in 2 Corinthians of his part in preaching the gospel, and he does not mention him to the Romans either, suggesting strongly that they were no longer co-workers beyond Illyricum.

Thirdly, and perhaps most importantly, we know the Romans, that is, the Roman Jewish congregation, were already Christians by the testimony of Rufinus, a presbyter of Aquileia. Rufinus purports to provide to his Lord Bishop Gaudentius a translation in Latin of the written memoir of Clement, the Bishop of Rome, which described Peter's teaching. This is one of the works known collectively as the Clementina. In his preface to the *Recognitions of Clement*, Rufinus explains:

> For some ask, "Since Linus and Cletus were bishops in the city of Rome before this Clement, how could Clement himself, writing to James, say that the chair of teaching was handed over to him by Peter?" Now of this we have heard this explanation, that Linus and Cletus were indeed bishops of Rome before Clement,

> but during the lifetime of Peter: that is, that they undertook the care of the episcopate, and that he fulfilled the office of apostleship; as is found also to have been the case at Caesarea, where, when he himself was present, he yet had Zachaeus, ordained by himself, as bishop.[219]

The suggestion of Rufinus that Peter appointed at different times all three of the earliest bishops of Rome is not at all unreasonable, considering that more than fourteen years have passed since Jesus was available in the flesh. Linus and Cletus must have been bishops of Rome previous to Clement. Peter is noticeably not described as one of the bishops of Rome. Later, it became important to name Peter as the first Bishop of Rome in order to establish the primacy of Rome over all other churches.[220] Linus is mentioned by Paul at Rome in 2 Timothy 4:21.

If the natural conclusions from all of this circumstantial evidence are correct, then Peter has already evangelized the Roman congregation. So, Paul could expect and probably knew that the congregation had accepted Jesus Christ. Yet, we should not ignore the obvious question of why Paul would need to evangelize the Romans if Peter already was there and had already established the Roman Church. Clearly, Paul had no confidence in Peter and his gospel; Paul's gospel was different.

Another possible reason for writing to Rome is suggested by the timing— just before Paul's return to Jerusalem: If Peter was in

---

[219] Rufinus, Bishop of Aquileia. *Recognitions of Clement.* Trans. Rev. Thomas Smith. Eds. Rev. Alexander Robertson and James Donaldson. The Ante-Nicene Fathers. Reprinted by Eerdmans in 1989.

[220] Eusebius lists Linus and Anacletus as Bishops of Rome after Peter, Paul, and Clement. So, in either list Clement was the third Bishop of Rome. It should be clear, however, from Rufinus and what we have discovered from Paul so far that Peter never assumed the responsibility of bishop anywhere. Peter was already an apostle and superior to any bishop in the hierarchy of the earliest Church except for James, the Lord Bishop of Jerusalem, who attempted to rule the whole Church. See the chapter on the Clementina for more discussion of this.

Rome at this moment, as the New Testament letters suggest, then he too would hear or read Paul's letter. This would give Paul the chance to preview his gospel and his criticisms to Peter, without explicitly saying so, before the inevitable showdown in Jerusalem, giving Peter a more extensive introduction to the nature of Paul's teaching and grievances. Perhaps, Paul believed that with sufficient discussion, the differences with the Jewish Christians could be overcome.

In the letter, Paul begins by thanking the Romans because their faith is being proclaimed in all the world. He says that he serves God in the Gospel of his Son. He tells them how much he has wanted to see them, although prevented, so that he might have some fruit among them as he has among the rest of the nations (gentiles). He says that he is in debt to both Greeks and barbarians. It is not clear whom he means by barbarians. Then, Paul leaves us another clue to the conflict by saying that he is not ashamed of the Gospel; clearly this suggests that someone is saying that he should be. He takes this statement right into the core of his preaching, which is salvation by faith, begging the question, "as opposed to what?"

Paul makes a subtle comparison with those who worship the law and those who worship idols. He appears to start talking about those opposing the truth, as he has just stated it, so we believe he is talking about the Jewish Christians; but then he continues into a discussion of idolatry and immorality into fornication and all manner of baseness. The effect is that he has equated his opponents' actions with the worst forms of immorality without even mentioning their names.

Paul then goes into condemning those who judge, which presumably his opponents do against him. Then through an exhortation to do good and avoid evil he segues into a discussion of the place of the law and of those who uphold the law. This brings him to address the Jews, asking, "if while claiming superiority because of the law [the Jews] commit crimes?" Paul ends with reference to the prophets: "The name of God through you is blasphemed among the nations." Clearly, this is a strong reprobation against his Jewish opponents. Immediately, Paul attacks circumcision as an unnecessary Jewish custom, and we first hear the phrase, "circumcision of the heart" as the true circumcision, a doctrine that will resurge as important at a later time in the Letter of Barnabas.

Interestingly, Paul attempts to give Jews some credit for circumcision, but his praise rings hollow as he is unable to give any example of a real advantage to their heritage or circumcision other than they were entrusted with the oracles of God. Of course, the uncircumcised also have these too now, so the advantage is moot. Ultimately, Paul concludes that no one is justified by the law but by the grace of God through the redemption in Christ. Then, Paul delivers the *coup de grace* in the example of Abraham, who was justified by faith before he was circumcised— Abraham, who was the "father of many nations," which is to say, "father of the gentiles." If I am correct that the Letter of James was one of those carried by some apostles to support their authority, then we should probably see this example from Abraham as a direct counterpoint to James' example of Abraham in his letter, where Abraham is justified by his works in attempting to sacrifice Isaac.

Here in Romans 5, Paul shows the full development of his doctrine of redemption through Christ's death and resurrection. He mentions briefly the theme of boasting as he expounded on previously in 2 Corinthians, but just as an aside. The single act of righteousness by Jesus Christ is sufficient to counter the original sin of Adam.

Paul then explains baptism as symbolically re-enacting the death and resurrection of Jesus Christ. He is arguing that freedom from sin also means avoiding sin. Continuing along this vein, he states that Christians have died to the law by joining the body of Christ. Finally, he comes to the conclusion that the law actually causes sin by teaching it! And moreover it creates an unresolvable conflict between the flesh and the spirit. The law of the spirit of life in Christ is set against the law of sin.

At this point, Paul says that God sent his Son in the "likeness" of sinful flesh. This turn of phrase is confusingly similar to the language of the Docetic doctrine; however, Paul also insists on the death and the Resurrection of Christ, which opposes Docetic doctrine.

Then Paul moves into a contrast of flesh and spirit. Here Paul does take on the adoptionist language in referring to all who are led by the spirit of God as sons of God by adoption. Does this mean that Jesus Christ was adopted as the Son of God, as well? Paul seems to maintain a definite dichotomy between the son-ship of Christ and the son-ship of Christians. Had Paul meant that Jesus Christ was merely adopted, this would have been the place to say it, showing that Christians are equal heirs, and he just does not. Consequently, for Paul, Jesus Christ is not human but the likeness of a human; Christ chose to put on the flesh of Jesus.

How is this different from the view of Christ seen in the Revelation of John? There is not much difference, in fact. John sees Jesus Christ as a heavenly spirit being, also called the Lamb of God. John, like Paul, seems to imply that Christ was a pre-existent being that put on the flesh of Jesus. Two points of difference are detectable: First, for John, Jesus Christ is called the Son of God, because God adopts him so in a metaphorical or symbolic sense, while Paul seems to insist that Christ was always the Son of God, perhaps metaphysically but not symbolically, even before Jesus. Second, it is obvious that John, with Peter and James, disagrees with Paul also on some of Jesus' teaching after the Resurrection, causing John to prophesy that Christ was separated from Jesus at the Crucifixion.

In Romans 9, Paul expresses his sorrow over his kinsmen, the Jews. He then makes an esoteric argument that not all descendants of Abraham would be chosen, but only through Isaac and Jacob. Descendants of Abraham outside of Isaac and Jacob means the Arabs, the traditional enemies of Israel, whom he calls children of the flesh as opposed to the children of the promise. In other words, Arabs, like other pagans, are not qualified for redemption. This statement was a patent repudiation of the universal gospel to all humans, setting the people of Isaac and Jacob against all others; yet eventually these same words will justify the mission to the pagans, out of context, focusing only on the statement that the children of the promise inherit not by birth nor by deeds but out of the calling by Jesus Christ.

Paul then returns to the explanation that the law did not avail because of the lack of faith, opposing completely the doctrine of salvation by works of James:

> But Israel pursuing a law of righteousness did not achieve law. Why? Because not out of faith but as out of works [did they act]. They stumbled on the stumbling stone just as it has been written.[221]

Recalling that Peter was at Rome and would have heard the letter read, Paul surely must have been aware of the pun on Peter's name and the potential double-meaning on who was causing the people to stumble.

Paul now prays for his kinsmen to be saved. It has always been clear that he meant the Jews; now we know that he means the Jewish Christians who are opposing him. It is precisely because he has been opposed that Paul is continuing his arguments at length to Hellenists that the Jews are doomed. But then he saves them again! Because he prophesies that they will return to obedience in the end. Paul makes clear that he expected eventual reconciliation and he even describes the current discord as predestined by God and necessary for the salvation of the gentiles. In fact, we learn from Paul himself that his mission to the gentiles was a direct result of the Jewish Christians rejecting the freedom from the law in the gospel of Jesus Christ. He even states twice that the purpose of preaching to the gentiles was to make the Jewish Christians jealous, so that through jealousy or zealotry (same word in Greek) the Jewish Christians would be encouraged to reconcile

---

[221] Rom. 9:31-33.

with him and his gospel.[222] For now, as regarding the gospel, Paul calls them enemies because of the gentiles, but the calling of the Jewish Christians is irrevocable and they will receive mercy.[223]

Chapters 12, 13, and 14 exhort the Romans to lead a godly life, including fulfilling the law, which Paul defined as loving one's neighbor. Paul also spends much effort discouraging the judging of others or exercising freedom thoughtless of one's brother. Concluding Chapter 14, Paul indicates that the controlling factor is one's own conscience. He says:

> But the one doubting whether he should eat has been condemned, because not out of faith [did he eat]; all which is not out of faith is a sin.

In Romans 15:20, Paul states that he does not wish to go where Christ has already been named in order to avoid building on another's foundation. This is in conflict with the conclusion that Peter has already been at Rome— unless Peter was not evangelizing the Gospel of Jesus Christ in Paul's point of view. It appears that Paul did not see Peter's gospel as the true Gospel.

In some fragments of a letter from Dionysius, one of the earliest bishops of Corinth, is retained an ancient tradition, probably accurate, that Peter and Paul suffered martyrdom at the same time. Interestingly, the same fragments also assert that the churches at Corinth and Rome were planted by both Peter and Paul, further substantiating our conclusion that the two apostles were proselytizing in close proximity and time.

> Therefore you also have by such admonition joined in close union the churches that were planted by Peter

---

[222] Rom. 11:11-15.

[223] Rom 11:28-31.

and Paul, that of the Romans and that of the Corinthians: for both of them went to our Corinth, and taught us in the same way as they taught you when they went to Italy; and having taught you, they suffered martyrdom at the same time.[224]

Hebrews

We do not know how the Letter to the Hebrews was preserved, but it was probably written initially in Aramaic from Corinth. Being written in Aramaic and later translated into the Greek explains why the language is different from the other letters. We should also make an allowance for a different audience, because Paul is addressing in this letter priestly Jews who are quite confident in their understanding of scripture, doctrine, and prophecy.

Did the Hebrews themselves preserve this letter? This seems possible because it was kept separate from Paul's other letters, suggesting it appeared at a later time and was added to the collection. Another reason it may have appeared later, however, is that its doctrines may have been considered secret and not for general dissemination. Or it may have been lost for a while because it was not originally Greek and would have required a person literate in Aramaic, presumably rare in Corinth, to discover its nature.

In any case, there is much about the doctrines and argumentation that do support that Paul wrote it. The divine son-ship is everywhere described in the same sense that Paul described in his other letters. Jesus Christ was the Son of God, and the spirit of Jesus was not different from the Christ— i.e., no doctrinal difference from the other letters is apparent. The author scolds the Hebrews for their unbelief in similar fashion to Paul's comments against Jews in other letters. It is really difficult to see who other than Paul would scold the Jews on their own scriptures for falling away from God, using the

---

[224] Roberts and Donaldson, eds. *Ante-Nicene Fathers: Translations of the Writings of the Fathers down to A.D. 325*. Volume VIII. Grand Rapids: Wm. B. Eerdmans, 1989. Page 765.

metaphor of milk versus solid food as Paul did in 2 Corinthians. Who other than Paul would argue to Hebrews that the old covenant had been valid but now has been made obsolete and would soon disappear altogether?

Some may have questions about who the Hebrews were. The reference to falling away indicates that once they had knowledge and then left it. Paul also states that he would skip over the more basic teaching and he lists: repentance from dead works, faith towards God, teaching about baptisms, laying on of hands, resurrection of the dead, and eternal judgment. Moreover, he speaks of the persecution that they endured in the early days. These statements make it certain that he is addressing Jewish Christians and not a general body of Jews without previous knowledge of Christ.

Titus

Paul left Corinth and passed through Crete on his way to Jerusalem. Paul had to leave Crete so quickly that he had not said goodbye to Titus, and he left him in Crete. In this letter, we can tell that things are going badly, because Paul's mood is angry and morose. Totally out of character, he is unreservedly insulting of the Cretans, whom Titus is evangelizing. He calls them rebellious, idle, liars, and gluttons. He does not praise the congregation, as was his custom even with difficult churches; in fact, he did not write a letter to the Cretans, only to Titus. Therefore, it is certain that nothing good happened for Paul in Crete.

Paul calls Titus his loyal child in the faith. However, this does not seem so much praise as it is exhortation. That Paul would ask and remind Titus about his duty to Paul, rather than simply loyalty to God, indicates a critical level of weakness. The indication is subtle, but we can be sure that Titus understood that Paul was appealing to his devotion. Moreover, we will see in the remaining letters that many trusted co-workers abandoned Paul, which explains his subsequent insecurity and concern for loyalty.

Another indication of how badly things are going is found in Paul's instructions on selecting important officers and on how to lead the congregation as an apostle. The fact that Paul does discuss these topics in a letter is a recognition that he might never have the opportunity to do so in person, which would be the more preferable way to investiture an apprentice with apostolic authority.

Yet another indication that he is losing his case is that he asks for Titus to send along Zenas, the lawyer. By lawyer, he can only mean a person learned in Roman law, because Jewish law was Paul's strength as a Pharisee and Jerusalem had no shortage of rabbis, scribes, and priests. This suggests that Paul has already lost his case with the Jewish authorities, and he was soon to face a Roman tribunal. Also, Paul asks for Apollos, who was at Ephesus with him, so it appears that he values him as a witness to the events there and elsewhere.

Paul reveals a bit more about his opponents. They are mainly "of the circumcision," which suggests that they are Jews and Judaizers. They are apparently following Jewish myths and commandments that do not agree with the gospel. They profess to be Godly, but they do not agree with Paul. He also implies that they involve themselves in stupid controversies, genealogies, dissensions, and quarrels over the law.

The whole letter describes proper behavior for church officers and members. Paul stresses good works to an extent that he has not before. Certainly, this was to counter and to allay charges that he advocated licentious, irreligious, and unlawful behavior.

Remember that the works versus faith debate was the main part of the exchange in the letters of Paul, Peter, James, and Jude. Also, recall that Paul has written that works cannot provide salvation and that, except for Jews, following the law is a denial of the gospel. It would not be unreasonable to come to the conclusion that Paul was apostate as a Jew, since he is teaching against the very things that had before made a person Jewish. So his Jewish trial and subsequent conviction must have been a quick matter.

We should note before we pass on to the remaining letters a few significant clues to the context: Firstly, Titus must remain at Crete and later meet Paul at Nicopolis.[225] From Galatians we know that the leadership in Jerusalem had already rejected Titus because he was uncircumcised; so, this is a possible reason that Paul has left Titus behind. Paul probably wanted to avoid putting Titus' life in danger. It does not seem merely coincidental that Paul is facing death in Jerusalem while his chief assistants are elsewhere. Secondly, apostles appointed elders and bishops— this is in contrast to later Christian practices that call for congregations to elect these officers. Apostles had great authority and responsibility in the beginning.

We should also note something important that does not appear in this letter: Paul does not forbid women to talk or to hold any office nor does he command any special rules for dress or comportment. He appears somewhat chauvinistic to our modern tastes in his prejudices, but entirely absent is the denigration of women as lesser citizens and incompetents that we find in some selected passages of other letters. If his opinions were so disrespectful of women, we should have expected their inclusion in such a letter. Rather, this letter is in agreement with Paul's treatment of women in most of his writings. This provides us a powerful reason for rejecting certain other passages as the later insertions of scribes.

1 Timothy
Paul's first letter to Timothy followed quickly on the letter to Titus, perhaps days to a week— certainly not longer than a week. In some ways it duplicates the content of Titus, although Paul does flesh out the details somewhat.

Again, Paul is insecure and reminds Timothy too of his loyalty. Paul asks Timothy to remain at Ephesus, and considering the situation in Jerusalem this is probably a selfless act to spare Timothy potential death. Paul was certainly in no position to protect him.

---

[225] There were numerous cities of the Roman Empire named Nicopolis, in Greek, "city of victory"; however, this is undoubtably a reference to *the* City of Victory in Illyricum— founded by Octavian in 31 BCE across the bay from Actium, the site of his great victory over Anthony and Cleopatra. Because it was well known to Titus, Paul did not have to explain which Nicopolis he meant.

Paul names directly some of his opponents for the first time. Paul "turned over to Satan" Hymenaeus and Alexander; by this we should understand that he accused them to the Sanhedrin, constituted mostly of non-Christian Jews of the other sects, so that they would then forward the pair to the Romans. For Jews of the middle first century, Satan was the ruler of the physical world, which was also an obvious description of Rome. Rome, besides ruling the world, occupied Judea and had its boot harshly on the throats of all Jews. However, we can see in the next letter that his accusations fell flat and landed ineffectual; Hymenaeus was not condemned.

Another thing that is important to notice here is that Paul expects Timothy to know Hymenaeus and Alexander, because he does not tell more than their names. Moreover, Paul appears to be concerned with their faith and somewhat surprised at their behavior. Using the word "shipwrecked" implies that before they were sailing well and their blaspheming represents a change. Therefore, Hymenaeus and Alexander were Christians who had previously agreed with Paul.

Paul's tone in 1 Timothy is more measured and studious than in Titus, probably indicating the acceptance of his fate. Again he exhorts Timothy to teach ethical and proper comportment. He praises the law but with a hollow praise. He says, essentially, that the lawless are those who need the law. Imagine how this would sound to a strict adherent of the law! This statement is keenly insulting to the Jews.

Paul does take a position of greater humility by admitting himself to have been a great sinner, and he was saved by the grace of the Lord "with the faith and love in Christ Jesus." Paul goes from humility, however, to being the foremost example of patience to the believers.

Again, as in Titus, Paul indicates that apostles have authority to choose bishops, also mentioning deacons and women as deacons. This flatly contradicts the statement, in 1 Timothy 2:11-15, that women must be silent and may not teach nor have authority over a man, which is certainly an insertion by a later copyist.

Paul also gives further clues to the teachings and practices of his opponents. He again mentions myths and genealogies, teachers of law, and asceticism. He says they are renouncing the faith with hypocrisy. They forbid marriage and demand abstinence from foods. This last remark suggests that Paul has even rejected kosher food laws! This does, however, agree with his position that the Mosaic law is now void.

Paul also describes his opponents as adhering to vain ideas that are the "opposing tenets of falsely named gnosis" (γνώσεως). This has been often interpreted to say that Paul was against gnosis, rejecting unorthodox teachings, but this interpretation is slightly inaccurate. Paul does not completely repudiate gnosis or Gnostics in general, but only the *false* gnosis of his opponents. Gnosis is still a valid category of knowledge to Paul, but it must be true knowledge and not foolishness. Paul indicates further that his opponents are motivated by desire for money, another insult of course; but, if Paul really believes what he says here, this would explain his conviction that the collection for the poor could overcome the controversies between the Jewish Christians and himself.

It is difficult to know if any of the other moral teachings in this letter are also interpolations of scribes, because Paul probably did agree on most points with his opponents. After all, they were all Christians, so they shared much in common. So we do not need to worry much generally, because Paul would have likely agreed with the scribes in most cases.

There are some interesting doctrinal statements in this letter. Paul does not condemn slavery. He does advocate young widows to marry in a positive manner that is an apparent reconsideration of 1 Corinthians; the contradiction suggests that 1 Timothy 5:14-16 could be an interpolation of a later scribe.

The instruction to Timothy to take a little wine is also suspicious as an insertion, because there is no apparent cause for the change in behavior. It does tell us that the earliest Christians abstained from wine, however, and we have to wonder if this included the earliest forms of the Mass. We cannot, however, say that the pericope gives the original tradition; the Gospels have too many references to wine to easily conclude that Jesus did not drink, but abstaining from wine was part of the regimen of a Nazarite.

Another interesting point is that Paul already seems to accept the authority of worldly powers, i.e. Roman and other pagan kings. Paul tells Timothy to promote praying for officials in high position. He calls Jesus Christ the Savior of all men, which appears to indicate non-Israelites too. These may have been later insertions, but we have no real basis in evidence for discrediting these verses.

Paul mentions Pontius Pilate momentarily, without offering any characterization, in saying that Christ Jesus witnessed before him the good confession. He appears to be referring to the statement of Jesus that he is the King of the Jews. He goes further calling Jesus "the blessed and only ruler, the king of kings and lord of lords." We should remember that these were titles traditionally reserved for God Himself.

Paul then goes on saying:

> ...until our Lord Jesus Christ's appearance, which in its own time will reveal the only One having immortality, inhabiting light unapproachable, Whom no man saw nor is able to see; to Whom honor and might eternal, amen.

Paul's statement here that only God has immortality seems to be an interesting difference with later orthodox Christian doctrine. We should not, however, jump to conclusions without reviewing the other ancient writings; we may see that this just adds another layer of depth to the theology of the ancient Christians.

Another point, obvious to modern Christians because it is a virtually universal dogma, is that Christ Jesus is the only mediator between God and humankind as stated in 1 Timothy 2:5. Also, in 2:6, Paul asserts that Christ Jesus gave himself as a ransom for all, showing a highly developed Christian theology, in agreement with the Letter to the Hebrews.

Are these statements later additions to Paul's letter in order to give new doctrines credibility? When in doubt, we must err on the side of the given text, accepting Paul's authorship until we have solid evidence against it. These verses do not appear to contradict Paul's belief elsewhere, nor any of the texts of the New Testament.

Can we associate these comments, however, with the rest of the chapter? We have already pointed out that the last part of the chapter is certainly not Paul, and the first verses have a poor transition from the previous chapter; because "first of all" is not appropriate after he has already covered several topics and issues. Remembering that chapters, paragraphs, and versification are conveniences added by later scribes, it seems likely that the entire Chapter 2 is an insertion added later to reap the advantage of Paul's credibility.

2 Timothy

Although this letter was written from Rome, much of its content concerns the trial at Jerusalem, which argues that only a short time has passed since 1 Timothy. Regarding his friends, Paul states that all who are in Asia turned away from him, except for Onesiphorus, who came to Paul in prison at Rome. He lists some known to Timothy who converted or abandoned him: Phygelus, Hermogenes, Hymenaeus, Philetas, Demas, Titus, and Alexander the coppersmith.

We do have some clues in this letter on the differences between Paul and his opponents. Paul so strongly states that he and Timothy were called according to the grace of the Lord and not according to works, that we know he is opposing James and Peter, whose letters extolled the value of works.

Paul gives some messages to Timothy in coded metaphor: He states that wrestlers must compete fairly to be crowned winners. This is probably a jibe at the Jewish Christian apostles who continued to convert the uncircumcised in violation of his understanding of the agreement that they made with him. Paul is telling Timothy furtively that he should not honor the authority of the Twelve. More interestingly, Paul says the hard-working farmer should have the first fruits. This statement is not to be taken literally, and it even contradicts Jewish law. Rather, Paul is telling Timothy that he is to separate finances from those at Jerusalem, and further gifts are to be retained to support the ministry of Paul and Timothy. This is effectively a schism.

Can we identify in 2 Timothy the source of dispute between Paul and the Jewish Christians? Paul's added emphasis in 2 Timothy 2:8 that Jesus was the descendent of David, according to his gospel, is a clear implication that his opponents found this statement objectionable. This agrees with the *Didache*, which, as we have seen, theologically nudged Jesus Christ off the pedestal of the Son of David Messiah, in favor of a dynastic understanding of the concept. Moreover, Paul, in his manner of discussing this issue in isolation from anything else, suggests that this was the only significant point of contention. Of course, he was wrong. The *Didache* is also clear that Jesus was only a man, no different than David himself, while Paul believed that Jesus Christ was divine.

This was not Paul's only underestimation of the conflict with the Jews. We have already seen that Paul's position on the law was absolutely incompatible with the Jews; however, Paul never loses faith that the Jewish Christians would share his understanding of the gospel; which means, of course, that he believed that the other apostles shared his opinion on the law. How could he possibly believe this after all of these conflicts? I can only speculate that, by this time, it was so clear that agreement with non-Christian Jews on disregarding Mosaic law was not going to happen, it was therefore standard practice by Christian authorities and missionaries not to confront Jews on this subject at all. Therefore, when the Jews became outraged at Paul and his fellow apostles did nothing or even agreed with them, Paul misinterpreted their motivation rather than realizing that the apostles were actually aligned with the Jews.

Paul carried the delusional belief that the Twelve, especially Peter, understood the gospel in the very same way that he did— in spite of so much evidence to the contrary. Apparently, Paul did not see his gospel as a change in doctrine in any sense, which is why he never grasped that his opponents did not agree with his teachings and actions. It also means that Paul learned his gospel from some highly respected Christian authority who was not Peter, James, or John, an authority equal or greater than these. Paul believed that his gospel came from Jesus himself, and it was certainly the theology of those in Arabia, whatever Paul meant by that. Perhaps, it just comes down to a matter of Paul's faith that all would happen according to God's plan, even if it looked impossible; Paul adamantly refused to accept the schism as permanent.

Several times, Paul attributes to his Jewish Christian opponents the motivation of greed. He may have come to believe this because his opponents repeatedly attacked him on matters of material support and money, giving him the impression that this was their real concern. His mistaken conclusion led him to believe that his way to reconciliation was to prove his loyalty through a financial gift, prompting him to arrange a large collection for the poor in Jerusalem. However, his gift appears to have angered the Jewish Christians even more.

Another point of contention is the claim by Hymenaeus and Philetas that the Resurrection has already taken place. By this Paul is referring to the eschatological resurrection of all the dead. The belief was that Elijah would inaugurate the Day of the Lord by resurrecting all who had died. Apparently, some thought this was a necessary element with the appearance of the Son of David Messiah. Paul is concerned about the effect of this claim, because naturally all Christians want to see their loved ones who had passed. If the Resurrection of the Dead on the last day has already occurred, what would it mean to the believers that their loved ones have not returned to them? They might think that they were permanently condemned by God or that they had been raised but could not find their way home— both very frightening possibilities to believers. In Chapter 3, Paul suggests that his two opponents are the worst kind of sinners and ends by comparing them to Jannes and Jambres opposing Moses.

Paul's dispute with the Jewish Christians hovered around three epicenters: the value of the law, the identification of the Son of David Messiah, and the divinity of Jesus Christ. Paul believed that faith in Jesus Christ had replaced the obligations and works of Mosaic Law; the Jewish Christians believed that Jesus Christ had intensified the obligations of the Torah. Paul believed that Jesus Christ was the one and only Son of David, whose return would inaugurate the Messianic age. The Jewish Christians maintained that the Son of David was a title conferred on the king of Israel in the Messianic age already begun with the appearance of Jesus Christ.

In accordance with their respective views, Paul believed that Jesus Christ was a divine being, the Son of God, and the Jewish Christians maintained that Jesus was purely human, although Jesus Christ referred to a spirit greater than the angels. The Jews and Jewish Christians also used the epithet, "Son of God," for Jesus Christ, but they meant by it someone special to God; especially they used it for the true anointed king in the tradition of the psalm. Therefore, the Son of God was not a supernatural being, as Paul taught, but a human especially favored by God. This understanding of Christ was the adoptionist point of view, believing that the spirit of Christ descended on Jesus after his purification by baptism. Paul may also have subscribed to the adoptionist doctrine to some degree, but with the differences described above.

The differences between these two visions were profound indeed. Yet, these two faiths seemed close enough and the language of spiritual doctrine supported both well enough that the chasm between them was not apparent until the mission to the gentiles dumped both Jew and Christian suddenly into the abyss of contention. When Paul and Peter met, they had different gospels and visions of the meaning of Jesus Christ; yet they conversed initially without knowing the gap between them. Although the differences seemed small and even technical, there was no possibility of reconciling these two visions.

A Prisoner for Christ

Paul is in chains at Rome. Recognition of the Ebionites by Paul. Letters to Ephesians, Colossians, Laodicaeans, Philemon, and Philippians. Death in Rome.

After the Trial in Jerusalem, Paul went to Rome. Contrary to the story in Acts, the trip was likely very short and uneventful, so Paul discusses nothing about it and Timothy is right where Paul left him. However, this did not end the controversies.

In Rome, Paul is immediately in chains, awaiting trial before a Roman magistrate, and writes 2 Timothy. Paul sent this letter and the Letter to the Ephesians with Tychicus to fetch Timothy.

In 2 Timothy 8-10 Paul gives us a further clue to the identity of his opponents. He says:

> Remember Jesus Christ having been raised from the dead, from the seed of David, according to my gospel, by which I have suffered unto bonds as an evildoer. But the word of God has not been bound. Therefore all things I endure because of the chosen ones, in order that they also may obtain the [reward] in Christ Jesus with glory eternal.

Reading this carefully, we can see with surprise that the chosen ones are not saved already, and Paul's heroics are in part directed for their salvation. They do not accept Paul's gospel and Paul writes here two points of contention, which of course is to him the true gospel and the faith necessary for salvation. How then can these Jews be described as "chosen" by Paul if they were not yet saved? The answer is that these are the Essene monks, the Ebionites, the Poor, the Saints, also called the Elect, who were the core of the Essene community and so also the core of the Jewish Christian church.

Notice that Paul recognizes the importance of the Elect. He justifies his imprisonment and suffering for their sake, and he expects Timothy to accept this reasoning. Unlike some groups, the Ebionites could not be ignored, because they were the foundation of the Messianic movement. They were the followers of John the Baptist and the primary target of Jesus' ministry. Consequently, their holding out against Paul was a devastating blow to his credibility and to his ministry.

Paul goes on to tell Timothy to remind them of his reason for suffering. Although he ostensibly is continuing his thought and so referring to the Ebionites, Paul means that he wants Timothy to witness for him to the Jewish Christian apostles, who were representing the position of the Ebionites. The Ebionites, dedicated to extreme purity and holiness, could not themselves venture among the gentiles, because even incidental contact with impure persons was polluting. So, Timothy's contact with the Ebionites could only be by proxy, through the Jewish Christian apostles.

Paul does not mention to Timothy anything about Peter. We really cannot make anything out of this fact. If Peter were being held in Rome also, awaiting his martyrdom, it is still unlikely that Paul would have acknowledged him. Had Peter already died in Jerusalem as a result of the conflict and trial, Paul would have not needed to mention it and it could not have helped his standing with Timothy. So, we will have to make what we can of silence.

Fortunately, however, silence may say a great deal here; because if Peter were alive, Paul would have needed to discuss his opinion of Peter's position. If Peter had sided with Paul and had become an ally, Timothy would need to know. Or, if Peter had sided against Paul as an enemy, Timothy would need to know not to trust him. Because of Peter's prominence in the Church, whatever his attitude might be, it would have been important enough to mention it to Timothy.

On the other hand, Paul's purpose in writing is to call Timothy to him; so, perhaps, he did not want to write something so sensitive and to send it by courier. When we consider the continued silence from Peter after this point, also the tradition that Paul and Peter died at the same time, and other writings written soon afterwards that indicate that Peter was dead, it seems very probable that Peter died at this point—whether at Jerusalem or Rome.

Ephesians

The Letter to the Ephesians is not a response to some challenge to Paul's authority or to his gospel. As this letter accompanied the one to Timothy, we might guess that this was simply a gesture of apostolic love for the congregation. Certainly, we should also see the letter to be support for his newly appointed apostle, Tychicus. Considering that Paul has just faced the trial in Jerusalem and was now a prisoner in Rome, we should also suspect that it is a subtle defense of his situation and a warning in anticipation of further attempts to undermine his gospel.

This letter is a treasure of theology. In Ephesians 1:4, Paul states that God had chosen the Christians before the foundation of the world. He goes on to state with absolute clarity that this means predestination, and he seems to imply pre-existence. In 1:20, Paul states that God raised Christ from the dead. In 1:22-23, he describes the Church as his body, elevating Christians to the level of Christ himself.

Paul declares openly and without hesitation that Christ abolished the law, the commandments, the ordinances. It is this change that makes it possible for the reconciliation and reunification of the gentiles with the Jews. Of course, we should remember that to his mind Paul was speaking to fellow Israelites, which is why he says "reconcile both in one body." It is only later that the term "gentile" began to be applied to all non-Jews, including pagans; however, the term went through the transition to the modern meaning quite seamlessly, perhaps because the non-Jewish Israelites were themselves little better than pagans.

188   Jesus Christ Divided: Solving the Mystery of the New Testament

Most of the letter, which is quite beautiful in style and sentiment, is simply exhortation to upright Christian behavior. Interestingly, Paul does not even mention the impending return of Jesus Christ, although this would greatly enhance his encouragements to the Ephesians. This is quite unlike Paul, whose other letters seem pregnant with expectation. Perhaps, we should read this to be a sign of despondency due to his incarceration, but this is the only hint that he is not entirely proud to be a prisoner for Christ, about which he boasts several times.

Colossians and Laodiceans
Apparently, the Colossians and the Laodiceans have strayed a bit from Paul's gospel by entertaining Jewish regulations and practices. From Paul's descriptions, it appears that he is referring to Mosaic law and other Jewish practices. He emphasizes that now circumcision is spiritual and not physical.

Paul also mentions "elements of the world" and "philosophy." This points to something that has been too much overlooked, which is the influence of Hellenistic philosophies on Judaism. Here the reference points directly to Stoicism, which had tremendous points of agreement with the Jewish Christians. For example, the Letter of James states that the smallest infraction of the law is an abrogation of all the law, which seems an extreme position to modern Christians; compare this with the strange Stoic belief that all immoral persons are equally immoral. Both views arrive at the same conclusion and are essentially equivalent in their guidance, suggesting that the Jewish Christians were enamored of and guided by Stoic philosophy. And Paul seems to be connecting the two as well.

Another indication that the Jewish Christians held to Stoic belief was that some ancient Jewish Christian baptismal liturgies invoke elemental powers. This seems to be what Paul is denouncing in Colossians 2:8 and 2:20.

Before moving on to the Letter to Philemon, which accompanied these letters, we should note some interesting points:

First, Tychicus is connected to these communities, which shows that he was over the entire area, not just a single community in Ephesus.

Second, as previously mentioned, the community is warned about Barnabas. The warning appears to be softened by a clarifying statement that he should be welcomed; however, even the softening comment does not entirely remove the sting. Moreover, the fact that he felt it necessary to tell the Colossians to welcome him shows that he thought that Barnabas might not be welcome.

Third, it is worth noting that Luke, the beloved physician, is with Paul.

Philemon

Everywhere that Paul mentions slaves, he states that they should obey and remain subject to their masters. Now, this is in apparent contradiction to Paul's rather democratic rhetoric that God is impartial and does not recognize earthly status. It is explainable, however, from the point of view that Paul favors no change in earthly matters. Seemingly, for Paul, the end was so near that no energy should be wasted rectifying what Jesus Christ himself would reconcile.

Consequently, the Letter of Philemon stands out and against Paul's preaching elsewhere, including in the Letter to the Colossians. It is a flat contradiction that Paul is asking Philemon to free Onesimus; however, Paul has a very good reason for asking. He says that he has become the father of Onesimus. What he means by this becomes clear only in a letter written by Ignatius to the Ephesians, where Onesimus is found to be the bishop of Ephesus. This is supported by the nearly equal status that Paul gives him with Tychicus in Colossians 4:8-9. Of course, a bishop, as ruler of the church, could not be subject to a lesser person, and so by necessity a bishop had to be free of any human master. So, Paul needed Philemon to free Onesimus to serve the Church.

Philippians

The last letter that Paul wrote, Philippians, seems to have been prompted by a desire to thank the congregation for gifts. These gifts were a great statement of confidence in Paul, and at the same time giving to Paul was a rebellion against the Jewish leaders. In the past, such gifts were sent to the Temple in Jerusalem. The Essenes, and then the Christians, however, had diverted many contributions away from the Temple, which they opposed, to support the Poor, the Ebionites. This was what Paul was referring to by his accusations that his opponents were motivated by money, and it is also why he believed that his gift would tip the scales in his favor. The Ebionites had to be motivated by money; else why would they try to recruit those whom they despised?

The Ebionites were as monks devoted only to spiritual pursuits and they avoided money and business as worldly and polluting, so they would have been greatly dependent on contributions from other Essenes and Christians for financial support. Therefore, after the events in Jerusalem, the sending of support to Paul instead of to James, Peter, John, and the Poor solidified the schism and declared the Philippians' allegiance to Paul.

This is Paul's last letter but it is also the first letter in which Paul addresses to bishops and deacons, again showing that the organization of the Church was already advanced. This raises the question of why Paul neglected addressing bishops and deacons in other letters. Of course, he did commend Phoebe, the deaconess, in the Letter to the Romans, yet this was to introduce her to them as Paul's agent in carrying his message. He also mentions Andronicus and Junia as apostles. It seems to us a strange lack of courtesy for Paul to neglect to acknowledge by title the presbyters, bishops, and deacons, who were part of every community Apparently, Paul did not emphasize rank, and this was probably a cultural aspect of Christianity, making a point that all were equal before God. So, it is a noticeable change in Philippians that Paul makes special mention of bishops and deacons, and we must wonder why and why now.

It is a reasonable speculation, because Paul is dying, that he has recognized that he will not be around to lead the congregations. Now that his communities were cut off from the Jerusalem with only Timothy and the few remaining Greek apostles to lead them, Paul must have realized that the bishops and deacons would have to take on more responsibility for the future of the gospel. They would have to stand strong independently against the Judaizers, who would inevitably attempt to dominate and convert them to their own gospel.

Paul describes his enemies as proclaiming Christ from envy and rivalry, from selfish ambition, and with insincerity. He even states that their intention in preaching is to cause him personal suffering. Obviously, a great hatred has come between Paul and the Judaizers, whom he calls dogs (an unclean animal), evil-doers, and mutilators, referring to circumcision. These are the people who are responsible for Paul's imprisonment.

Paul boasts that his suffering has furthered the gospel. Specifically, he states that he has evangelized the praetorium and the emperor's household. Again, however, this does not mean that Paul is converting non-Israelites. The emperor's household would contain many slaves, and some slaves would be Jewish. Likewise, the Roman legions were not populated entirely by Latins, but most troops were recruited from the many conquered peoples, including Judeans and other Semitic peoples. Of course, we should also remember that the definition of who was an Israelite could be quite flexible outside of Judea.

Paul's death was painful enough that he compared his suffering to that of Christ, yet he gave thought to the future of the gospel and the faith of his congregations. Paul remained miraculously steadfast in his faith to the very end in spite of the fact that, in his time, he largely failed. He had failed to convince the Jews, the most prominent apostles hated him, and the Church had broken into pieces. He had preached to many communities and few remained loyal to him. Most of his trusted companions deserted him. He had been condemned and turned over to the Romans as a criminal. Today, however, we have no doubt that he was ultimately successful, because Christianity still lives on in a form very similar to the way he taught it.

The Gospel of Paul

Search for doctrines and theological statements within Paul's letters.

Paul tells Timothy to retrieve some scrolls, "especially the parchments," from Troas (Troy). The word "Bible" comes from βιβλία, the Greek word for "scrolls," and very likely Paul carried some of the books of the Bible with him. Possibly, Paul had all the books that we have in the Old Testament today, but that would have required a large shipping container. More likely, he had certain fundamental texts or anthologies of quotations. He may even have had other books that are not in the Bible, apocryphal texts that for unknown reasons were left out of the canon.

The reference to "parchments" is intriguing, because this word may be an early reference to a codex, which has the modern form of a book instead of a roll. Often the word is translated as "notebooks." Because we know that Paul's mission was to evangelize, that is, to preach the gospel, these parchments could have contained notes and references from the Old Testament used to prove that Jesus Christ was the Messiah. They may have included doctrinal statements and formulas, which Paul sometimes quotes; and they probably included sayings of Jesus recorded for posterity, some also quoted by Paul. He also could have used a passion narrative to indicate the importance and meaning of the Resurrection. Therefore, it is likely that Paul's parchments or notebooks contained most of the elements that we associate with the Gospels today, although I doubt that he had one document that we would call a gospel.

It is clear that no authoritative written gospel existed for the early apostles proselytizing to the Hellenistic/Roman world, because Paul and his opponents can have two different messages without at first realizing it, and no one had the authority to correct the dissonance—the dispute could not be immediately resolved by checking the text. Moreover, this explains why so many contradictory writings could later acquire the status of an authoritative "gospel."

The disputes that split the Church into factions were already active prior to the existence of written texts of the Gospels; it was precisely the variations in understanding the Gospel that caused the proliferation of texts and sects later. If Paul had a written gospel with him, its importance would have demanded that the communities friendly to Paul retain it, just as they did his letters. Indeed, part of the reason that Paul's letters were so valuable at the time was that no other such reference materials were available. Therefore, we can be confident that no written gospel had currency before 55 CE, although I think that one or more were written in that year.

From the conflicts and the splits that we know did occur, I think that we can reasonably see this period, the time of Paul's mission and before, as a formative period in the Church. It was a time when the founders of the Christian religion were searching for the meaning of Jesus Christ, his teachings, and the events of his life; for, Jesus Christ did not conform to the preconceptions of the Messiah held by the various Jewish authorities and peoples. Under the pressure of competing visions, Paul and his contemporaries sought the Holy Spirit with extravagant abandon, and they finally succeeded with much pain and effort in producing a coherent religious understanding that has stood the test of time. Yet, it is important to recognize that the result was greater than the expectations of any one apostle or group.

The oral gospel that Paul preached, to which he refers many times in his letters, is one of the earliest expressions of the Christian truth. Because he evangelized so close in time to Jesus, we should expect that his teaching and thought was very close to that original gospel message. Moreover, Paul's confidence, in the face of his differences with the authoritative Jewish Christians, actually reinforces that his message was an authoritative understanding of Jesus Christ. Paul's authority as an apostle rested on only two things: his own revelation of Jesus Christ and the truth of his gospel. Paul could not have innovated without drawing question to his authority, and by this accident of history we can rest assured that Paul understood well the true gospel, the original meaning of Jesus Christ.

It was the Jewish Christian apostles, those pillars of established authority within the Church, who had the power to innovate. They changed the radical message of Christ Jesus, molding it to a form that would fit closer to the orthodox views of Pharisees, the violent aspirations of the Zealots, and the ascetic purity of the Ebionites (the poor, the Essenes). James the Just may even have attempted to appease the Sadducees by denying the Resurrection of the Dead. The Jewish Christian gospel message was a political platform for a new government, inclusive but more thoroughly Jewish. They rejected the spiritual freedom and diminished the generous forgiveness of Jesus Christ in favor of obedience to the law, to ritual, and to the hierarchy—a materialist view of the Kingdom. Most of all, they rejected the uncircumcised and non-kosher gentiles from fellowship in Jesus Christ.

Obviously, understanding Paul's preaching is of tremendous importance to our understanding of the early development of Christianity. From the letters of Paul, we should be able to piece together Paul's gospel, at least, approximately.

Originally, the meaning of the word "gospel" was simply "good news." A gospel was the formal announcement of the appearance and installation of a new ruler. We have inscriptions showing that the Romans employed the word in announcing the emperor Augustus, and reasonably we might expect that they were following traditions far older than themselves. For the Jews, of course, the gospel also announced the new ruler who would be the anointed king of Israel, who by the tradition from David in the Psalms was the beloved Son of God.

The political concept of a gospel also had religious significance, of course, both for Romans and for Jews. Religion and politics were closely connected for all ancient peoples, but perhaps far more for Jews who in agony and oppression waited for God to personally take over control of the world. Religion and politics for Jews were one and the same thing, because God was their political leader. Consequently, a gospel was both a political announcement and a statement of spiritual revelation.

The purpose of spreading a gospel or good news was more than just advertizing and informing. We have inscriptions in durable stone, because the announcement was a political act and part of the process to validate and establish the rightful authority of the new ruler. We do not need much imagination to see that such an announcement would impose obligations on the hearers to declare their acceptance and loyalty to the new lord, by word and gesture. A gospel demanded a decision. Failure to declare loyalty could be seen as an expression of opposition, which could prompt negative responses by the new authority. We should expect that at minimum a government official who did not support the new ruler would quietly resign their position. Such resignations would be both dangerous and costly, inviting suspicions and reprisals, and therefore they were probably rare. Spreading the good news demanded a political decision of the hearers; but also the announcers would have the obligation of thoroughly spreading the gospel to everyone. No one could be uninformed, and everyone could be held accountable for declaring their loyalty.

This is so similar to the Christian meaning of the idea that it is difficult not to see the idea of a gospel as a cultural borrowing from Rome; although, it could have originally entered Judaism from even more ancient cultural contacts. Any ruler in any time would have to consolidate their authority to rule. With Christians, however, spreading the good news, "evangelizing," became a verb— "to good news someone." This word appears as early as Jesus Christ himself, according to the New Testament Gospels, in reference to announcing that the Kingdom has arrived. The knowledge that the Messianic king had appeared and had been anointed required a response, both political and spiritual, declaring a promise of faith, loyalty, and obedience to the new king.

Paul's use of the word, "gospel," however, approaches our own modern sense of the word. He writes about "my gospel," that he taught, distinguishing it from gospels preached by others. His gospel contained specific ideas, teachings, and dogmas more nuanced than the simple announcement of the king. The gospel of Paul was his understanding of the meaning of Jesus Christ, perhaps more spiritual than political.

As discussed earlier, some passages of Paul's letters are clearly interjections by others, attempting to arrange Paul's position in support of their own. Some of these passages are recognizable because they are found in different places in various manuscripts, revealing that they were not original. Also, some are so blatantly contrary to Paul's statements elsewhere, that they are easily identified as non-Pauline. We will have to identify these insertions of an editor in order to distinguish from Paul's teaching.

However, we begin to tread on boggy ground when we try to determine which passages were from Paul and which were not. People often appear to contradict themselves; and sometimes it is a logical error on their part, and sometimes it only appears to be contradictory when the author is straddling two concepts in apparent, but resolvable, contradiction. Sometimes, honest and thoughtful people hold contradictory opinions, even though such contradictions could damage their credibility. So the question for us becomes three-fold: Is the contradiction due to an error or fault of understanding by Paul? Is it an apparent but resolvable conflict of ideas, if we only understood better? Or is it an addition by others?

The only practical solution to the problem is to leave the less obvious contradictions intact and to correct only the most obvious and direct. We can justify being reticent to distance from Paul anything that is not patently an interpolation, because error is part and parcel of dealing with ancient thought from a different culture. Moreover, subtle errors are by definition minor distinctions.

Therefore, we should ask, what does Paul say about his gospel? I will proceed in discussing indications within Paul's letters about his beliefs and teachings, but I also want to anticipate a potential problem:

It will be tempting for us to see in the letters a development of thought from the earlier letters to the later. This is a natural impression created as we learn with more specificity— as more details of Paul's thought are revealed; however, this is almost certainly a false impression. Paul's letters were written over a very short period of time, about two years, which would not have been sufficient to create or evolve new theology. Rather, Paul simply revealed more of his spiritual understanding about Jesus Christ, as he saw the need and, perhaps, as the dramatic conflict forced him to ignore previous taboos about secrecy.

1 and 2 Thessalonians
Paul's first theological statement is to describe the Thessalonian church as *in God the Father and the Lord Jesus Christ*.[226] Firstly, we should understand that Paul's grammar seems to equate God the Father with the Lord Jesus Christ, seeming to evoke Trinitarian doctrine. Moreover, he also elevates the Thessalonians to a share in the Deity and in Jesus Christ, suggesting that the Thessalonians too share his divinity.

Of course, 2 Thessalonians 3:11 describes the Lord Jesus Christ directing his way, just like God. I will now leave off describing each similar occurrence, because these kinds of references and use of Jesus Christ are numerous in Paul's writing. He rarely mentions God without also giving equal position and identical purpose to Jesus Christ.

Paul exhorts the Thessalonians to morality, for God called them to holiness. God gives the Holy Spirit to the Thessalonians.[227] They have been taught by God to love one another.[228]

Paul writes that Jesus died and rose again. Through Jesus, God will bring those who previously died in Christ, and *the Lord himself,*

---

[226] 1 Thess. 1:1.

[227] 1 Thess. 4:7-8.

[228] 1 Thess. 4:9.

apparently meaning Jesus Christ, will give a cry of command.[229] We should notice how much more active Jesus Christ is than God the Father in controlling events.

Paul states that the Day of the Lord will come like a thief in the night. Sudden destruction will come like labor pains to a pregnant woman and no one will escape.[230]

In 2 Thess. 1:5, Paul mentions the Kingdom of God, but is unclear whether it already exists or is soon to come. Paul gives a vision of Lord Jesus exacting retribution, eternal punishment, from those not knowing God and not obeying Paul's gospel of Lord Jesus.[231] Interestingly, the method of punishment is simply separation from Jesus and his glory.

Paul prophesies that the Man of Lawlessness must appear before the end in 2 Thessalonians chapter 2; but this was a reaction to events and does not appear essential to his gospel, because it was never repeated in other letters to other churches. Also, Paul calls the Thessalonians the first fruits for salvation, because they were the first to believe in Paul's gospel, suggesting that Paul's gospel was a recent development.[232]

From chapter 3, we learn that part of Paul's teaching was that his spiritual children should imitate Paul and his compatriots— not to live in idleness or off the efforts of others. This seems to be in contrast with the practice of Paul's opposition. Although Paul asserts that he did have the rights of an apostle, he wanted to set an example.

1 Corinthians

In 1 Corinthians 1:9, Paul calls Jesus Christ the Son of God. The following verses reveal a great deal: The divisions within the church

---

[229] 1 Thess. 4:14-17.

[230] 1 Thess. 5:2-3.

[231] 2 Thess. 1:8-10.

[232] 2 Thess. 2:13-15.

show that there had already been among the Corinthians, prior to Paul's preaching, an idea that baptism implied a relationship of discipleship or servitude. Paul rejects this idea, but in the discussion he reveals that Jesus had baptized some from Corinth. Another interesting fact can be gleaned in the mention of Apollos, who is described in Acts as knowing only the baptism of John the Baptist phrased in a manner that suggested inferior authority. However, Paul here argues vigorously against any such distinctions and gives equal status to all Christians regardless of who baptized them. Of course, this suggests that many of the Corinthians were already Christians even before receiving Paul's gospel, some of them for nearly two decades!

In 1 Corinthians 1:18, Paul states that the message of the cross was a fundamental part of his gospel. He indicates that Jews and Greeks both had difficulty with this message. Paul later states: "For I decided not to know anything among you except Jesus Christ and this one crucified." This is a plain statement of the simplicity of his initial gospel message. In 4:15, Paul emphasizes that he is their spiritual father through the gospel.

It is apparent that Paul preached a kind of freedom in Christ, which was easily misunderstood by his children, because, just as he had to admonish the Thessalonians to abstain from immorality, the Corinthians seem to have gone even farther.[233] Paul quotes his gospel: "All things to me are lawful," but he adds wisdom by stating that not all things are beneficial nor should anyone allow himself to be dominated by anything. His gospel of freedom needed some clarification.[234]

In Chapter 10, Paul overtly equates "the Lord" of the Old Testament with Christ, as a mystical source of spiritual nourishment. Paul may be describing Moses as Christ. On the other hand, nowhere does Paul declare Moses to be Christ; rather, he calls Christ "the

---

[233] 1 Cor. 5:1.

[234] 1 Cor. 6:12-20.

spiritual following rock" from which the Israelites drank, but God was not well pleased with most of them. This metaphor is strange and may well be a play on Peter's name, suggesting that those who receive Christ through Peter are in danger of not pleasing God. Nonetheless, however, Paul is clearly implying that Christ is a supernatural being who transcends time, and this does lead inevitably towards the doctrine of the Trinity.

In 10:16-17, Paul reveals the sacramental meaning of the cup and bread: the cup of blessing is sharing in the blood of Christ and the bread is the body of Christ. He explains that the sacraments symbolize the unity of the Church in Christ. He does not mention any idea of Christ's death as a sacrifice, but his following up immediately with a comparison to the sacrificial cult is suggestive. In 11: 23-26, he adds the remembrance of Christ, saying that by the sacrament they declare the Lord's death, but he does not explain the significance of declaring the crucifixion.

Chapters 12-14 are tremendously important, because it makes certain that the Corinthians were already Christians when Paul preached to them. We can be certain because had Paul taught them the spiritual practices, he would not have needed to explain their use and practice in a letter.

In Chapter 15, Paul declares his gospel: Christ died for our sins according to the scriptures. He was buried and raised on the third day in accordance to scriptures. This is the most explicit statement of Paul's teaching. Unfortunately, some parts of this chapter are somewhat suspicious. He does not mention the women who, in the canonical Gospels, were the initial witnesses to the Resurrection. He names James as receiving an individual revelation before the other apostles, giving James unusual prominence, although we know that James was his primary opposition. He denigrates his own revelation, which makes no sense at all in light of his opposition to the Jewish Christians and the confidence in his own mission that he displays elsewhere. Consequently, I am doubtful of the authenticity of verses 5-11.

Paul argues that because Christ was raised there would therefore be a general Resurrection of the Dead. His use of the metaphor of the first fruits implies that this event would happen imminently.

Paul's statement in 15:28 shows a view at variance to the modern view of the Trinity, one God in three equal persons, because the Son cannot be equivalent with the Father if subject to him. A way around this might be to argue that God is subject to himself, which answers the objection but in an unsatisfactory way; because it fails to account for Paul's emphasis and reasoning in making this statement.

The position of 1 Corinthians 15:50-54 flatly denies the ascension of ordinary flesh to heaven and creates the idea of a spiritual body— a soul? This too contradicts modern Christology, demanding that Jesus' ascension to Heaven was complete and bodily, whatever that might mean.

Galatians
When Paul talks about the Galatians forsaking his gospel in favor of another, he is speaking about the legal requirements and most of all about circumcision. One explanation for his vehemence could be that through circumcision, the Galatians left his dominion, as "apostle to the uncircumcised." This would mean that according to Paul's agreement with Peter, the Galatians would literally belong to Peter and his gospel, as the "apostle to the circumcision." We have already discussed that Paul's understanding of the agreement was metaphorical, but the reality of Jewish gentiles actually undergoing the operation and adopting the purity laws changed the situation. Now, any of Paul's communities could be converted to Peter.

I see no reason to degrade Paul's spiritual commitment by reducing the conflict to a simple question of hegemony and financial support: Paul probably realized that the gospel that he knew and believed to be from Jesus Christ could be overtaken and eliminated by the increasingly popular asceticism of James. Apparently, this movement was accompanied by an intensified apocalypticism and new

Gnostic teachings. The move towards circumcision and excessive Ebionite purity was a move away from the original gospel of Jesus Christ, and Paul hated the change with honest religious fervor as a corruption of the gospel.

> "I do not deny the grace of God; for, if through the law [comes] righteousness, then Christ for nothing died."[235]

Here we have the most succinct expression of Paul's particular teaching: the law is useless and Christ has done away with its literal import.

2 Corinthians

It may not have been integral to Paul's gospel, but his letters do stress suffering for Christ a great deal, but to a much lesser extent does he emphasize Christ's suffering for humans. Christ's suffering is not precisely the idea of a God-Man sacrifice for sin:

> Because one for all died, thus all died. And, for all he died in order that the living no more for themselves live but for the one having died and having been raised for them.[236]

Paul is saying here that Christ has saved them all by absorbing death to himself on behalf of all and defeating death through Resurrection. Death has already happened for Paul and his followers through the death and Resurrection of Christ. However, this is still not saying directly that Jesus had to die to expiate sin.

Yet, Paul soon makes a statement that is nearly plain:

---

[235] Gal. 2:21.

[236] 2 Cor. 5:15.

> Therefore, if anyone [is] in Christ a new creation, the old things passed away; behold! they have become new. And all things [are] from God, who having reconciled us to himself through Christ and having given to us the ministry of reconciliation, so that God was in Christ reconciling the world to himself, not counting their trespasses against them, and placing in us the commandment of reconciliation.[237]

God reconciles the world to himself in Christ— but not explicitly by Christ's death but through the ministry of reconciliation. God does not count sins against the sinners, although Paul emphasizes that this is out of forgiveness and mercy rather than from the retribution of a blood debt. However, we can see Paul as nearly all the way to the sacrifice of Christ for sin.

However, we now must consider:

> The one not knowing sin, for us a sin [Jesus] made, in order that we might become the righteousness of God in him.[238]

Several other translations of this passage are possible, because the subject of each of the first two clauses is not explicit; however, I think that the best possibility is that Jesus is the subject of both. Most translators treat sin as an abstract noun throughout, without the indefinite article, but the above translation is more likely. In translating abstractly, with Jesus as an embodiment of all sin, requires assuming that God transformed Jesus into sin— which is a terribly unlikely idea— or that Jesus created or committed sin. To claim that Jesus Christ was sin itself would be blasphemous, even metaphorically

---

[237] 2 Cor. 5:18-19.

[238] 2 Cor. 5:21.

speaking. Saying that God did this is blasphemous also. Saying that Jesus created or committed sin invalidates the sanctity of the event. In this translation presented here, including the indefinite article, which is only implied in Greek, the sin refers to the murder of Jesus through crucifixion by the Jews, which *constituted* a sin. This could suggest a preordination of the event; but that is not a necessary interpretation. This reading, however, does not demand that Jesus be a sacrifice for all sins.

In Chapter 12, Paul speaks about the third heaven, the highest level according to the Secret Book of Enoch, suggesting that the apocryphal document structured his thinking on spiritual matters. This should not be a surprise, since the Letter of Jude even quotes from this extra-canonical book:

> But even prophesied to them seventh from Adam Enoch saying: "Behold came the lord with his holy myriads to exact judgment against all and to rebuke all the wicked about all their works of wickedness which they wickedly did and about all the obstinacies which spoke against him [the] wicked sinners.[239]

This suggests that Paul had the very same views of most doctrines that the Jewish Christians had, and that the differences, the conflicts, were isolated to a select set of ideas.

Romans
Certainly, Paul knew that Peter was at Rome. He may have seen Peter's letters from Rome, scribed by Sylvanus, and Paul's Italian friends visiting in Corinth would have brought him news. Although Paul had never been there, the Roman church had certainly heard of his activities. Consequently, Romans is a diplomatic statement of his

---

[239] Jude 14-15.

gospel; and we should imagine that Paul is writing directly to Peter, because he knew that Peter would hear his words.

Paul everywhere declares equality between Jew and Greek, yet he also with some contradiction states over and again the formula, "Jew first, then the Greek." He preaches strongly against judging and hypocrisy and sums up his whole position in one sentence, quoting Habakkuk 2:4, "the righteous by faith will live."

Paul states a very interesting proposition in Romans 2:14 in saying, "whenever the gentile not having the law does naturally things of the law, these, not having law, unto themselves are a law." We should see here a delicate dance where the law is neither criticized nor praised outright. Paul states that Jesus Christ will judge men's hearts according to their consciences: their righteous acts reveal their knowledge of righteousness and accuse or excuse their sinful acts. He then embarks on a diatribe against Jews in an accusing tone suggesting hypocrisy. This leads into the statement that real circumcision is of heart, in spirit, and not in letter nor in flesh.

Of course, Paul's real argument is that we cannot be justified by the law, only by faith in Jesus Christ. Through faith we die and are raised anew in Christ's Resurrection, a sacrifice of atonement. The law condemns our inability to comply with it. By dying with Christ, we die to our desire for sin, and, in reward for our faith, out of mercy and with the intercession of Christ Jesus, God forgives our sin. Without faith, redemption does not happen. With faith, all will be saved. The faithful demonstrate their inner redemption by outward goodness.

Perhaps, the lynchpin of Paul's argument is his use in Romans 4:3 of Genesis 15:6:

> *For what does scripture say? "And believed Abraham [in] God, and it was reckoned to him as righteousness."*

This is perhaps the most succinct statement of Paul's scriptural foundation, uniting his faith in Jesus Christ with the law and at the same time negating the law with the forgiveness received by faith alone.

We should remember that Paul's use of Abraham as an example was not merely a convenient use of a suitable scripture to support his position. He was preaching to Jews, both gentile and kosher, who defined themselves by their ancestry. He held to the belief that a fundamental mystery of the gospel was that it distinguished the righteous Hebrew from the unrighteous— only the righteous called by the Holy Spirit and pre-destined by God would turn to belief in Jesus Christ, the King of the Jews, and by definition the righteous would be Jews, subjects of the king of Israel. At this point, no effort was made to convert pagans, which is why Paul never wrote to the churches that they should go out and preach to non-Hebrews. If a pagan had accepted the gospel, swearing loyalty to Jesus Christ as lord and master, this would be an impossibility and would reveal that the pagan was not really a pagan but one of the lost tribes of Israel. Nonetheless, it is easy to see that if faith is the definition of the elect, which is Paul's argument later in chapter nine, this leaves open the possibility of negating even ancestry in defining who would be "children of the promise." Paul nearly makes this leap in Romans 9:17-18, but he does not go so far as to consider Pharoah righteous, but only as a tool of God. We should also realize that, in the Greek, calling Abraham the father of nations is the same wording as calling him the father of gentiles.

In chapter five, Paul compares the Fall of Adam with the sacrifice of Jesus, the latter negating the former. Paul indicates here that the purpose of law was to increase sin; a truly radical departure from Judaism! Perhaps it was not his intention, but this statement could only inflame his Jewish opposition.

Perhaps, the most significant statement of Paul revealing his interpretation of salvation is in Romans 5:9 when he mentions "justification in his blood." This is not explained and is almost formulaic, as though he expects the Romans to know what he is talking about. It could be just a thought slipping in that he did not intend to explain, but that accident may actually indicate even more strongly that Paul understood Jesus' death as a human sacrifice to God in expiation of human sin.

In chapter six, Paul redefines the meaning of baptism into a re-enactment of the death of Jesus Christ. Originally, baptism had been a purification ritual, so the parallel is that Jesus died to purify the faithful. Paul seems here to also redefine sin, which in Judaism was the abrogation of law, but Paul's definition of sin is not at all clear. Certainly, he means disobedience to God, but the law had been the means of knowing the will of God in Judaism. Now, it seems only one's conscience defines sin and therefore righteousness. The only clear reference to any behavior as sinful is sexual, employing bodily parts to uncleanness and lawlessness unto lawlessness. Paul literally uses the Greek word for "lawlessness," which would naturally be confusing in midst of the argument that sin is not defined by, and is even increased by, the dictums of law.

Nonetheless, Paul continues his rejection of the law through an analogy with marriage. He claims that Jews died to the law through the body of Christ in order to bear fruit to God. Startlingly, he identifies law as the very cause of lustful passions, operating as a physical force within our bodies. He counters his overreach immediately, though, denying that the law is sin, but claims that sin, as an evil force, uses the law to create temptation and death, even though the law Paul declares holy. Paul seems to be equating sin with our inclination to push beyond imposed limits in the same way that an obstinate child will immediately rebel at guidance from their parent. Sin appears to be aroused by the imposition of limits, the restriction of freedom.

Paul proceeds to explicate in a deeply psychological manner his angst caused by the opposition of the law of God by the law of sin. It is a war between the mind and the flesh, where the passions, especially sexual passion, rule his flesh and goodness rules his mind. The law of God is goodness and the law of sin is sexual passion.

While his argument seems to be meandering and confused, Paul has set up beautifully his next turn, which is to argue that people can escape sin and fulfill the law only by living according to the Spirit and ignoring the flesh. We must focus our attention not on the flesh, which is the subject of the law, but upon the Spirit. The law failed to save us because of the opposition by our flesh, but we can still be saved by focusing our attention on the Spirit of God within and God will give life to our mortal bodies. Paul goes further to claim that all led by the Spirit of God are children of God and joint heirs with Christ, since we suffer with him in order that also we may be glorified with him.

Paul then moves into an apocalyptic personification of creation as a suffering creature similar to the elect of Israel awaiting salvation. He answers anticipated doubts by pointing out that hope is by definition unseen, and he adds that even the lack of faith and imagination is mitigated by the Spirit interceding for us at the behest of God. So then, failure cannot be a possibility.

In chapter nine, Paul continues his argument for the superiority of faith over the law. He ends strongly in identifying Jesus Christ with the stumbling stone in Isaiah, implying that the reliance on the law blinded the Jews, i.e., the Pharisees and Sadducees, to faith in Jesus Christ. Certainly, Paul could not have failed to recognize the pun on Peter's name and the potential double-meaning in this context? He then goes on in chapter ten to state his disagreement with the Jewish leaders, that through arrogance they have substituted their own form of righteousness for that of God. He then picks apart the scriptures in detail to exalt the gentiles over the Jews.

If the point has not been made thus far, I should repeat again the duality between the ideas of justification by law and justification by works. The law requires works, that is, it requires specific behaviors. Works or behaviors are justified by being in accordance with law. So, in chapter eleven when Paul states in Romans 11:6 that those chosen were by grace and not by works, he is continuing the argument against reliance on the law. In the same way, James' argument that salvation comes by works was also an argument in favor of obedience to the law. Also, we might see in Paul's statement a certain relationship between the ideas of grace and faith, where one cannot exist without the other, just as one cannot accept the gospel without the gift of the Holy Spirit.

Romans 11:11 may be an important clue to Paul's motivations in his mission to the gentiles. Paul seems to imply that the rejection by the Jewish Christians of the gospel of freedom from the law caused him to take the Gospel to the gentiles, "to make them [the Jewish Christians] jealous [or zealous]." This may be an inordinately blunt statement of his intentions, but it does appear likely that Paul genuinely believed his efforts with the gentiles would prompt a reconciliation with the Jewish Christians.

It would be interesting to learn if the gentile Romans understood the priestly metaphor of the dough, but anyone can appreciate the beautiful analogy of the wild olive shoot being grafted to the tree. Paul expresses clearly his hopes that he expects the Jewish Christians will repent, but he does not shy from calling them the enemies of the gospel because of the gentiles, although beloved because of their ancestors. Paul makes another revelation of about his faith in the gospel by saying that the gifts and calling of God are irrevocable. He has total faith that the Jewish Christians will join with him again and that the Church will remain whole, even describing the current discord as necessary to the plan of God.

Paul states, "I know and have been persuaded in the Lord Jesus that nothing [is] common [unclean] through itself; only by reckoning [is] anything to be common [unclean]."[240] Succinctly, let your conscience be your guide (and not the law). And more strongly put, "whatever [is] not from faith, sin it is."[241]

Hebrews

The Letter to the Hebrews, however, is a more serious problem than the other letters, because we can be sure that it was originally composed in

---

[240] Rom. 14:14.

[241] Rom. 14:23.

Aramaic and later translated into the Greek. As any experienced translator can attest, the translating process is not the simple exchanging of words from one language to another. It often requires interpretation and elucidation, which means that the opinions of the translator may influence the resulting text. Such additions, deletions, and commentaries will be impossible to detect, unless they blatantly conflict with Paul's other letters; however, no such conflicts are obvious in Hebrews.

The fact that the translator of Hebrews discarded the greeting and the thanksgiving is an indication that the letter was translated at a time when the conflict between Paul and the Jewish Christians was an embarrassment. On the other hand, Hebrews 5:11 is sufficiently critical of the Jewish Christians to give us confidence that purposeful editing of the letter for soothing the embarrassment was limited, perhaps only to the truncation of the introductory paragraphs.

However, we cannot be sure that the translator did not include inadvertent errors of understanding, perhaps by unintentionally introducing later, more developed theology. Certainly, the translation occurred much later than the initial collection of Paul's letters. We can guess that the schism between Pauline and Jewish Christians would have been a very disturbing event and that some would want to rectify it as soon as possible. A later, compromise gospel, however, might contain and influence doctrine in Hebrews which was not original to Paul. Although Hebrews does not contain any blatant contradictions with Paul's other letters; in translation, the subtle differences of spiritual and of theological exposition might not be detectable. Consequently, we are going to have to remain aware that our conclusions based on the Letter to the Hebrews are not entirely solid.

Much depends upon how much later the translation was made, because the closer in time the translation was made to the time of Paul's writing, the closer in understanding to Paul's original thought. Since the Letter to the Hebrews can be associated in time with the attempt to reunify the Church, it may have been close in time with the Acts of the Apostles and the interpolations added to Paul's letters. We do have some clues to the likely time period. The Acts of the Apostles clearly references and associates itself with the Gospel of Luke, and it was therefore written after that gospel. While the Gospel of Luke has usually been dated between 80 and 95 CE, I would argue for an earlier date, 62-69 CE, because of the prominence of Cleopas in Luke's resurrection story, included to lend support to his following James as the primate of the Church.[242] This should have been during the leadership of Simon Cleopas, not too long after James' death in 62 CE. The Acts of the Apostles, however, ignores Cleopas completely, suggesting that he no longer had any role whatsoever for the Church— that he was dead. This places Acts after the destruction of Jerusalem, but still soon enough that reconciliation between the Jews and the gentiles was still thought possible— meaning that gentiles were still considered non-kosher Jews at this point and not permanently separate from the Jewish Christians. This points to a time shortly after the Roman conquest of Masada in 73 CE. The Letter to the Hebrews would have been translated from Aramaic into Greek about this time as well. The main difference for Jews, both Christian and non-Christian, is that the hope for military victory over the conquerors had recently been crushed, which was not something that motivated Paul.

Hebrews is the most important letter in understanding Paul's gospel, even with the problems mentioned. It was originally written directly to Jews who were largely hostile to Paul, but Paul wants very much to persuade them to his way of thinking. Moreover, the Jewish Christians were learned in the Jewish scriptures and belief, so that Paul discusses his reasoning in greater theological depth and specificity than in his letters to gentile communities and his approach is thoroughly Jewish and priestly.

---

[242] Simon bar Cleopas or Simeon bar Clopas was a cousin of Jesus and James. He took over leadership after the assassination of James in 62 CE, moving the Jerusalem church to the area near Pella. However, if we can identify him with the Simon bar Giora mentioned by Josephus, he died in 69 CE; so after that year any importance to his witness of the Resurrection.

Paul begins with an explicit statement that the Son of God, who has spoken in these last days, was the co-creator of the aeons, meaning eternity. This statement explicitly connects Jesus Christ with the cosmic Christ, and with God in a nearly Trinitarian doctrine. In saying that the Son of God is the exact representation of God's being, sustaining all things, we can see that the Christ is nearly equal to God, which Paul goes on to confirm by placing him above the angels.

It is interesting that Paul describes Jesus Christ as being inferior to the angels until suffering death crowned him with glory and honor, having made a purification of sins. Notice that he emphasizes here the suffering, which is a flat confrontation with the Docetic theology that did not allow for Christ to suffer nor to die. Paul equates those sanctified with Jesus Christ as brothers and sisters, sharing flesh and blood in every respect— another jibe against Docetism. Jesus Christ came to help the descendants of Abraham.

Paul next makes a distinction between Moses and Jesus Christ. He follows with another interesting digression that appears to be an apocryphal quote which Paul specifically designates as from the "Holy Spirit," warning the Hebrews against hardening their hearts, comparing contemporary Jews with those following Moses. Apparently, he is anticipating recalcitrance.

In Hebrews 4:12, Paul seems to equate Jesus Christ with the Logos of God, judging thoughts and intentions of the heart, "before [him] whom to us [is] the Logos." The word λογος has many potential variants of meaning, but in this paragraph the best fit seems to be "reckoning," which speaks to both the incisive reasoning of God and to the perspicacious judgment of our hearts.

Equating the Logos with a high priest, Paul continues into a statement and argument that Jesus, the Son of God is the great high priest, is merciful because he has shared our humanity. Paul recruits for his proofs the Psalms related to David's kingship, which also alludes to Melchizedek, who although a king was also a priest of the Most High God and who blessed Abraham. Adroitly, in the phrase "according to the order of Melchizedek," Paul supercedes the need for a priest to anoint the king, showing that the king could himself also be a priest, superior even to Abraham.

Paul then insults his hearers by saying they have become dull in understanding. He says they need milk and not solid food, which is to call them babies who are unable to distinguish good from evil. I doubt that his message was very convincing here.

Paul then goes on to enumerate the basic teachings which had made up his gospel: repentance from dead works (which could mean sin and might also signify useless adherence to the law), faith toward God, instruction about baptism, the laying on of hands, the Resurrection of the Dead, and eternal judgment. He says that he will skip these basics, because those who have fallen away are hopeless. Paul then backs off by suggesting that the hearers are not completely lost, because they have made efforts. What follows are the more advanced teachings that Paul probably did not include in his gospel to the gentiles at all.

Paul explains the meaning of Genesis 14:18-20, when King Melchizedek, whose name means "righteous king," who was king of Salem, blessed Abraham and received tithes from Abraham, as a priest would. A key point to his argument on these grounds is in Hebrews 7:12, stating that a change in the priesthood requires a change in the law. Paul's argument here is weak, although sincerely made; and he applies the kingly priesthood example to Jesus Christ, who naturally was descended from Judah, David's tribe. From this change, he argues that the law must change, because it was weak and unprofitable. As high priest, Jesus Christ offered one sacrifice for all time. Paul offers proof that Jesus Christ's priesthood supercedes the prior by stating that the Psalms came later than the Torah, the five books of Moses. "In saying 'new' he has made old the first and that being made old and growing old [is] near vanishing."[243]

Paul then compares Jesus Christ to a permanent high priest, not in an earthly sanctuary but in heaven, purified by his own blood offered

---

[243] Heb. 8:13.

to God through the "Eternal Spirit." Consequently, Jesus Christ is a mediator of a new covenant. Paul makes an analogy between the covenant and a will, requiring a death to put it in force. And he then argues that without the shedding of blood there is no remission of sins. Paul's emphasis here is probably to counter the stigma associated with Jesus' death by violence. The sacrifice of Jesus Christ was perfect and superior to those of the priesthood under the law and was required only once. Paul went so far as to state that the blood of goats and bulls cannot remove sin— which completely denied the validity of the Jewish Temple service. However, Paul's argument is scripturally strong in his use of Psalms 40:6-8 and Jeremiah 31:33-34.

Then Paul continues into exhortations of faith and constancy using as examples Abel, Enoch, Noah, Abraham, and Moses. In discussing Moses, Paul inserts Christ as the object of his faith, equating him with Yahweh. He continues by including all the heroes and prophets of the Old Testament, first the victorious blending into the scorned, scourged, killed, and destitute— which of course invited comparisons with Jesus Christ.

Then, Paul returns to exhortations and warnings for the Hebrews. We do not need to see criticism of the Hebrews in all Paul's exhortations. More likely, he was attempting to endear himself by demonstrating that he shared their values. However, from repetitions in 1 Timothy, we should see at least his addressing marriage and food restrictions as admonitions.

Paul includes in his final exhortations a small argument that the Hebrews should join Jesus Christ outside the "camp," as a metaphor for the city of Jerusalem. This use of "camp" is reminiscent of the language of the Dead Sea Scrolls evoking the image of the Israelites sojourning in the wilderness. The interesting point here is that Paul wants the Hebrews to join Jesus Christ outside the camp metaphorically, meaning they should abandon the law and bear the same reproach imposed upon him.

Titus

Paul describes God as un-lying, which is not surprising. He states that he is an apostle according to the faith and full gnosis (knowledge) of truth of God's chosen ones. Paul here calls Jesus Christ the Savior, although in other letters he calls God the Savior through Jesus Christ.

In 2:13, Paul fully calls Jesus Christ both God and Savior. In a Jewish context, where only one God was tolerable, such a statement demands a Trinitarian view of some kind. Paul calls Jesus Christ in 3:4 "the kindness and the love of humankind from God our Savior." He states that Jesus Christ poured out the Holy Spirit upon the Christians, having been justified by his grace and becoming heirs to hope of eternal life. This further reinforces Jesus Christ as God.

Before concluding, Paul proposes that Christians should do good works but avoid foolish inquiries, genealogies, and legal disputes.

1 Timothy

Paul calls God the Father and Christ Jesus the Lord. He begins by preaching against myths and genealogies and speculations. He makes the statement that the law is good, but for the lawless and disobedient who act contrary to the gospel of God. Christ Jesus came into the world to save sinners, like Paul.

2 Timothy

"Grace, mercy, [and] peace from God the Father and Christ Jesus our Lord" equates God and Jesus Christ as the co-sources of these blessings.

In 2 Timothy 2:8, Paul states that Jesus Christ was from the seed of David. He emphasizes that this is his gospel, suggesting that others had claimed something else, which Paul says was the reason for his imprisonment. We do not know precisely what the others claimed or on what basis that they denied that Jesus was the Messianic Son of David, although we have seen that evidence points to a claim by James, the brother of Jesus. Paul described an apocalyptic interpretation of the situation in chapter three.

Ephesians

Paul calls God the Father of our Lord Jesus Christ. Stating in this manner appears to imply more than adoptionist language of God choosing his son.

God chose those believing in the heavens before the foundation of the world, just as he chose them in Christ. Paul is stating that the Church and the members of the Church were preexistent and predetermined in heaven. Christians are his children by adoption through Jesus Christ, and this was sealed by believing the Gospel. The plan of God is to gather all things in Christ. In Ephesians 1:23, Paul states that the Church is Christ's body.

In chapter two, Paul argues that the gentiles were saved by grace and not by works, although created for good works as a way of life. In Christ's flesh, Jew and gentile have been joined as one, because he has broken down the dividing wall. The gentiles have become fellow heirs and members of the same body through the gospel.

In Ephesians 4:17-24, Paul speaks of the nations referring to non-Jews, aliens from God, as a counterpoint to his desire for their own godliness. He continues on exhorting the Ephesians to behave well and describing what that should be.

In 6:12, Paul states that the enemies are not flesh and blood but cosmic powers and forces of evil. This is a flat rejection of the zealot cause that had been a primary mover in Jewish apocalypticism. It is a stunning admission that Paul did not adhere to the military vision of the Messiah, which was paramount in the Essene scriptures. In Paul's understanding, Jesus Christ was not a warrior except in spiritual terms.

Philemon

Again, grace and peace equally come from God the Father and the Lord Jesus Christ. Although Paul elsewhere instructs slaves to serve their masters, here Paul asks for Philemon to free his slave, who was probably a runaway ("formerly useless to you"). From Ignatius letters, we see that the slave became bishop of Ephesus.

Colossians

God Father of our Lord Jesus Christ. In 1:13, Paul writes of the kingdom as a present reality.

Jesus Christ is described as the image of the invisible God. He is the firstborn of all creation, and in him all things were created both visible and invisible. He is before all things and in him all things hold together. He is head of the body, the Church. All the fullness of God dwells in him, a patently Trinitarian statement.

In chapter two, Paul warns the Colossians and the Laodiceans against philosophy. In so doing, Paul finally makes an unambiguous affirmation of the Trinity: "Because in him dwells all the fullness of the Godhead bodily."[244] Ironically, he was denouncing what can only be a Gnostic heresy, and he chose the Gnostic doctrine of the *Pleroma*, the fullness, to prove his case.

Baptism in Christ is spiritual circumcision. In 2:16-23, Paul warns against human regulations and foolishness, much of which sounds like Ebionite practices.

Philippians

In Philippians 1:1, Paul gives his first greeting to bishops and deacons. Again, Paul gives a level of equality to God and Jesus Christ, although God has always been mentioned first in similar circumstances.

Philippians 1:21-25 is very interesting because, whether by accident or by intention, Paul describes the moral dilemma of the Bodhisattva, whether to go to bliss or to stay for the benefit of others. This is nearly identical to a statement in Laodiceans.

In the formulaic passage of chapter two, the plain statement of equality with God in 2:6 cannot be overlooked; yet, God still retains a level of superiority.

What Paul did not write is as interesting as what he revealed. Paul makes no mention of the ascension, although the question hangs

---

[244] Col. 2:9.

heavily why Jesus Christ has returned to heaven and why he delays return. There was some question about the Day of the Lord, whether it had already come or would come, and Paul was adamant that Christ would return when that time came. Yet, Paul did not describe the moment of Christ's return to heaven, although he was clear that Jesus was Christ through the Resurrection.

Paul also does not distinguish any teaching of Jesus as from before or after the Resurrection. Presumably, he did not know of any change in emphasis or direction within the teachings.

Also, and perhaps surprisingly, Paul did not exalt the flesh of Jesus in any significant way. Yes, Jesus was without sin and he was a descendent of David, but he was not as a human different from other people.

We should notice that, in spite of the conflict that we have discussed in this book, Paul's vision of Jesus Christ was not greatly different from the Jewish Christian vision of Jesus Christ, a heavenly being who had shared the flesh of Jesus. Paul, however, insists that Jesus remained Christ through the Resurrection and, for Paul, Christ was not just an angel but God.

The Gospel of James

Reconstruction of Jewish Christian doctrines from several sources.

However convenient we may find the label of "Jewish Christian" to describe James, Peter, John of the Twelve, and their followers, we must remember that the label is somewhat arbitrary. The gentile Christians considered themselves Israelites, descendants of Abraham, and adherents to a form of Judaism. We can see easily through the narrative formed by the Pauline epistles that Paul actually failed to hold on to many of the communities to whom he preached; those communities falling away from Paul chose to follow his opponents, who were preaching Judaism. Paul's narrative implies many of his failures: Damascus, Antioch, Galatia, Thessalonika, Athens, Troas, and Crete. Corinth vacillated and Paul struggled in Ephesus. Many communities were more loyal to Judaism than to Paul's gospel. And Paul himself, in spite of his gospel, boasted that he was a Jew. James, Peter, and John started out as Jews and renewed their zeal in Judaism. Closely associated with James were the group called the Ebionites, and their name suggests monks. The Ebionites, however, were only one faction of the Essenes. We know of at least one group from the Essene division of Judaism which never accepted Jesus as the Messiah and remained loyal to John the Baptist instead. Undoubtedly, there were other groups among the Essenes with various interpretations. All of these could have been considered to be Jewish Christians because of their Messianic religion.

At the time of James, the Essenes as a whole including all the Christian groups and non-Christians fell mostly outside of the largest Jewish division of Pharisees, although some Pharisee rabbis may have been Essene in their sympathies. However, the Essene religion represented by their writings and the Jewish Christian writings (including the New Testament) had already left mainstream Judaism even before Jesus Christ. John the Baptist had preached purification by baptism alone, apparently rejecting the Temple cult and animal sacrifices. The Essenes redefined Jewish membership and even the priesthood according to the Damascus Document. The monks rejected marriage and sex and strictly regulated all concessions to the physical body to the point of asceticism. They, like Jesus, reinterpreted the Torah as symbolic and even flawed, evidenced by the elimination of polygamy and animal sacrifice. Much of the reinterpretation of the Bible continued to be maintained by James and his followers even as they pushed for a return to Judaism. However, this would not be sufficient for a complete reconciliation. The Sadducees and many of the Pharisees would never accept the new kind of Judaism that James was promoting, even though his reforms to the gospel sought to support some of the ancient Jewish practices like circumcision.

In this book, we are looking at only a snapshot of the situation with incomplete information. Some of the sources that we have for the Jewish Christians were actually written later than James and seem to have differed with him on some points, possibly reflecting that the Jewish Christians had developed either further or a slightly different direction. The later Jewish Christian writings downplay the importance of James, as do the three largely Jewish Christian Gospels of Mark, Matthew, and Luke. Instead, they focus on the importance of Peter, since he became a less controversial and unifying figure after his death.

Consequently, using the term "Jewish Christian" generally as a term to describe James and his followers is inaccurate unless we first agree that we are talking about a narrow time period and a limited sense applying only to Christians who wished to maintain a select interpretation of Judaism as part of the Christian religion. I think it is reasonable to consider most of the Essenes outside of the gentile churches as Jewish Christians, even though they may not all have accepted James as their lord at first, because later they almost certainly did support him enough that he gained some control over the Temple around 62 CE.

We should not, however, separate the Essenes too far from the Pharisees, because at this early time an orthodoxy did not really exist in Judaism. Sadducees (and the Samaritans) did not recognize any scripture but the Torah, the five books of Moses. Pharisees recognized as scripture many of the books respected by the Essenes; however, there were wide variations of interpretation even amongst the Pharisees. After the final destruction of Jerusalem and the renunciation of all hopes to restore the Temple, the Pharisees constructed the Mishnah, which was a codification of the "oral law" given to Moses. A plain reading of the Mishnah, without reconciliation through the commentaries of the Talmud, shows wide diversity and conflicting opinions among the early rabbis. Consequently, although Jewish Christians, as part of the Essene tradition, were outside of what would become mainstream Judaism, we cannot claim that they were far different in thought from the Pharisees of their time.

Recognizing the limitations in our understanding of the Jewish Christians, we can identify many sources that provide us some information on the gospel that James preached. First, and best, we have the letters of Paul, when he described his opponents and his disagreements with them. The Jewish Christian letters of the New Testament give us some information, especially in the Revelation of John, but these require careful scrutiny and interpretation. We also have the Gospels of Mark, Matthew, and Luke, which are replete with Jewish Christian ideas, although the versions that we have in the New Testament have been edited and reworked into forms acceptable to the later gentile churches. The Gospel of John is largely against the James and Peter group, and in agreement with Paul. A group of apocryphal writings known as the *Clementina*, offer us some of the plainest views of the Jewish Christian doctrine, although from a later date and with some alteration to make them more Catholic. The descriptions of the Church fathers Irenaeus, Eusebius, and Epiphanius are also valuable, if we remember that they had certain interests and ideas to protect. The many apocryphal gospels and histories offer some hints. Gnostic texts, especially those of the Nazoraeans and the Manicheans, are important.

We could consider Arianism, and Christian religions still in existence, such as the Nestorian and Assyrian churches, the Druze, and St. Thomas Christians (Nasrani). Finally, the Qur'an provides us significant information about Jewish Christianity, because both the Judaism and the Christianity of the Qur'an reflect a close relationship with Jewish Christians. Consequently, if we can remember that James represented one significant revelation, but not all of Jewish Christianity, we can trace backwards through Jewish Christian sources to reconstruct the gospel of James.

The Qur'an is particularly important and a good starting point for several reasons. First, the Jewish Christians lived in areas east of the Jordan River frequented by Mohammed's caravans from Mecca to Damascus. The Jewish Christians seem to disappear coincidental with the Qur'an and the rise of Islam; consequently, the Qur'an seems to represent the end result of the arc of the Jewish Christian sect. As already noted, the religion of the Qur'an agrees with the religion in even very early texts from Jewish Christians. For example, in the Qur'an, Jesus is accepted as a true prophet, the Messiah, and servant of God; he was born of a virgin, Mary; but he was human and not God, nor the Son of God; and he verified the Torah but designating some parts as allegorical and changing others. The Qur'an shows the disciples calling Jesus "Lord," and Allah planned the Crucifixion. Jesus is the likeness of Allah in the same manner as Adam. The Gospel was true, but it was not any of the texts that we commonly know, i.e., not the Gospels of the New Testament. Most significantly, Jesus did not die upon the cross, but only appeared to be killed and so was not resurrected. However, he was raised exalted to heaven. Also, in the Qur'an, Jesus is not regarded as the Son of David.

Other aspects of the Qur'an also agree with the Jewish Christian gospel. Good works are essential and always accompany belief. John the Baptist was a prophet greater than any before. Both John the Baptist and Jesus had miraculous births. The Qur'an echoes belief in the prophets and that the Jews killed the prophets. The Qur'an insists on the singularity of God and His ineffable nature. The Qur'an considers itself a final clarification of the "Book," which refers to the Hebrew Bible, in the same way that the Jewish Christians interpreted the revelation of Jesus Christ. In the Qur'an, Muslims believe in an Antichrist, which points to the early prominence of Jesus Christ in Islam. Also, Muslims believe in Heaven and Hell, a Resurrection of the Dead, a Kingdom of God, and a Day of Judgment. Another interesting parallel between the Qur'an and Jewish Christian texts is that, while forgiveness is praised and recommended highly, it is not an explicit commandment for Muslims in the Qur'an.

While the Qur'an nowhere discusses Saint Paul directly, the following passage very much resembles the Jewish Christian position against Paul:

> Those who disbelieved from among the Children of Israel were cursed by the tongue of David and Jesus, son of Mary. This was because they disobeyed and exceeded the limits. They forbade not one another the hateful things they did. Evil indeed was what they did. Thou seest many of them befriending those who disbelieve. Certainly evil is that which their souls send before for them, so that Allāh is displeased with them, and in chastisement will they abide. And if they believed in Allāh and the Prophet and that which is revealed to him, they would not take them for friends, but most of them are transgressors. Thou wilt certainly find the most violent of people in enmity against the believers to be the Jews and the idolaters; and thou wilt find the nearest in friendship to be those who say, We are Christians. That is because there are priests and monks among them and because they are not proud. (5:78-82)

In this passage, we can see a reflection of the Jewish Christian conflict with Paul in the references of "exceeding the limits" and "forbade not

. . . hateful things," suggesting Paul's view on freedom in Christ. "Befriending those who disbelieve" suggests the conversion of the gentiles. The mention of "the most violent of people . . . the Jews and the idolaters" calls to mind both the Jewish persecution of the Jewish Christians and the conflict with the gentiles, whom Paul also considered to have been idolaters originally and who continued controversy by eating meat sacrificed to idols. Contrasting with the Jews and idolaters, the Christians, referring specifically to the Jewish Christians, are nearest in friendship to Muslims because they include educated clergy and practice humility— probably an allusion to asceticism. Together with the mention of monks, we see a reflection of James and the Ebionites.

The Qur'an further emphasizes in the strongest terms the close friendship with the Nazareans:

> And when they hear that which has been revealed to the Messenger thou seest their eyes overflow with tears because of the truth they recognize. They say: Our Lord, we believe, so write us down with the witnesses. And what (reason) have we that we should not believe in Allāh and in the Truth that has come to us, while we earnestly desire that our Lord should cause us to enter with the righteous people? (5:83-84).

To cement the identification of these "Christians" with the Jewish Christians, the Qur'an also reflects the skepticism about the Resurrection found in the Revelation of John:

> And for their [the Jews] saying: We have killed the Messiah, Jesus, son of Mary, the messenger of Allāh, and they killed him not, nor did they cause his death on the cross, but he was made to appear to them as such. And certainly those who differ therein are in doubt about it. They have no knowledge about it, but

> only follow a conjecture, and they killed him not for certain. (4:157)

Immediately, this is followed by an excellent approximation of Docetism: "Nay, Allāh exalted him in His presence. And Allāh is ever Mighty, Wise." (4:158) Considering the similarity in the doctrines of the Qur'an to the Jewish apostles, we can find great significance that the disciples are also described as loyal believers of Jesus.

The apocryphal *Clementina* literature is even a stronger source for revealing the conflict between Paul and the Jewish Christians. In the Epistle of Peter to James:

> And this I know, not as being a prophet, but as already seeing the beginning of this very evil. For some from among the Gentiles have rejected my legal preaching, attaching themselves to certain lawless and trifling preaching of the man who is my enemy. And these things some have attempted while I am still alive, to transform my words by certain various interpretations, in order to the dissolution of the law; as though I also myself were of such a mind, but did not freely proclaim it, which God forbid!

Obviously, as we have already uncovered in Paul's letters, this is an accurate description of Paul and his followers, although Paul sincerely believed that Peter agreed with him in the beginning. Of course, Peter did not write this letter, but it does show the concerns and the hostility with which the Jewish Christians held Paul.

The *Clementina* is mostly made of the two large narratives, the *Recognitions* and the *Homilies*, which share much similarity of structure and content. After Clement, following Barnabas, meets with Peter at Caesarea Maritima and travels with him to witness a series of debates against Simon Magus, who seems to be an exaggerated representation of Paul as a Greek magician and polytheist. Peter is on his way to Antioch and both narratives leave off just before he arrives there, which suggest that the narratives are playing off the known confrontation of Peter and Paul there.

The origins of the texts are not really datable with any precision. The introduction by Rufinus of Aquileia provides an upper limit of the middle fourth century. I would suggest that the earliest date is sometime after the Acts of the Apostles, although the basis for the narrative may have been earlier. The reason that the story may have an earlier source is that Simon Magus, an obvious antitype to Simon Peter in these narratives, appears in Acts 8:9-24. The reason, however, that these texts must be later than Acts is an interesting scene in *Recognitions* that shows an unnamed person who is obviously Paul attempting to incite a riot and to murder James. The events occur in front of Gamaliel, whom Paul does not greet nor show respect. This seems to be a refutation against the idea that Paul was truly a student of the famous and highly respected rabbi, an idea which is claimed in the Acts of the Apostles.

The identification of Simon Magus as a type of Paul is not immediately obvious because the caricature is so exaggerated, but it does become clear on a closer reading. The ultimate destination being Antioch is an important and inescapable clue. The fact that Paul is not named is another. Also, the description of Simon Magus being the disciple of John the Baptist and then of John's successor, Dositheos, whose name means "gift of God," clearly a code for Jesus Christ, alerts us both to the identity of Simon as a top apostle, competing with the position of Peter in succession, and to the hostility of the Jewish Christian authors to Jesus Christ himself. The portrayal of Dositheos in the *Homilies* is outrageously insulting.

In the *Homilies*, we also see other hints of hostility against Paul and his teaching. Peter declares:

> "Our Lord and Prophet, who hath sent us, declared to us that the wicked one, having disputed with Him forty days, and having prevailed nothing against Him,

promised that he would send apostles from among his subjects to deceive. Wherefore, above all, remember to shun apostle or teacher or prophet who does not first accurately compare his preaching with that of James, who was called the brother of my Lord, and to whom was entrusted to administer the church of the Hebrews in Jerusalem,— and that even though he come to you with witnesses; lest the wickedness which disputed forty days with the Lord, and prevailed nothing, should afterwards, like lightning falling from heaven upon the earth, send a preacher to your injury, as now he has sent Simon upon us, preaching, under pretense of the truth, in the name of the Lord, and sowing error."[245]

Thus, Peter establishes the teaching of James as the standard of truth. He also does this in the *Recognitions*:

"Wherefore observe the greatest caution, that you believe no teacher, unless he bring from Jerusalem the testimonial of James the Lord's brother, or of whosoever may come after him."[246]

These statements take on high significance when we recall 2 Corinthians 3:1:

Or do we begin again to commend ourselves [to you]? Or do we not need, like some, commendatory letters to you or from you?

---

[245] Page 291-292.

[246] Page 142.

Consequently, it appears we can see the same events from two antagonistic perspectives.

The Clementina has some significant correlations with the gospel of James. For example, in the *Homilies*, Peter implies that those who believe that Christ is the Son of David are wrong. In explaining the text of Matthew 11:27 (see also Luke 10:22):

> "For, first, the statement can apply to all the Jews who think that David is the father of Christ, and that Christ himself his son, and do not know that He is the Son of God. Wherefore it is appropriately said, 'no one knows the father,' since, instead of God they affirmed David to be his Father;"[247]

Peter then goes on to state that the Son gave the revelation of the Father to the patriarchs. It is difficult to see how this does not imply some deification of the Son. It is consistent with representing Christ as an angel, however. When the Clementina is considered as a whole, this seems to be the best understanding.

The Clementina does not discuss the birth of Jesus nor the origin of Christ. Christ is called the Son of God, but without explanation. Most significantly, the Crucifixion and Resurrection are not even mentioned and so play no part in the teachings of Peter. The role of Jesus Christ is limited to being the true prophet, who reports the correct doctrine. This doctrine is extremely simple: there is one God, the creator, greatest in all respects, entirely righteous, who will render justice to everyone according to their deeds. There is a brief mention of the two paths, which calls to mind the *Didache* and the Epistle of Barnabas. Wealth is declared sinful, as in the Letter of James.

Now leaving the Clementina moving closer still to the New Testament, we should mention again the *Didache*, which I have identified as from James, the brother of Jesus. We have already seen

---

[247] Page 328.

that this document dismisses that Jesus was the Son of David. Jesus is also the servant of God more than the Son of God. No mention nor significance is granted to the Crucifixion nor the Resurrection.

There are several commandments in the *Didache* that probably reflect antagonism against Paul. One states that if an apostle or prophet passing through stays more than two days, he is a false prophet. This was something that Paul frequently did. Also, the *Didache* orders the gentiles not to listen to someone asking for money, which probably refers to the collection by Paul.

In the Epistle of James, we find a denouncing of the rich and the extolling of works and the law. Abraham was justified by works. The Crucifixion and the Resurrection are not mentioned at all.

The Crucifixion and the Resurrection are both significantly mentioned with emphasis in 1 Peter, where we can see great similarity to the words of Paul. Peter pointedly calls God "the Father of our Lord Jesus Christ." And, Jesus Christ as a sacrifice, "who our sins he himself bore in his body upon the tree."[248] (Notice the emphasis upon Jesus' body as the repository for sins.) Peter speaks of the "Resurrection of Jesus Christ from the dead." This similarity to Paul and difference from later doctrines of the Jewish Christians raises the question that Peter may not have realized how radical James and John had become. On the other hand, looking closely at the language shows that 1 Peter describes the Resurrection as a direct translation into heaven, which may or may not agree with Paul.[249]

This underlines an interesting and probably crucial question of what the living Jesus did after surviving the Crucifixion, not mentioned by Paul, not respected by Peter, and reviled by John. Even the Gospels do not provide consistent testimony except that Jesus, at the height of his credibility, taught nothing new or significant, with the ascension noticeably not described in any detail. The tradition maintains that the

---

[248] 1 Pet. 2:24.

[249] 1 Pet. 1:4, 3:18. Heb. 10:12.

risen Jesus Christ appeared to his disciples on several occasions; yet, we do not have any record of significant teaching after the Resurrection. Therefore, either Jesus taught nothing significant or the teachings were too controversial to repeat publicly. By rejecting Jesus after the Resurrection, calling him a beast, a spawn of Satan, the Revelation of John declares the latter— that Jesus did teach significantly but, although initially accepted by most of the Church early on, the teachings fell out of favor later with those who supported James, while Paul made no distinction from Christ before the Resurrection.

Second Peter was almost certainly directed against Paul and his followers, although this is never made explicit. The reference to cleverly designed myths suggests that Peter did object ardently to something in Paul's doctrine. The fact that Peter indicates that his own death may be near suggests that this letter was written after the confrontation in Jerusalem. However, no mention appears of the Crucifixion nor of the Resurrection.

First and Second Peter are too small a sample to make a strong statement about Peter's beliefs, but we have to notice that, outside of his acceptance of Judaizing practice, very little in these letters can be seen to oppose Paul's teaching and what we have come to know as orthodoxy. Indeed, 1 Peter appears to vary more in belief from John and James, in describing the Crucifixion as a redemptive sacrifice, precisely as Paul does.[250] Nonetheless, we must recognize that Peter never describes Christ as God, which was the most important part of Paul's doctrine.

Of course, as we have discussed, the Revelation denies the importance of the Crucifixion, contradicts the death of Jesus Christ, and transforms the Resurrection into a spiritual exaltation. Jesus is not the Son of David, and there is barely a hint that he might be the Son of God.

---

[250] 1 Peter 1:18-19, 3:18.

The letters of Paul describe opponents, some who deny the Resurrection. The opponents insist on Jewish practices that Paul believes have been superseded. They insist on works over faith. They insist upon adherence to the Jewish law. They deny that Jesus was the Son of David. The opponents attack Paul for not forbidding idolatrous meats, for promoting fornication, for lawlessness and immorality, for disobedience to their own authority, and for revealing secrets. Some of Paul's opponents are promoting innovations, such as genealogies and element worship. Taking the complaints of Paul together, remembering the short time frame, we should recognize that Paul's opponents had various opinions and doctrines, suggesting that Jewish Christians had various opinions and doctrines even while working together against Paul.

The Aftermath

Paul and Peter have been martyred. Continuation of the conflict between gentiles and Judaizers. Letters from Bishop Clement of Rome, Bishop Ignatius of Antioch, and Bishop Polycarp of Smyrna.

From the totality of the evidence we have examined so far, a natural conclusion appears that both Saint Peter and Saint Paul died as prisoners in Rome at the end of 55 CE. However, this end for them did not mean an end to the conflict between the Judaizers and the non-Judaizers in the gentile churches.

We will turn now to three authors already mentioned to illustrate the next stage of the struggle: Ignatius of Antioch, Polycarp of Smyrna, and Clement of Rome. All three of these authors were bishops. Previously, scholars dated the letters of Ignatius and Polycarp to the early second century and 1 Clement to 60 to 100 CE, because they show highly developed structure within the Church, going back to the same complaints against the authenticity of some of Saint Paul's letters.

In light of the new evidence of this book, we can say that these letters, like Paul's, are also much earlier, only weeks to months after the deaths of Paul and Peter, because we see exactly the same fight continuing— Judaizing Christians denying that Jesus Christ came in the flesh and denying the Resurrection of the Dead. Astoundingly, in spite of the similarity to Paul's conflicts, Ignatius mentioned Paul to the Ephesians only once and without any reference to the current situation. Perhaps, the similarity was so obvious that any discussion would have been superfluous. Nonetheless, only two brief insignificant mentions of Paul in his letters, to the Ephesians and to the Romans, and no allusion at all in letters to the Smyrnaeans, Trallians, Magnesians, Philadelphians, and Polycarp; this must be seen as incredible given the conflict that he was describing. The only sensible explanation is that Ignatius did not yet know Paul's letters, his story, nor the honor that Paul's memory would soon command; in other words, Ignatius is suffering almost immediately after Paul's death in Rome.

Also pushing for an extremely early date, Ignatius calls for the churches of Asia Minor to take part in the council at Antioch. That Ignatius needs to tell the Asian churches to send representatives suggests that the council itself was still a new development, meaning almost no time has passed from the mention of the Nicolaitans in the Revelation of John. Another piece of evidence of the early date is that Ignatius and Polycarp commend some followers of Paul: Crescens, Onesimus, and Rufus. Clement also asks the Corinthians to send him Fortunatus, who may have been with Paul at Ephesus but who also was known to the Corinthians, although this was likely a very common name.

Ignatius suffered a revolt within his church at Antioch, deposing him, although he states that the church regained its proper state, nonetheless. I see in this statement that the Judaizers were overcome, although Ignatius and others were casualties of the conflict, turned over to the Romans for disposal. Ignatius, just like Paul, was in chains traveling to Rome where he expected a violent death. Because his captors took him overland instead of by sea, we can expect that it was winter.

Although Ignatius wrote to Asian churches and to Rome, he did not write to the Corinthians, which may mean the church there was not friendly to him. He did not write to the Philippians either, but he might not have seen the need since his path took him through Neapolis, which was the port for Philippi. From there, he may have been carried overland or south to Corinth. If he went through Corinth, that also would explain why he did not write them, since he may have known his road to Rome.

In his letters to the Trallians, the Philadelphians, the Magnesians, the Ephesians, and the Smyrnaeans, Ignatius strongly exhorts these churches to obey and honor their bishop like Christ. In his letter to the Romans, Ignatius noticeably does not repeat this lesson. He also does not preach against the Judaizers and their doctrines, although he does praise as food the flesh of Christ from the seed of David and as drink the blood of Christ.

> I delight not in food perishable nor in pleasures of this life. Bread of God I choose, which is the flesh of Christ, of him from the seed of David, and drink, I choose his blood, which is love incorruptible.[251]

Except for this one pointedly orthodox sentence, however, he avoids controversy with the Judaizing Christians. He does refer to both Peter and Paul as apostles and authorities, but mentioning them only in passing. He may have avoided exhorting the Romans to support their bishop and he may have evaded more criticism against Judaizing because Clement, who was bishop at Rome, was himself a supporter of the Jewish Christian gospel of James. In other words, Clement of Rome was almost certainly on the opposing side of the conflict that was ending Ignatius' life.

Polycarp wrote his letter to the Philippians following the passage of Ignatius, responding to their request for the letters of Ignatius. Like Ignatius, Polycarp condemned those who did not acknowledge that Jesus Christ came in the flesh and died on the cross. Polycarp at times seems to reference 1 Clement; however, Polycarp may simply have similar source teachings, because there is nothing that is convincingly lifted from Clement's Letter to the Corinthians.

Nonetheless, the extremely extended argument of 1 Clement, fits the pattern of events shown in the letters of Ignatius. Clement argues that the Corinthians did wrong by deposing their bishop, who had been appointed by the apostles— a fact which also argues for an early date. He wants them to restore their previous bishop, who must have been of the Judaizing faction, probably installed after Stephen

---

[251] Letter of Ignatius to the Romans 7:3.

was murdered in Judea.[252] This suggests that the newest bishop was a follower of Paul, and, as we have mentioned before, this was likely Dionysius from Athens, the "Areopagite." Clement lauds Peter and Paul as victims of jealousy, praising emphatically especially Paul as an example of patient endurance.[253] No hint here of any conflict with the apostle to the gentiles.

Indeed, like Peter, in a cursory reading, Clement often appears to agree with Paul's doctrine. "The Lord Jesus Christ, whose blood for our sake was given, let us reverence."[254] He accepts resurrection from the dead and that Jesus Christ was resurrected. Abraham attained righteousness through faith. Further he states strongly:

> And we therefore through his will in Christ Jesus calling not through themselves being justified nor through our own wisdom or understanding or piety or works which were produced in devoutness of heart, but through the faith, through which all those from the beginning almighty God justified; to whom be the glory forever and ever. Amen.[255]

This sounds exactly like Paul.

However, Clement calls Jesus Christ the servant of God and calls him the Son of God only in the adoptive sense. God chose the

---

[252] Flavius Josephus: Antiquities Book XX, Chapter V, and Wars of the Jews Book II, Chapter XII. Acts 6-7. Josephus states explicitly in both mentions of Stephen that he was robbed, which could indicate that the robbery was memorable— perhaps, the collection from Paul for the poor of Judea? This event also included the destruction and desecration of a Torah by a Roman soldier, causing a riot among the Jews. I must note, however, that Josephus associated this event strongly with the time of Cumanus, around 52 CE, three years earlier than the dating that I propose for the delivery of the collection. However, I count it more likely that Josephus used poetic license in connecting the event to Cumanus than for John to have had a revelation that Christ would not return until Claudius and Nero had both passed and a little time into the next emperor's reign.

[253] I Clement 5:4–6:1.

[254] I Clement 21:6.

[255] I Clement 32:4

Lord Jesus Christ, which emphasizes his human and not godly nature. He does not call Jesus the Son of David. He declares that only at the Temple in Jerusalem can there be atonement for sin, a statement which is not found in other Christian writings. He does not indicate any expectation that Jesus Christ would return, although it would have added significant urgency to his argument. Adding to this that we know his honored status among later anti-Pauline Jewish Christians, we should expect that Clement was allied with James, the brother of Jesus; however, he does not state this.

On a final note regarding these three authors, we should recognize that in two instances the word "gentiles" refers exclusively to pagans distinguishing them from themselves as both Christians and Jews.[256] This shows that these non-Judeans saw themselves as children of Abraham and distinct from the pagans, in spite of the fact that they did not practice Judaism.

Paul must have succeeded, because James failed. Orthodox Christianity became what it is, mostly of Pauline origin. The Jewish Christians and later apostles lost credibility with communities outside of Israel, while Paul's legacy grew in stature.

The Jewish authorities in Jerusalem assassinated James, taking advantage of a lapse in Roman oversight. According to Eusebius' History of the Church, Simeon Clopas, his successor, retreated from Jerusalem to the region of Perea across the Jordan River. From Josephus, we learn that three generals of the First Jewish Revolt in 66 CE were Niger of Perea, Silas of Babylonia, and John the Essene. I suspect that John the Essene refers to the same John who was one of the Twelve Apostles, the "Son of Thunder" and author of Revelation, since the church was still at that time known as the sect of the Essenes to other Jews. He had spent most of several decades in Jerusalem, and he would have been well known by then. Josephus tells us that John the Essene fell at the battle of Ashkelon. Silas of Babylonia probably was

---

[256] 1 Clement 55:1. Polycarp to the Philippians 11:2.

the same Sylvanus that accompanied Paul and Peter. According to Acts 13:1, there was a certain prophet, Simeon, with the nickname "Niger" at Antioch, who was almost certainly the same Simon called Niger mentioned by Josephus at Jerusalem. The three names being together in Josephus' account is strong circumstantial evidence that Christians were instrumental in the Jewish Revolt.

Josephus discusses also a Simon son of Gioras, whom he describes as one who was fond of innovations, a euphemism for a heretic. "Giora" means a proselyte or sojourner, perhaps in this context meaning an exile since Josephus says that he came from Gerasa in Perea, where Simon Clopas had retreated after the assassination of James according to Eusebius and Hegesippus. It is undoubtably significant that the High Priest sent an army after Simon to Masada and continued to pursue him until the High Priest died. This conflict with the High Priest sounds remarkably similar to the situation around James the Just. We know that this Simon bar Gioras had Messianic pretensions, minting coins with the slogan "Redemption of Zion," occupying the Temple, and appearing publicly in purple and white. Consequently, if this is not all a huge coincidence, we should recognize Simon bar Gioras to be Simon Clopas and that Jewish Christians were very active in the rebellion against Rome.

More significant, however, is who did not participate in the Jewish Revolt. Jews and Christians outside of Judea and Alexandria notably are not reported to have joined in a general uprising, in spite of the tremendous successes of the Jews early in the war. The lack of reports does not mean nothing happened, but significant problems likely would have been mentioned by Josephus and other Roman historians. Roman suppression held the peace, but the Messianic gravity of the situation should have generated stronger sympathetic reactions. That apparent lack of sympathy probably indicates a real split between Judeans and the Greek Diaspora before 66 CE.

Presumably, the orthodox Christians had successfully separated from the Jewish Christians and built their own church hierarchy on the foundation of Saint Paul's vision of Jesus Christ. Without the Jewish nationalism and without the purity laws, Christians in the empire had little reason to keep themselves entirely separate from the pagans, although it may have required decades to break that barrier completely and redefine "gentile." What was the difference in a Christian church between a gentile claiming Jewish descent and God-fearing heathen? The usage of the word "gentile" as a reference to Jews, applied to non-kosher Jews by kosher Jews and Jewish Christians, made no sense in this new situation where no one was kosher. The word meant "of the nations," and in the new context, outside Judea and absent the Judaizers, the only possible reference was the outsiders surrounding them. This required a reinterpretation of Paul's letters, which was amazingly easy as it turned out. We must recognize a miraculous ambiguity in the manner that Jews spoke about each other: Precisely because strict Jews ostracized other Jews as though they were aliens, aliens becoming members of the true community was already written into the scriptures, sanctioned, and quickly came to be accepted as natural. Soon, Christians were themselves mostly gentiles, now meaning non-Jews, i.e., anyone at all, and Christianity became a truly universal religion, available to everyone regardless of race or nation.

Afterword

The incidental details within the letters of Paul are sufficient to determine the chronological order of the letters. Putting the letters in order allows a close inspection of Paul's missionary journey and even the reconstruction of much of his itinerary. Also, we find many clues about the timing of his activities, suggesting that his journey after he left Antioch was around two years total. This is far shorter than we had thought before.

Because of the compact time period, we must look at the conflicts described within the letters, not as isolated events, but as an ongoing struggle. These were not occasional disputes with many different Jews but a concerted challenge to Paul's apostleship by an authoritative group. We can see now that Paul told us with whom he battled: the Jewish Christian apostles, including Peter, John, Barnabas, and James. He told us why: the Jewish Christians were demanding that gentiles follow the Jewish purity regulations according to their standards, which Paul opposed. In spite of violence, Paul sought reconciliation and he had a plan that he believed might succeed: he would travel throughout the Israelite communities in the Diaspora, who were affiliated with the Essenes, to gather them to Jesus Christ. As a tribute of his loyalty, he also arranged the collection of a monetary gift for the group behind his opposition, the Ebionites, i.e., the Poor. The Ebionites were ascetic supporters of James and, as their name suggests, they were probably monks, living on donations from the larger organization. Paul may have believed that greed could sway their puritanism, since, as he said in Romans, he had preached to the gentiles only to make the Jewish Christians jealous.

The gentiles of Paul's letters were usually themselves Israelites by faith and culture, living far from Jerusalem, and not observant of Jewish proscriptions and prescriptions of law. Most importantly, they were not circumcised and they ate meat, which had been consecrated in idolatrous sacrifices to pagan gods.

The Jewish Christian apostles followed Paul around and even managed to anticipate his mission. The conflicts in the various churches were vigorous debates and sometimes turned violent. Nonetheless, in about two years, Paul managed to accomplish a collection and he returned to Jerusalem to deliver it. The conflict at Jerusalem and the trial resulted in Paul being sent to Rome as a prisoner, where he died within weeks.

Because Paul's missionary journey was so short, we now know that Paul spent more than half his time as a Christian in Arabia for unknown reasons. We can also see that there were small but significant differences in his gospel from the gospel of the Jewish Christians. Most importantly, the Jewish Christians attempted to maintain certain Jewish practices, while Paul rejected any requirements other than faith and obedience to Jesus Christ.

While it might be tempting at first to see an evolution of his gospel in Paul's letters, the short time span of his journeys really precluded such development. Rather, besides the simple unfolding of more information that is made available to us, Paul appears to have become more explanatory as he encountered more opposition and greater misunderstandings. We might have the illusion that Paul developed the doctrines, but he merely revealed more as he saw the need.

While the impression to modern readers might be that Paul was innovating, that could not have been the case, because Paul's authority was seriously in question during his mission to the gentiles. He was being attacked by the authoritative Jewish apostles on many counts, but they did not denounce his representation of Jesus Christ as different from that taught by Jesus himself; rather the Jewish Christians denounced Paul and the resurrected Jesus Christ equally. This strongly implies that Paul's representation of Jesus Christ as both the Son of God and the God of Moses agreed with the Gospel of Jesus.

We see in Paul's letters several different approaches to Christ, which were not necessarily contradictory but nor did they form a single coherent structure. Paul had enough confidence in his metaphors to split them, but he did not have enough confidence to insist on any single projection of the meaning of Christ. Surprisingly, nineteen years or more after the Resurrection, no consensus had yet been reached on the meaning of Christ.

The highly developed doctrine in Paul's letters corresponds with the implication that Paul was not working with blank slates. The communities he visited were already churches or synagogues with established leaders and organization. They had deacons and priests, called presbyters. There were already other apostles among them such as Junia and Apollos, who did not seem to owe their authority to Christ nor to his disciples. Each church would have had a bishop, although not exactly as we know bishops today, because these overseers were not priests at this early time. The churches also had prophets, teachers, nuns, and monks. All of this existed before Paul's arrival; Paul merely taught the three things that made up his gospel: Jesus was/is the Christ, Jesus Christ was crucified, and he was resurrected by God. He assumed that the gentiles knew the other things necessary to live as Christians, but he repeatedly found that the gentiles were not as well educated as he presumed, causing shocking problems.

Of course, this brings up many questions that we have not yet examined thoroughly and will have to leave for future discussion. Where did these communities come from and how did Paul know about them? Why did it take more than fifteen years to begin to spread the gospel outside of Judea? How could Christians and established churches exist without knowing about Christ? How did Jesus become the Christ and how did Christianity emerge from Judaism?

Appendices

Details of Paul's Journey from the Epistles

1 Thessalonians

1:1	Paul, Silvanus, and Timothy are together.
1:4-6	Paul, Silvanus, and Timothy preached the gospel in Thessalonika.
1:7	Thessalonika became example to Macedonia and Achaia.
1:8	Thessalonika's fame has spread beyond Macedonia and Achaia.
1:9	The people of the regions of Macedonia and Achaia and beyond report about how Paul, Silvanus, and Timothy evangelized successfully at Thessalonika.
2:1-2	Paul and companions had previously been mistreated at Philippi before coming to Thessalonika.
2:9	Paul says again that they preached the gospel, working among the Thessalonians.
2:14-15	Thessalonians imitated churches of Judea and suffered similar to Jesus and the prophets. The Jews killed the Lord Jesus and the prophets and drove Paul, Silvanus, and Timothy out.
2:16	The Jews are hindering their mission to the nations.
2:17-18	Paul, Silvanus, and Timothy have been away from Thessalonika for a short time. Paul wanted to return to Thessalonika but was impeded again and again.
3:1-2	Paul stayed alone in Athens and sent Timothy to Thessalonika.
3:6	Timothy has just returned to Paul and Silvanus from Thessalonika. Paul longs to see the Thessalonians.
3:10	Paul again says that they long to visit the Thessalonians.

Appendix I: Details of Paul's Journey from the Epistles

4:13-18	Paul must discuss the fate of some who have died. Therefore, the Thessalonians have been Christians a very short time, and they were taught very little dogma.

2 Thessalonians

1:1	Paul, Silvanus, and Timothy are together.
2:5	Paul asks if the Thessalonians remember his telling of the coming events.
2:6-12	Extensive description of the situation in present tense indicates that Paul is referring to current events.
2:15	Paul says the Thessalonians were taught by them.
3:7-10	Paul says that they were among the Thessalonians.
3:17	Paul writes with his own hand.

1 Corinthians

1:1	Paul is with Sosthenes.
1:2	The Corinthians are called saints.
1:11	Chloe's people reported quarrels in Corinth to Paul.
1:12-13	Some at Corinth are forming factions according to who baptized them. Some are of Apollos, Cephas, Christ, and Paul.
1:14-16	Paul mentions Crispus, Gaius, and Stephanas as being among the Corinthians.
2:1	Paul went to Corinth to preach.
3:2	Paul fed them milk, not solid food.
3:5-6	Paul says that he planted and Apollos watered in Corinth.
3:10	Paul laid the foundation but another is building on it.
4:15	Paul became the Corinthians' father in Christ.
4:17-18	Paul sent Timothy, his "beloved and faithful child," but Timothy's authority was rejected and Paul has heard of the events.
4:19	Paul says he will come to Corinth soon.

5:3	Paul says he is absent from Corinth in body.
5:8	Festival approaching— an allusion to the Feasts of Passover and the Unleavened Bread.
5:9	Paul has written a letter (no longer extant) previously to the Corinthians.
7:1	Paul has received a letter from Corinth.
7:25-40	Detailed instructions regarding sex and marriages suggests that Corinth has not been Christian long nor have they received extensive teaching.
9:3-7	Paul mentions Barnabas together with himself as apostles with full rights in response to the letter from the Corinthians.
15:1	Paul preached the gospel at Corinth.
15:32	Paul mentions contending with beasts at Ephesus.
16:1	Paul mentions the collection for the saints. Paul says the Corinthians should follow the instructions that he gave to the churches of Galatia. Paul either went to Galatia or sent someone to Galatia with instructions for the collection and the Corinthians should follow the same instructions.
16:2	They should collect small amounts over time. Paul intends to go to Corinth for the collection.
16:3-4	Paul's travel plans are not fully set.
16:5	Paul intends to pass through Macedonia before arriving at Corinth.
16:6-7	Paul wants to spend the winter in Corinth.
16:8-9	Paul will stay at Ephesus until Pentecost due to an opportunity to preach the gospel and face adversaries.
16:10-11	Timothy is not with Paul and may not know where Paul is, but he may pass through Corinth.
16:12	Apollos was at Ephesus with Paul. Paul urged him to visit but Apollos refused for now.
16:15	Stephanas was among first converts in Achaia.
16:17	Stephanas, Fortunatus, and Achaicus visited Paul.

16:19	Churches of Asia send greetings. Aquila and Prisca send greetings.
16:21	Paul writes with his own hand.

Galatians

1:2	To the churches of Galatia.
1:6	Paul expresses surprise that the Galatians have forsaken him so quickly. Paul had called the Galatians.
1:13	Paul had previously persecuted the Church as a follower of Judaism.
1:14	Paul had advanced in Judaism beyond his years because he was zealous.
1:15-16	Paul received a revelation of God's son.
1:16-17	Paul did not immediately go to Jerusalem, but he went at once to Arabia. Afterwards he returned to Damascus.
1:18	After three years, he went to Jerusalem to visit Cephas and he stayed fifteen days.
1:19	Paul did not see any other apostle at this time in Jerusalem except James the brother of the Lord.
1:20	Then Paul went into the regions of Syria and Cilicia.
1:22-24	Paul was still unknown by sight to the churches of Judea, although his conversion brought him some fame.
2:1	Through fourteen years, Paul visited Jerusalem again with Barnabas and Titus.
2:2	In response to a revelation, he laid before acknowledged leaders in a private meeting the gospel that he would proclaim among the nations, in order to make sure that his preaching was acceptable.
2:6-9	Acknowledged leaders including Cephas and James gave approval to Barnabas and Paul, agreeing that Paul should minister to the uncircumcised and they to the circumcised.

2:10	They stipulated only that Paul should remember the poor.
2:11-12	When Cephas came to Antioch, Paul opposed him openly, charging hypocrisy regarding the fellowship status of gentiles, after certain people came from James.
2:13	Other Jews including Barnabas joined Cephas in excluding gentiles from fellowship.
4:13	Paul taught at Galatia because of a weakness of the flesh.
4:20	Paul wishes he could come to the Galatians, because he is perplexed about them.
6:11	Paul writes in his own hand.
6:17	Paul carries the stigmata of Jesus on his body.

2 Corinthians

1:1	Paul and Timothy are together. To the church in Corinth including all the saints in Achaia.
1:6	Paul indicates that he and Timothy are being afflicted.
1:8	Paul and others are being severely afflicted in Asia.
1:10	Paul indicates that he and Timothy escaped peril.
1:15-16	Paul says he wanted to visit Corinth on his way to and from Macedonia, but did not.
1:19	Paul recounts that Timothy, Silvanus, and he proclaimed the gospel to the Corinthians.
1:23	Paul did not visit Corinth.
2:1	Paul again says he did not come to Corinth.
2:3-4	Paul wrote to the Corinthians previously.
2:12	Paul went to Troas.
2:13	Paul did not find Titus in Troas, so he went on to Macedonia.
3:1	Paul refers to letters of recommendation carried by opponents.

4:8	Paul says that he and Timothy are afflicted in every way.
4:17	Paul says it is a light affliction.
7:5	Paul and others were harrassed in Macedonia.
7:6	Titus just joined Paul.
7:8-12	Paul previously wrote harshly to the Corinthians.
7:13	Titus came from Corinth.
8:1-5	Paul praises the generosity of the Macedonians regarding the ministry to the saints.
8:6	Paul is sending Titus to Corinth to administer the collection at Corinth.
8:10-11	Paul says the Corinthians began the collection last year.
8:17	Titus will go to Corinth.
8:18-20	A famous brother will accompany Titus who was appointed by the churches to observe the collection of the gift to verify that Paul is blameless in this task.
8:23	Titus is Paul's partner and co-worker. The brothers are apostles of the churches.
9:2	Achaia has been preparing their collection gift since last year.
9:4	Paul hypothetically indicates that he may follow Titus and the brothers to Corinth.
11:5	Paul refers sarcastically to the "super-apostles" indicating that they have been at Corinth.
11:24	Paul recounts that he five times received the thirty-nine lashes.
11:25	Paul adds three times he was beaten with rods, once he suffered a stoning, three times he was shipwrecked, once he was adrift for a night and a day.
11:32-33	Paul recounts that in Damascus, the ethnarch under King Aretas guarded the city in an attempt to seize Paul, but he escaped through a window in the wall, being let down in a basket.

12:2	Paul, referring to himself in third person, had a revelation of Christ fourteen years ago.
12:14	Paul intends to return to Corinth for a third time.
12:18	Paul sent Titus and the brother to Corinth previously.
13:1	Paul states clearly that this is the third time he is coming to Corinth.

Romans

1:7	The Romans are beloved of God and called saints.
1:10	Paul has not been to Rome but wants to go there.
1:13	Paul repeats that he wanted to go to Rome but was prevented.
15:19	Paul has preached from Jerusalem to Illyricum.
15:23-24	Paul has no more places to preach in the East and desires to stop at Rome on his way to Spain.
15:25	Paul is enroute to Jerusalem for the ministry of the saints.
15:26	Collection is completed in Macedonia and Achaia.
15:30-32	Paul's enemies are the unbelievers in Judea and Paul seems to connect the collection with his own survival.
16:1-2	Paul is commending to the Romans Phoebe, a deacon of the church of Cenchreae, so they may welcome her.
16:3-4	Paul sends greetings to Prisca and Aquila, who work with him and risked their necks for him.
16:5	Prisca and Aquila have a church in their house in Rome.
16:5	Epaenetus is in Rome who was the first convert in Asia.
16:6	Mary in Rome.
16:7	Andronicus and Junia, compatriots of Paul, had been in prison with him and are now in Rome. They are notable apostles.
16:8	Amplias is in Rome.
16:9	Urbanus, a coworker, and Stachys are also in Rome

16:10	Apelles and the family of Aristobulus is in Rome.
16:11	Herodian, a compatriot, is in Rome. Also, some of the family of Narcissus.
16:12	Workers in the Lord Tryphaena and Tryphosa and Persis are in Rome.
16:13	Rufus, an elect one, and his mother are in Rome.
16:14	Asyncritus, Phlegon, Hermes, Patrobas, and Hermas, are in Rome.
16:15	Philologus, Julia, Nereus and sister, and Olympas and all the saints that are with them.
16:21	Timothy is with Paul. Lucius, Jason, and Sosipater are Paul's compatriots.
16:22	Tertius is the scribe of the letter.
16:23	Gaius is Paul's host and to the whole church. Erastus, the city treasurer, and Quartus are with Paul.

Hebrews

13:19	Paul hopes to be restored to them soon.
13:23	Timothy was arrested and has been freed. If he comes in time, he will travel with Paul to the Hebrews' church.
13:24	Paul has some with him from Italy.

Titus

1:1	Paul calls Titus his loyal child in the faith we share.
1:5	Paul is explaining why he left Titus behind in Crete.
3:12	Paul intends to send Artemas or Tychicus. Paul intends to winter in Nicopolis.
3:13	Paul wants Titus to send Zenas the lawyer and Apollos on their way.

1 Timothy

1:1	Paul calls Timothy his loyal child.

1:3	Paul urges Timothy to remain at Ephesus like he did when he was on his way to Macedonia.
1:20	Paul turned over to Satan certain persons including Hymenaeus and Alexander for blasphemy.
1:14	Paul hopes to come to Timothy soon.
4:13	Paul is expecting to return to Timothy.

2 Timothy

1:1	Paul calls Timothy his beloved child.
1:5	Timothy's grandmother Lois and his mother Eunice were Christians.
1:8	Paul is a prisoner.
1:15	Paul tells that all who are in Asia turned away from him including Phygelus and Hermogenes.
1:16	Onesiphorus and household is with Paul.
1:17	Paul is in Rome.
1:18	Onesiphorus had been in Ephesus with Timothy at some time.
2:17-18	Hymenaeus and Philetus have gone astray.
3:11	Timothy saw that Paul had been persecuted at Antioch, Iconium, and Lystra.
4:9	Paul requests Timothy to come to him.
4:10	Demas has deserted Paul and gone to Thessalonika. Crescens to Galatia. Titus to Dalmatia.
4:11	Only Luke is with Paul. Paul wants Timothy to bring Mark.
4:12	Paul sent out Tychicus into Ephesus.
4:13	Paul wants Timothy to bring his cloak, scrolls, and especially his codices that he left with Carpus in Troas.
4:14	Alexander the coppersmith did Paul great harm.
4:16	Paul faced his first defense and no one supported him.
4:19	Paul greets Prisca and Aquila and the household of Onesiphorus.

Appendix I: Details of Paul's Journey from the Epistles

4:20	Erastus remained in Corinth. Trophimus was left ill in Miletus.
4:21	Paul wants Timothy to come before winter. Eubulus, Pudens, Linus, and Claudia are with Paul.

Ephesians

1:1	To the saints who are in Ephesus and are faithful.
1:15	Paul has heard of the faith of the Ephesians in the Lord Jesus and of their love toward all the saints.
2:11	The Ephesians are called the uncircumcision by those who are called the circumcision.
3:1	Paul is a prisoner of Christ Jesus for the sake of the Ephesians who are of the nations.
3:2	Paul reminds them that he was commissioned.
3:3	Paul had received a revelation of the mystery.
3:21	Paul refers to the church in the abstract.
4:1	Paul again says that he is a prisoner.
4:11-13	Paul says that the Church is a work in progress and not yet unified.
6:20	Paul says he is an ambassador of the gospel in chains.
6:21	Paul sent Tychicus to Ephesus and calls Tychicus a dear brother and a deacon.

Philemon

1	Paul is a prisoner. Timothy is with him.
2	Apphia is with Philemon, as is Archippus, whom Paul calls a fellow soldier. Philemon has a church in his house.
8	Paul indicates that he has authority over Philemon.
10	Paul has become a father to Onesimus during his imprisonment.
11	Onesimus was useless to Philemon.
12	Paul is sending Onesimus back to Philemon.

13	Paul wanted to keep him near to serve Paul during his imprisonment.
14	Paul wanted Philemon's consent.
15	Onesimus was separated from Philemon.
16	Onesimus was a slave and Paul wants him freed.
19	Paul is writing with his own hand.
21	Paul reinforces his command.
22	Paul hopes to go to Philemon.
23	Epaphras is with Paul and sends greetings.
24	Mark, Aristarchus, Demas, and Luke, who are Paul's fellow workers, are with Paul and send greetings.

Colossians

1:1	Timothy is with Paul.
1:2	To the saints and faithful brothers and sisters in Colossae.
1:7	Epaphras ministered at Colossae.
1:24	Paul is suffering for the Church, "completing what is lacking in Christ's afflictions for the sake of his body, the Church."
1:25	Paul became servant of the Church by God's commission.
2:1	Paul is struggling for the Colossians and the Laodiceans, and he indicates that they have not seen his face.
2:5	Paul says again that he is absent from Colossae.
4:3	Paul asks the Colossians to pray for his mission at his present location. Paul indicates that he is in prison.
4:7	Tychicus is carrying the letter and is a faithful minister and slave in the Lord.
4:8	Paul sent Tychicus.
4:9	Tychicus is coming with Onesimus, the faithful brother who is one of the Colossians.

4:10	Aristarchus is a fellow prisoner and greets the Colossians. Mark, the cousin of Barnabas. The Colossians have received instructions about Barnabas— "the Colossians should welcome him."
4:11	Jesus called Justus greets the Colossians. These are the only ones of the circumcision among Paul's coworkers for the kingdom of God and they are Paul's friends.
4:12	Epaphras is a Colossian and sends greetings.
4:13	Epaphras has worked hard on behalf of the Colossians and for those in Laodicea and Hierapolis.
4:14	Luke, the physician, and Demas send greetings.
4:15	Paul sends greetings to the Laodiceans and to Nympha who has a church in her house.
4:16	Paul says that the Colossians and the Laodiceans should read each others letters.
4:17	Paul sends instructions for Archippus to complete his task.
4:18	Paul writes in his own hand and asks that they remember his chains.

Laodiceans (extra-biblical)

1	To the brethren in Laodicea.
5	Paul calls the Laodiceans his converts.
6	Paul's bonds are manifest.
17	Paul says that all the saints salute the Laodiceans.
19	Paul says that the Colossians and the Laodiceans should read each others letters.

Philippians

1:1	Paul and Timothy are together. Paul addresses all the saints at Philippi with the bishops and deacons.
1:4	The Philippians had shared in the gospel from the first day until the present.

1:12-13	Paul's imprisonment has caused the gospel to be known throughout the whole praetorian guard.
1:14	Paul's imprisonment has encouraged the brothers and sisters to speak the word.
1:15	Paul says that some are proclaiming Christ intending to increase his suffering in his imprisonment.
1:19	Paul needs deliverance.
1:20-25	Paul's life is in grave danger.
1:30	The Philippians are facing the same struggle that they had witnessed Paul facing and that they now hear that he continues to face at present.
2:17	Paul is dying, possibly from torture.
2:19	Paul hopes to send Timothy soon.
2:20-21	Paul praises Timothy profusely.
2:22	The Philippians know Timothy's worth.
2:23	Paul hopes to send Timothy as soon as Paul's situation is resolved.
2:24	Paul says that he trusts in the Lord that he will also be able to come soon.
2:25	Paul thinks it necessary to send Epaphroditus, his brother and co-worker.
2:26	Epaphroditus has been longing for the Philippians and was distressed that they heard he was ill.
2:27	Epaphroditus had been ill but has recovered.
2:28	Paul is sending Epaphroditus.
2:30	Paul tells the Philippians to welcome Epaphroditus because he nearly died for Christ, giving service to Paul.
3:5	Paul was circumcised according to Mosaic law, member of the people of Israel, the tribe of Benjamin, born of Hebrews, a Pharisee.
3:6	Paul was so zealous that he became a persecutor of the Church, and blameless under the law.
3:8	Paul has suffered the loss of all things.

3:10	Paul wants to know Christ and the power of his resurrection and the sharing of his sufferings by becoming like him in his death.
3:18	Paul tells them now with tears about the enemies of the cross of Christ.
4:2	Paul exhorts Euodia and Syntyche.
4:3	Paul addresses his loyal yoke-fellow who struggled with Paul, Clement, and his other fellow workers.
4:10	The Philippians have rekindled their concern for Paul.
4:14	The Philippians were distressed for Paul.
4:15	No other churches shared financially in Paul's mission except Philippi.
4:16	Paul had received support from Philippi while he was at Thessalonika.
4:17	Paul received gifts from Philippi through Epaphroditus.

Details of Paul's Journey in the Acts of the Apostles

7:58	Saul is at Jerusalem for the stoning of Stephen.
8:1-3	Saul persecutes the church in Jerusalem.
9:1-8	Saul persecuting Christians, has revelation of Jesus Christ on the road from Jerusalem to Damascus and is brought to Damascus.
9:20-22	Saul preaches at Damascus confounding the Jews.
9:23-25	Saul escapes the Jews of Damascus, being lowered in a basket through a window in the wall.
9:26-27	Saul returns to Jerusalem, but the disciples are afraid of him. Barnabas takes Saul to the apostles.
9:28-29	Saul preaches in Jerusalem, arguing with Hellenists who try to kill him.
9:30	Believers foil the Hellenist plan to kill Saul by taking him to Caesarea and sending him off to Tarsus.
11:20-21	Some Hellenists are converted.
11:25-26	Barnabas goes to Tarsus to retrieve Saul and bring him to Antioch, where they taught the church for a year.
11:27-28	Prophets come from Jerusalem to Antioch and one Agabus predicts famine over all the world, and this happens during the reign of Claudius.
11:29-30	Apparently in response to the famine, the disciples determine to send relief to the believers of Judea, and they send it with Saul and Barnabas.
12:25	After completing their mission, Barnabas and Saul return to Jerusalem with John called Mark.
13:1-3	Barnabas and Saul receive a commission by the Holy Spirit through prophecy.

Appendix II: Details of Paul's Journey from the Acts of the Apostles

13:4-5	Barnabas and Saul, with John assisting, go to Cyprus via Seleucia preaching in Salamis at the synagogues of the Jews.
13:6	Barnabas, Saul, and John go through all of Cyprus to Paphos.
13:9	Saul is also known as Paul.
13:13	Paul and companions sail from Paphos to Perga in Pamphylia, but John leaves them and returns to Jerusalem.
13:14-15	From Perga, they reach Antioch in Pisidia, where Paul preached in a Synagogue.
13:50-51	After one week, Paul and Barnabas are persecuted and driven out, and they go to Iconium.
14:1	Paul and Barnabas preached in a synagogue in Iconium.
14:2-7	Unbelieving Jews stirred up the gentiles against them, and they fled to Lystra and Derbe in Lycaonia, and to surrounding area, proclaiming the gospel.
14:8-18	People of Lystra try to worship Barnabas and Paul as pagan gods.
14:19	Jews from Antioch and Iconium convince the people of Lystra to stone Paul.
14:20	The next day, Paul and Barnabas go on to Derbe.
14:21	After making many disciples, they return to Iconium and Antioch.
14:24-26	They pass through Pisidia, Pamphylia, and Perga to Attalia. From there they sail back to Antioch.
15:1-2	Then some from Judea came to Antioch demanding that brothers be circumcised. Paul and Barnabas argue with them and are appointed to go to Jerusalem to discuss the matter with the apostles and elders.
15:3	They pass through Phoenica and Samaria.
15:4	At Jerusalem, they are welcomed by the church, the apostles, and the elders.

15:22-30	Paul, Barnabas, Silas, and Judas called Barsabbas are sent back to Antioch with a letter from James and the apostles.
15:33	Judas leaves.
15:34	"But it seemed good for Silas to remain there." (omitted by Nestle).
15:35	Paul and Barnabas remained in Antioch.
15:36-39	Paul and Barnabas quarrel over taking John called Mark on a visit to the churches they founded, and Barnabas leaves with Mark to Cyprus.
15:40-41	Paul takes Silas with him through Syria and Cilicia.
16:1-2	Paul finds Timothy in Derbe or Lystra.
16:3	Paul chooses Timothy as an assistant and has him circumcised because of the Jews who knew Timothy's father was a Greek.
16:6	They went through Phrygia and Galatia, forbidden by the Holy Spirit from speaking the word in Asia.
16:7	At Mysia, the Spirit of Jesus prevented the from entering Bithynia.
16:8	They went to Troas instead.
16:9-11	Due to a vision, "we" set sail from Troas to Macedonia, going first to Samothrace, the following day to Neapolis.
16:12	Then to Philippi for some days.
16:16-40	Paul and Silas were flogged and imprisoned and miraculously released.
17:1	They passed through Amphipolis and Apollonia and came to Thessalonika, where there was a Jewish synagogue.
17:2-4	Paul preached three successive Sabbaths in the synagogue, and some are persuaded including many leading women.
17:5-9	The Jews become jealous and try to turn them over to Roman authorities, causing a riot.

Appendix II: Details of Paul's Journey from the Acts of the Apostles

17:10-12	Thessalonian believers send Paul and Silas to Beroea, where they go to the synagogue and the Jews are more receptive. Many believed including Greek women and men of high standing.
17:13-14	Because Thessalonian Jews come stirring up and inciting crowds, the believers send Paul to the coast, but leave Timothy and Silas.
17:15	Paul is taken to Athens, and he sends word back that Silas and Timothy should join him as soon as possible.
17:16-17	Paul argues with Jews and others in the marketplace.
17:18-34	Paul debates philosophers at the Areopagus and some are converted.
18:1	Paul left Athens for Corinth.
18:2-3	Paul meets Aquila, a native of Pontus, recently arrived from Italy with his wife Priscilla, because Claudius had ordered all Jews to leave Rome. Paul stays with them because they shared a trade— as tent-makers.
18:4	Every Sabbath Paul argues in the synagogue and tries to convince Jews and Greeks.
18:5	Silas and Timothy arrive from Macedonia, while Paul is evangelizing.
18:6	Paul declares that he will go to the gentiles from now on.
18:7	Paul leaves synagogue and goes to house of Titius Justus.
18:8	Crispus, the official of the synagogue, and many other Corinthians became believers.
18:11	Paul stayed there a year and six months.
18:12-17	The Jews take Paul before the proconsul of Achaia, Gallio, but he refuses to hear their complaint. So they beat Sosthenes, the official of the synagogue, in front of the tribunal, but to no effect.

18:18	Paul sails for Syria accompanied by Priscilla and Aquila, but at Cenchreae Paul has his hair cut under a vow.
18:19-21	Paul leaves Priscilla and Aquila at Ephesus. Paul enters the synagogue to have a discussion with the Jews. He is well received, but he leaves Ephesus.
18:22	Paul lands at Caesarea and goes up to Jerusalem to greet the church, and goes down to Antioch.
18:23	After some time he goes through Galatia and Phrygia strengthening disciples.
18:24-28	A Jew named Apollos, a native of Alexandria, came to Ephesus. He had been instructed in the Way of the Lord, but he knew only the baptism of John. Priscilla and Aquila heard him preach in the synagogue and instructed him, more accurately. Apollos went to Achaia and refuted Jews in public.
19:1	While Apollos was in Corinth, Paul passed through the interior regions and came to Ephesus.
19:8	Paul entered the synagogue and preached for three months.
19:9-10	When some spoke evil of the Way before the congregation, he left them to argue daily in the lecture hall of Tyrannus. This continued for two years so that all the residents of Asia, Jew and Greek, heard the word of the Lord.
19:21	Paul resolves to go through Macedonia and Achaia and then to Jerusalem. After this he intended to go to Rome.
19:22	Paul sends Timothy and Erastus to Macedonia.
19:23-41	Riot at Ephesus.
20:1	Paul sent for the disciples, and leaves them for Macedonia.

Appendix II: Details of Paul's Journey from the Acts of the Apostles

20:2-3	After going through those regions, he stayed for three months in Greece. A plot by the Jews caused him to return through Macedonia.
20:4	Paul is accompanied by Sopater, son of Pyrrhus of Beroea, by Aristarchus, and by Secundus from Thessalonika, by Gaius from Derbe and by Timothy, as well as by Tychicus and Trophimus from Asia. These went ahead and were waiting for "us" in Troas.
20:5	"We" sailed from Philippi after the days of Unleavened Bread and in five days joined them in Troas, where "we" stayed for seven days.
20:13	"We" set sail for Assos intending to meet Paul there, by arrangement, in order to go by land from there.
20:14	Paul boarded and "we" took him to Mitylene.
20:15	On the following day "we" arrived opposite Chios. The next day "we" touched at Samos, and the next "we" came to Miletus.
20:16	Paul had decided to sail past Ephesus, so that he would not have to spend time in Asia, being eager to be in Jerusalem by Pentecost.
20:17	From Miletus he sent a message to Ephesus for the elders of the church to meet him.
21:1	When "we" had parted from them and set sail, we came by a straight course to Cos, and the next day to Rhodes, and from there to Patara.
21:2-3	"We" set sail for Phoenicia and came within sight of Cyprus, leaving it on "our" left, sailing to Syria and landing at Tyre for the ship to unload cargo.
21:4	"We" stayed there seven days.
21:7	"We" continued from Tyre to Ptolemais and stayed one day.
21:8	Leaving the next day, "we" came to Caesarea and stayed at the house of Philip the evangelist for several days.

21:15	After these days, "we" started for Jerusalem with some disciples from Caesarea who brought "us" to stay at the house of Mnason of Cyprus.
21:17	When "we" arrived in Jerusalem, the brothers welcomed "us" warmly.
21:18	The next day Paul went to visit James and all the elders who were present.
21:19-26	Paul is persuaded to pay for shaving the heads of some who are taking vows.
21:27-32	When the seven days were almost complete, Jews from Asia stirred up the crowd to riot and try to kill Paul.
21:33	Paul is arrested.
23:12-23	The Jews' plot to kill Paul is discovered.
23:23-35	The tribune Claudius Lysias sends Paul to the governor Felix at Caesarea.
24:1-23	Five days later Paul faces a Roman hearing.
24:24	Some days later Felix arrives.
24:27	Paul is held at Caesarea for two years.
25:1	Three days after Porcius Festus arrived in the province, he went to Jerusalem.
25:6	After eight to ten days, Paul is brought before Festus.
25:13	After several days, King Agrippa comes to Caesarea.
25:23	On the next day Paul is brought before King Agrippa.
27:1-2	"We" set sail for Italy via the ports along the coast of Asia accompanied by Aristarchus a Macedonian from Thessalonika.
27:3	The next day "we" put in at Sidon.
27:4	"We" sailed under the lee of Cyprus.
27:5	After "we" sailed across the sea that is off Cilicia and Pamphylia, "we" came to Myra in Lycia.
27:6	On an Alexandrian ship bound for Italy.

27:7	"We" sailed slowly for a number of days and arrived with difficulty off Cnidus under the lee of Crete off Salmone.
27:8	Sailing past it with difficulty, "we" came to Fair Havens near Lasea.
27:9	The fast had already gone by.
27:12	The pilot made for Phoenix, a harbor of Crete.
27:13-16	"We" began to sail past Crete but a violent northeaster drove "us" to the lee of a small island called Cauda.
27:17-44	"We" shipwrecked on Malta.
28:11	Three months later "we" set sail.
28:12	"We" put in at Syracuse and stayed for three days.
28:13-14	Then we came to Rhegium and on the second day to Puteoli, where "we" stayed with believers for seven days. And so we came to Rome.
28:16-31	Paul is at Rome for two years, a prisoner in name only, proclaiming the gospel.

Proposed Chronology for Paul's Career in Christianity

41 CE	Paul receives revelation of Jesus Christ at Damascus.
41–50 CE	Paul immediately goes into Arabia and stays there eight or more years.
49–50 CE	Paul returns to Damascus.
52 CE	Paul is driven out of Damascus by the ethnarch who had been appointed by King Aretas IV (9 – 40 CE), escaping by being lowered in a basket from the Jewish Ghetto.
52 CE	Paul travels to Jerusalem to meet with Peter and James, the brother of the Lord, and spends fifteen days.
52 CE	With Barnabas, Paul goes into Syria and Cilicia—through Caesarea, Ptolemais, Tyre, and Sidon to Antioch and Tarsus, finally basing their mission at Antioch— requiring probably two to three months.
52–53 CE	With Barnabas and Titus, Paul returns to Jerusalem to seek clarification of the position of gentiles within the Church, requiring two to three weeks including travel time.
53 CE	Paul returns to Antioch. He then soon leaves with Barnabas on a journey through Seleucia, across Cyprus, including Salamis and Paphos. From there they go on to Pamphylia, Pisidia, and Lycaonia. Then they return to Antioch. This would probably require between six and twelve months.
53–54 CE	At Antioch, Peter arrives and a confrontation ensues when the Jews discover that many at table are

	uncircumcised. With Sylvanus and Timothy, Paul is driven out and he is forced to start toward Macedonia.
54 CE	Possibly due to severe mistreatment at Antioch, Paul suffers infirmity and has to stop in Galatia, where he evangelizes.
54 CE	Paul hurries on toward Macedonia.
54 CE	In Macedonia, Paul probably preaches at Neapolis, Philippi, Amphipolis, and Apollonia, while staying at Philippi. He overcomes some resistance. This likely required four to five weeks.
54 CE	In Thessalonika, Paul, Silvanus, and Timothy are mistreated but prevail over the resistance. Including nearby areas, this would require about a month.
54 CE	Paul and the others go to Beroea, then Paul continues on to Athens (late summer).
54 CE	Sending Timothy to Thessalonika, Paul's gospel is rejected at Athens and he goes then to Corinth.
54 CE	While in Corinth, Paul writes 1 & 2 Thessalonians with Sylvanus and Timothy.
54 CE	Paul continues his systematic coverage of the Greek peninsula, journeying around as far as Illyricum. However, he quickly turns back eastward to Achaia, perhaps because he learns that the Jews have been expelled from Rome.
54 CE	On returning to the cities of Corinth and Cenchreae in Achaia, Paul meets many from Italy, including Prisca and Aquila. Paul resolves to make a collection for the saints of Judea and writes a letter to Galatia, which has not survived to us.
55 CE	Paul goes to Ephesus with Prisca and Aquila. Paul contends with "wild beasts" and nearly dies. He also says in 1 Corinthians, however, that an opportunity has opened for preaching the gospel, probably referring to the persons who are with him from the

	churches in Asia (early spring, Passover). Paul writes Galatians.
55 CE	Paul visits other nearby churches of Asia on his way toward Macedonia, and he is shadowed by some Judaizers. He goes first to Smyrna and then to Pergamum. At Pergamum, he sends a woman (Prisca? Thecla?) south and eastward to Thyatira, Sardis, Philadelphia, and Laodicea, and she is also followed by Judaizers (early summer).
55 CE	Paul continued north to Troas.
55 CE	Paul is driven out from Troas, leaving his cloak and notebooks behind, possibly to Macedonia.
55 CE	Paul in Macedonia writing 2 Corinthians and completing the collection for the saints there.
55 CE	Paul returns to Corinth and Cenchreae. Those from Italy are preparing to return to Rome, and Paul writes Romans. Paul sends Timothy to Ephesus, probably to administrate their contribution to the collection, but Timothy is imprisoned for a short while. Expecting Timothy's release, Paul writes Hebrews in anticipation of his return to Jerusalem (late-summer).
55 CE	With Timothy still at Ephesus, Paul returns to Jerusalem by way of Crete, but he is driven out so violently that he is forced to leave Titus behind (late-summer).
55 CE	Paul probably lands at Syria and learns that his mission will not be favorably received in Jerusalem, writing Titus and 1 Timothy (early fall).
55 CE	At Jerusalem, Paul is ruled an apostate Jew and turned over to the Romans for trial. Paul is sent as a prisoner to Rome (fall).
55 CE	At Rome, Paul is held prisoner until he dies, writing 2 Timothy, Ephesians, Colossians, Laodiceans, Philemon, and Philippians (late fall).

New Testament Apocrypha

Epistle of Paul to the Laodiceans

{1.} Paul an Apostle, not of men, neither by man, but by Jesus Christ, to the brethren which are at Laodicea.

{2.} Grace be to you, and peace, from God the Father and our Lord Jesus Christ.

{3.} I thank Christ in every prayer of mine, that you may continue and persevere in good works looking for that which is promised in the day of judgment.

{4.} Let not the vain speeches of any who pervert the truth trouble you, because they may draw you aside from the truth of the gospel which I have preached. {5.} And now may God grant that my converts may attain to a perfect knowledge of the truth of the gospel, being beneficent and doing good works which accompany salvation.

{6.} And now my bonds which I suffer in Christ are manifest, in which I rejoice and am glad. {7.} For I know that this shall turn to my salvation forever, which shall be through your prayer and the supply of the Holy Spirit. {8.} Whether I live or die: for me to live shall be a life to Christ; to die will be a joy.

{9.} And our Lord will grant us his mercy that you may have the same love and be like-minded. {10.} Wherefore, my beloved, as you have heard of the coming of the Lord, so think and act reverently, and it shall be to you life eternal. {11.} For it is God who works in you {12.} and does all things without sin. {13.} And what is best, my beloved, rejoice in the Lord Jesus Christ, and avoid all filthy lucre.

{14.} Let all your requests be made known to God, and be steady in the doctrine of Christ. {15.} And whatsoever things are sound and true, and of good report, and chaste, and just, and lovely— these things do. {16.} Those things which you have heard and received, think on these things, and peace shall be with you.

{17.} All the saints salute you. {18.} The grace of our Lord Jesus Christ be with your spirit. Amen. {19.} Cause this epistle to be read to the Colossians, and the epistle of the Colossians to be read among you.

Didache (Teaching of the Twelve Apostles)

Teaching of the Lord through the Twelve Apostles to the nations:
{I.} There are two ways: one of life and one of death. But [there is] much difference between the two ways. {2.} Amen, therefore, [here is] the way of life: First, you will love the God [who] made you; second, [you will love] your neighbor as yourself. But every thing whatsoever you might possibly desire not to be for you, then you do not do to another. {3.} However, from these words the teaching is this: Bless the ones cursing you and pray for your enemies. Fast for those persecuting you. For what grace [is there] if you love those loving you? [Are] not also the nations doing the same? However, you love those hating you, and you will not have an enemy. {4.} Abstain from the fleshly and bodily lusts. If someone should give you a slap onto your right cheek, turn to him also the other; and you will be perfect. If someone should force you one mile, go with him two. If someone should steal your mantle, give to him also the tunic. If someone should take from you [what is] yours, do not demand [it] back. For neither are you able [because of the commandment]: {5.} "To all asking you give and do not demand back." For the Father intends to give everything out of his own graces. Blessed [is] the one giving according to the commandment, for he is unpunished. Woe to him receiving. For if one having need receives, he will be unpunished; but the one not having need will give justice for what he received and why. However, being in prison, it will be searched out concerning the things he performed, and he will not come out, not until he might repay the last cent. {6.} But also about this, however, it has been said: "Let your alms sweat in your hands, until perchance you might know to whom you should give."

{II.} However, the second commandment of the teaching [is]: {2.} You will not murder. You will not commit adultery. You will not

Appendix V: Didache (The Teaching of the Twelve Apostles) 273

corrupt boys. You will not fornicate. You will not steal. You will not do magic. You will not do sorcery. You will not abort a child nor will you destroy a begotten being. You will not covet things of [your] neighbor. {3.} You will not break an oath. You will not give false testimony. You will not speak evil. You will not remember evil. {4.} You will not be double-minded nor double-tongued. For being double-tongued is a snare of death. {5.} Your word will not be false, not empty; but having been filled, you will execute [them]. {6.} You will not be covetous nor rapacious nor a hypocrite nor malicious nor haughty. You will not receive evil plans against your neighbor. {7.} You will not hate any man. Verily, you will not rebuke them, except about things which you pray for; but you will love them above your soul.

{III.} My child, flee from everything of the evil one and from all likeness of him. {2.} Do not become prone to anger, for anger leads to murder. Neither [become] a zealot nor a quarreler nor a hot-head. For out of all these murders are born. {3.} My child, do not become lustful, for lust leads to fornication. Neither [become] foul-mouthed nor an eye-lifter. For out of all these adulteries are born. {4.} My child, do not become a bird-soothsayer, since it leads to idolatry. Neither [become] an enchanter nor an astrologer nor a magician nor will you intend to see them. For out of all of every one of these idolatry is born. {5.} My child, do not become a liar, since falsehood leads into theft. Neither [become] avaricious nor vainglorious, for out of every one of these thefts are born. {6.} My child, do not become a grumbler, since it leads to blasphemy. Neither [become] arrogant nor evil-minded, for out of every one of these blasphemies are born. {7.} But be humble, since the humble will inherit the earth. {8.} Become patient and merciful and guiltless and tranquil and good and trembling at the words because of all that you heard. {9.} You will not exalt yourself nor will you permit shamelessness in your soul. Your soul will not associate with the haughty, but with the righteous and the lowly you should live. {10.} You should accept all things befalling you as good, knowing that apart from God nothing is born.

{IV.} My child, by the one speaking to you the word of God you will be remembered night and day. Then you will honor him just like the Lord; for where the lordship is, there the Lord is. {2.} Then you will seek out everyday the faces of the holy ones, so that you may rest upon their words. {3.} You will not make a schism, but you will make peace with those quarreling. Judge justly— you will not consider the person to convict for a transgression. {4.} You will not be double-minded whether it will be or not. {5.} Do not be extending-out-the-hands in receiving but tight-fisted in giving. {6.} If possibly you might obtain [it] by your hands, you will give a ransom for your sins. {7.} You will not hesitate to give nor in giving will you grumble; because you know who is the excellent paymaster of the reward. {8.} You will not turn away the needy; but you will share everything with your brother, and you will not say, "[it is] to be mine." For if in the deathless you are partners, how much more so in dead things. {9.} You will not withhold your hand from your son or from your daughter, but from young age you will teach the fear of God. {10.} You will not command your slave or maiden, who hope upon the same God, in your bitterness, lest ever they lose the fear of the God over both [of you]. For He does not come to call according to appearance, but upon whom the Spirit prepared. {11.} But you slaves be subordinate to your masters just as to a type of God in shame and fear. {12.} You will hate all hypocrisy and all which [is] not pleasing to the Lord. {13.} By no means should you forsake a commandment of the Lord, but you will observe that which you adopted, neither adding to nor removing from. {14.} In church, you will confess your transgressions, and you will not approach your place of prayer in bad conscience. This is the way of life.

{V.} But the way of death is this: First of all it is evil and full of doom— murders, adulteries, lusts, fornications, thefts, idolatries, magic, potion-making, robberies, false testimonies, hypocrisies, double-purposes, deceit, haughtiness, wickedness, arrogance, avarice, obscenity, jealousy, willfulness, pride, pretension; {2.} persecutors of innocents, haters of truth, lovers of falsehood, unknowing the reward of righteousness, not cleaving to good nor to righteous judgment, not vigilant unto the good but unto evil, being far from humility and patience, lovers of useless thing, pursuers of repayment, not merciful of a beggar, not troubled because of an oppressed person, not knowing the One making them, murderers of children, corruptors of God's forms, turning away the needy, oppressors of the afflicted, advocates of friends, lawless judges of the poor, utterly sinners. Keep safe, children, from all these.

{VI.} Do not heed one who will seduce you from this teaching of the way, when other things of God he teaches you. {2.} For if indeed you are able to bear the whole yoke of the Lord, you will be perfect. But if you are not able [to do all]; what you can [do], do this. And about eating, bear what you are able. But absolutely keep from the idolatrous meat; for it is worship of dead gods.

{VII.} Then about baptism. Thus you baptize; all these things saying beforehand, you baptize: "in the name of the Father and the Son and the Holy Spirit" in living water. {2.} But if perchance you might not have living water, baptize in another water— if not cold, in warm. {3.} But if perchance you might not have either, pour water onto the head thrice in the name of the Father and Son and Holy Spirit. {4.} But before baptism let fast in preparation the baptizer and the one being baptized and permit those others able. But command the one being baptized one or two [days] before.

{VIII.} But your fasts, do not let them be in the company of hypocrites. For they fast the second [day] from the Sabbath and the fifth [day]. But you will fast the fourth and preparation day. {2.} Neither pray as the hypocrites, but as commanded the Lord in his gospel. Thus you pray: "Our Father, who [is] in heaven, holy be your name. Let come your kingdom. Be done your will as in heaven also on the earth. Give us this day our daily bread. And forgive us our debts as also we forgive our debtors. And may you not bring us unto trial, but rescue us from the Evil One." {3.} Thrice per day thus you pray.

{IX.} Then about the Eucharist, thus give thanks. {2.} First about the cup: "We give thanks to you, our Father, for the holy Vine of David, your servant, which you revealed to us through Jesus, your servant. To you the glory forever." {3.} Then about the pieces [of bread]: "We give thanks to you, our Father, for life and gnosis, which you revealed to us through Jesus, your servant. To you the glory forever." {4.} Just as this fragment was dispersed over the hills and, gathered in, it became one; so let be assembled your Church from the ends of the earth into your kingdom. Because from you is the glory and the power through Jesus Christ forever." {5.} Then let no one eat nor drink from your thanksgiving, but those baptized in the name of the Lord. For also about this the Lord has said: "Do not give the holy to dogs."

{X.} Then after the Eucharist, thus give thanks: {2.} "We give thanks to you, Holy Father, for your holy Name, which dwells in our hearts and for the gnosis and faith and deathlessness, which you revealed to us through Jesus, your servant. To you the glory forever. {3.} You, almighty, you created all things for the sake of your Name. Food as well as drink you gave to men for enjoyment, so that they might give thanks to you. Then you granted us spiritual food and drink and life eternal through your servant. {4.} Before all things we give thanks to you because you exist. To you the glory forever. {5.} Be mindful, Lord, of your Church, that it be rescued from anything of the Evil One, and perfect it in the love of You, and gather it from the four winds, sanctify it into your kingdom, for which you prepared it. For from you are the power and the glory forever! {6.} Come grace and pass away this world. Hosanna! to the God of David. If someone is holy, let [them] come; if someone is not, let [them] repent. *Maran atha!* Amen." {7.} Then permit the prophets to give thanks for whatsoever they want.

{XI.} Therefore, whosoever coming might teach you all these things aforesaid, welcome him. {2.} However, if perchance the teacher, himself being turned, may teach another teaching to abrogate [this teaching], you should not listen to him; but in order to add righteousness and gnosis of the Lord, welcome him as the Lord. {3.} But concerning the apostles and prophets according to the doctrine of the gospel thus do: {4.} Every apostle coming to you let him be received as the Lord, {5.} but he shall not remain but one day; or if perchance it be a necessity, also another. But if perchance three he remains, he is a false prophet. {6.} However, the departing apostle nothing let him take except bread until he might be lodged. But if silver he may request, a false prophet he is. {7.} Also, any prophet speaking in the spirit you will not test nor judge; for every sin will be forgiven, but this sin will not be forgiven. {8.} However, not everyone speaking in the spirit is a prophet, except he may have the manners of the Lord. Therefore, from the manners will be discerned the false prophet and the prophet. {9.} And any prophet ordering a table in the spirit will not eat from it; otherwise a false prophet he is. {10.} But any prophet teaching the truth, if what he teaches he does not do, a false prophet he is. {11.} But any prophet having been proved trustworthy making up a becoming mystery of the Church, but not teaching to do whatsoever he himself does, he will not be judged against you. For after God, he has the authority. For likewise did also the ancient prophets. {12.} But whoever may say in spirit, "Give me money or something else," do not listen to him. But if perchance about others needing he may say to give, let no one judge him.

{XII.} And let all coming in the name of the Lord be welcomed, but thereupon proving him you will know. For insight you have, right and left. {2.} Indeed if the one coming is traveling through, help him as much as you can. But he does not remain with you except two or three days, if it be necessary. {3.} Or if he wants with you to dwell, being a tradesman, let him work and let him eat. {4.} But if he does not have a trade, according to your insight, take care how you will not let a Christian live idle. {5.} Then, if he does not want to do so, he is a Christ-merchant.

{XIII.} However, any true prophet intending to dwell with you worthy he is of his food. {2.} Likewise, a true teacher is worthy himself as well, just as the laborer, of his food. {3.} Therefore, any first portion of produce of a winepress and a threshing floor, of oxen and also of sheep, receiving [it] you will give the first portion to the prophets. For they themselves are the high priests of you. {4.} But if you might not have a prophet, give to the poor. {5.} If you should make grain, receiving the first portion, give according to the commandment.

{XIV.} Now about the Lord's day, being gathered, break bread and give thanks having already confessed your transgressions in order that your sacrifice may be pure. {2.} However, any having a quarrel with their friend, do not let come with you, not until they reconcile, so that your sacrifice might not be defiled. {3.} For this is that spoken of by the Lord: "In every place and time [you are] to offer me a pure sacrifice, because a great king am I, says the Lord, and my name [is] a wonder among the nations."

{XV.} Therefore, elect for yourselves bishops and deacons worthy of the Lord— men meek and generous and creditable and having been proven. For to you they minister also the office of the prophets and teachers. {2.} Therefore, do not overlook them, for they are those having been honored from you among the prophets and teachers. {3.} But reprove one another not in anger but in peace, as you have in the gospel. And [about] any error against an outsider let no one speak nor beside you let [him] listen until he convert. {4.} But your prayers and the almsgivings and all the practices do in the same way as you have in the gospel of our Lord.

{XVI.} Be awake! for the sake of your life. Your lights will not be quenched and your loins will not be weakened, but be ready; for you know not the moment in which our Lord will come. {2.} Be often gathered [together] seeking things fitting to your souls. For the whole time of your faith will not help you, if in the end you might not be perfect. {3.} For in the end of days will be increased the false prophets and the corrupters, and they will change the sheep into wolves, and love will turn to hate. {4.} For from the increasing lawlessness they will hate and pursue and turn over one another. [There will be] signs and portents, and the land will turned over into his hands, and he will make wicked things, which never have existed in eternity. {5.} Thereupon the creation of men comes into the conflagration of trial, and many will be made to stumble and will be utterly destroyed. Then the remaining ones in their faith will be saved by the Cursed One.

{6.} And thereupon he will reveal the signs of the truth: First, [there will be] a sign of the sound of a trumpet and raising one-third of the dead—but not all. Rather, as was said, "The Lord will come and all the holy ones with him. {7.} Thereupon, the world will see the Lord coming above the clouds of heaven."

Epistle of Barnabas

{I.} Rejoice! sons and daughters, in the name of the Lord [who] loved us, in peace.

{2.} Assuredly great and rich are the ordinances of God among you over whom I am then overwhelmingly overjoyed because of your blessed and glorious spirits; so implanted is the grace you received from the spiritual gift. {3.} Wherefore all the more I congratulate myself, hoping to be saved, because I truly see in you the spirit having been poured out over you from the riches of the fount of the Lord. Such being the case, the yearnful sight of you sailed me away. {4.} Therefore, having been persuaded of this and convinced, that I spoke much among you because the Lord journeyed with me on the way of righteousness— and assuredly I was even compelled into this— to love you more than my own soul, because great faith and love dwell in you [who are] the hope of His life. {5.} Therefore, I was reckoning on this: if there were an interest to me about your portion which you shared from whence I received, then it will be for me that these kinds of spirits will translate into a boon. I endeavored every moment to dispatch to you so that along with your perfected faith you may have gnosis.

{6.} Now three commandments are of the Lord: hope of life, the beginning and end of our faith; and righteousness, the beginning and end of discernment; love rejoicing and exulting , the testimony of works of righteousness. {7.} For the master revealed to us through the prophets those things having passed away and those things having been at hand, even giving us first fruits of the taste of the things impending; of which as every single thing is being set in motion just as he said, we ought the more abundantly and more highly to seek the fear of him. {8.} However, not as a teacher but as one of you, I will show a little of those things being present through which you will be gladdened.

{II.} Accordingly, the days being evil and his, the active one seizing dominion, giving heed to ourselves we ought to seek out the ordinances of the Lord. {2.} Therefore, fear and perseverance are helpers of our faith. But those contending together with us [are] forebearance and self-control. {3.} With these dwelling in purity before the Lord, rejoicing together through him are wisdom, understanding, mastery, and gnosis.

{4.} For he has declared to us through all the prophets that he desires nothing of sacrifice nor whole-offerings nor oblations, when he so says:

> {5.} What to me are your multitude of sacrifices, says the Lord. I am full of whole-offerings. And of the fat of lambs, and of the blood of bulls and goats I desire not, not even if you should be allowed into my presence. For who sought these things from your hands? Do not continue to trample my courtyard: if you bring the finest flour, [it is] vain; incense, it is an abomination to me; your new moons and Sabbaths I do not accept. (Isaiah 1:11-13)

{6.} Therefore, these things he annulled in order that the better law of our Lord Jesus being without the yoke of obligation, the man-made oblation may not hold. {7.} Rather, he says again:

> I did not direct your fathers departing from the land of Egypt to offer me whole-offerings and sacrifices. 8. But instead I directed them this: (Jeremiah 7:22-23)

> Let not any of you carry in the heart malice against your neighbor and love not a false oath. (Zechariah 8:17)

{9.} Therefore, not being heathens, we ought to understand the resolve of our Father's goodness because he tells us, not intending on leading us astray in this, to pursue how we may draw near to him. {10.} Therefore, he tells us in this way:

> The sacrifice to God [is] a broken heart. (Psalm 50:17)

> The fragrance of a sweet odor to the Lord [is] a heart glorifying its maker. (?)

{10.} Therefore we ought to accurately inquire, brothers, about our salvation in order that the Evil One may not, forming a subtle way into us by deception, cast us out from our life.
    {III.} Therefore, again it tells in His name about these things:

> To what purpose do you fast to me, says the Lord, as today your lamentation was heard in a wail? I have not requested this fast, says the Lord, of a man having starved his soul. {2.} Neither if you bow your neck as a bulrush and you would put on sackcloth and you throw down ashes, neither in this way will you call a fast acceptable. (Isaiah 58:4-5)

{3.} But toward us he says:

> Behold! this [is] the fast that I have requested, says the Lord, loose any bond of iniquity, dissolve the bindings of violent treachery, and send forth, having been torn to pieces in deliverance, any unjust contract. Break your bread to the hungry. And if you see a naked [person], clothe; of a houseless one, usher him into your house. And if you see a poor man, do not exalt yourself over him nor [discern] from the household of your seed. {4.} Thereupon the light of you will break

forth early and effects your cure quickly, and your righteousness will proceed before you, and the glory of God surrounds you. Thereupon you will cry out and God will be heard by you. {5.} Even at your mentioning him he will say, "Behold, I am here!" If you would be cut off from your bond [of iniquity] and hand stretching and murmuring utterance, and you would give to the hungry your bread from your soul, and a soul having been humbled, you would be pardoned. (Isaiah 58:6-10)

{6.} Therefore, brothers, in this the Patient One was foreseeing [that] without hint of impurity will that people, whom he prepared in his bosom, believe. He foretold to us about everything in order that we would not beforehand shatter ourselves like potter against their law.

{IV.} Therefore, it is necessary for us, most profoundly investigating about the things at hand, to seek out those things capable of saving us. Therefore, we fly completely from all the works of the lawless, lest ever the work of the lawless might capture us. And we hate the wandering of the present time in order that in the imminent [age] we may be loved. {2.} We should not give our soul a rest so as to have in [our soul] liberty to run together after sinners and evil doers, lest we might resemble them. {3.} The perfected stumbling-block has drawn near about which has been written, as Enoch says:

For this purpose the master has cut short the time and the days, in order that quickly the beloved of him, even unto the inheritance, might arrive.

{4.} So then just as he says, and the prophets:

Ten kings over the land will rule, and will be raised up after them a little king, who will bring low three under one of the kings. (Daniel 7:24)

{5.} Likewise concerning him Daniel says:

> And I saw the fourth beast evil and mighty and more ferocious than any beast of the land and as out of him he raised up ten horns, and out of them a little horn, an excrescence, and in like manner he brought low under one three of the great horns. (Daniel 7:7-8)

{6.} Therefore you ought to understand.

But further even than this, I ask you as being one of you but personally loving all [of you] beyond my soul, to attend to yourselves and not to resemble some, piling up your sins, saying that our covenant continues to be in fact the former one. Rather, the former in the manner known to all he utterly destroyed it, removing [it] already from Moses. {7.} For the scripture says:

> And Moses was on the mountain fasting forty days for the Lord, tablets of stone having been written by the finger of the Lord's hand. (Exodus 34:28)

{8.} But [on their] returning to the idols he destroyed it, for as everyone knows the Lord says:

> Moses, Moses, go down quick, because your people which I lead forth out of the land of Egypt broke the law. (Exodus 32:7)

and Moses understood and he hurled down the two tablets from out of his hands and it was broken, their covenant, so that the one of the beloved, of Jesus, might be stamped into the heart of us in the expectation of his faith.

{9.} But much [I am] intending to write, not as a teacher but as is proper to one loving [you], not to leave out from the things we keep. I, your offscouring, hastened to write so that we may beware in the final days. It will profit us nothing the whole time of our faith, if we do not now in the lawless time and in the stumbling-blocks imminent, as is proper to sons of God, resist, in order that the black one might not be creeping in.

{10.} Let us flee from all vanity; let us hate utterly the works of the evil way. Do not by yourselves, creeping in, stand alone like you have already been justified. Rather, [do] the opposite, assembling together inquire concerning [what is] advantageous in common. {11.} For scripture says:

> Woe! the wise [are] to themselves and in their own
> eyes knowledgeable. (Isaiah 5:21)

We should become spiritual persons. We should become a perfect temple for God. While he is in us, we attend to the fear of God. We fight to observe his commandments in order that in the vindication of him we might rejoice. {12.} The Lord will impartially judge the world: each one just as he created, he will receive. If he was good, his righteousness will precede him; if he was evil, [he has] the recompense for wickedness before him; {13.} lest ever that resting upon ourselves as called ones we may fall asleep to our sins and the evil ruler obtaining power against us will thrust us away from the kingdom of the Lord.

{14.} But still this also, my brothers, mark:

> When you see, after so great the signs and wonders
> having occurred in Israel and under such
> circumstances, to have forsaken yourself of them.

Let us pay attention lest ever, as it has been written:

> many [are] called, but few [are] chosen

we might be found out.

{V.} For this purpose the Lord endured to deliver the flesh into corruption in order that in the remission of sins we might be purified, which is in the blood of his sprinkling. {2.} For there has been written concerning it things, certainly towards Israel and towards us. Moreover, it says in this manner:

> He was wounded because of our transgressions and he has been bruised because of our sins, by his stripes we were healed. As a sheep to slaughter he was lead, and like a lamb mute in the presence of the one shearing him.

{3.} Therefore do we not owe the Lord? That, one, he revealed to us things having passed, and to those things present he enlightened us, and into the things impending we are not ignorant. {4.} Furthermore, scripture says:

> Not unjustly are the nets stretched out for the birds.

He says this because with great justice a man was sent who, having gnosis of the way of righteousness, he kept himself utterly from the way of darkness. {5.} But still more this, since the Lord endured to suffer on account of the soul [from] the foundation of the world:

> Let us make man according to our image and according to our likeness.

Therefore, how did he endure to suffer under the hand of man? Learn ye. {6.} The prophets, receiving grace from him, prophesied about it. Then, he, in order that he might nullify death and he might be seen rising from the dead because it was necessary for him to appear in flesh, he endured [it] {7.} so that he might recompense the promise to the fathers, and he, preparing the new people for himself, he might show, being on the earth, that the rising-up he was making, he will judge. {8.} Further still, teaching Israel, and so great the wonders and signs doing, he used to proclaim, and he exceedingly loved [Israel]. {9.} Then when he chose the proper apostles to come to proclaim the glad tidings of him, being more lawless than any sin, in order that he might point out that:

> he came not to call the righteous but sinners.

Thereupon he manifested himself to be the Son of God.
{10.} For if he did not come in the flesh, neither would possibly, by any means, men be saved seeing him, although the one impending (not being the sun, a work coming into existence by his hands), those men seeing clearly cannot bear up against the rays from him. {11.} Therefore, did not the Son of God for this very purpose come in the flesh? So that the greatest of sins might be under one head to those persecuting to death his prophets. {12.} Therefore, did not for this very purpose he suffer? For God says [about] the stripe of his flesh that out of them:

> Whenever striking the shepherd of themselves,
> thereupon will perish the sheep of the flock.

Moreover, he intended to suffer in this way. For it was binding that on the cross he might suffer. For the one prophesying says because of him:

> Spare my soul from the sword;

> They were nailing down my flesh because evil-doing synagogues raised up against me.

{14.} And again he says:

> Behold! I have set my back to the whips, moreover my jawbone into the blows, but my face I set as hard as stone.

> {VI.} Therefore, when he made the precept, what does he say?

> Who to me [is] the one being judged? Let him approach to the child of the Lord.

> {2.} Woe to you! because you all like a garment shall become old, and a moth shall devour you.

And again the prophet says, when like a hard stone it was set into shattering:

> Behold! I will cast into the foundations of Zion a precious stone; a select, prized, cornerstone.

{3.} Then what does he say?

> And whoever will hope on him will live forever.

> Therefore, our hope [is] on a stone? Of course not! Rather, because in strength the Lord has set his flesh. For he says:

> And he set me as a hard stone.

{4.} Moreover, the prophet says again:

> A stone which the builders rejected, this was made into the principal cornerstone.

And again he says:

It is the day great and wondrous which the Lord has made.

{5.} Most sincerely I, the off-scouring of your love, am writing to you so that you may understand completely. {6.} Therefore, what does the prophet say again?

A synagogue of evil-doers surrounds me; they encircled me like bees [do] a honeycomb.

And:

Over my garment they cast a die.

{7.} Therefore, in his flesh coming to be manifested and to suffer, the suffering was previously revealed, for the prophet says against Israel:

Woe to their soul! because they have counseled an evil design down upon themselves saying: "Let us bind the righteous one because he is disagreeable to us."

{8.} What does the other prophet, Moses, say to them?

Behold! This says the Lord God: "Enter into the good land which the Lord promised to Abraham and Isaac and Jacob, and by lot divide it, a land flowing milk and honey.

{9.} But what does gnosis say? Learn ye. You hoped on the one impending to appear to you in the flesh, Jesus. For a man is earth suffering; for the face of the earth the shape of Adam was made. {10.} What, therefore, does he mean [by], "into the good land, a land flowing milk and honey"? Our blessed Lord, brothers— the wisdom and understanding residing in us of his secrets. For the prophet gives a parable of the Lord:

> Who perceived, if not a wise man knowing and loving his Lord?

{11.} Therefore, because he recreated us in the remission of sin, he made us another type so to have the soul of babes, as in an actual remolding of us by him. {12.} For scripture says concerning us, as he says to the Son:

> Let us make man according to our image and according to our likeness, and let them rule over the beasts of the earth and over the birds of heaven and over the fishes of the sea.

And the Lord says, seeing our excellent form:

> Be increased and be multiplied and fill up the earth.

The same things applying to the Son.
{13.} Again I will show you how regarding us he says he made a second creation in the end times. Moreover, the Lord says:

> Behold! I make the last things as the first things.

Therefore, for this reason the prophet proclaimed:

> Enter into the land flowing milk and honey and subdue it.

{14.} Look! We therefore have been reformed, just as again in another prophet it says:

Behold! says the Lord, "I chose from these."

That is to say, from those whom the Lord's spirit was foreseeing:

> the stony hearts and I will put into [them] flesh ones.

Because he in flesh was about to come and to dwell in us. {15.} For a sacred temple, my brethren, for the Lord [is] the dwelling of our heart. {16.} For the Lord again says:

> And in whom will I be revealed and glorified for the Lord my God? I will profess you in the church of my brethren and I will sing you among the churches of [the] saints.

Are we not, therefore, of those whom he lead into the good land? {17.} What, therefore, [is] the milk and the honey? Because first the babe by honey, next by milk, is made to live. Therefore, in this manner we shall live both by faith in the promise and by the word, life-producers subduing the land. {18.} Now we have already stated above:

> And let them be increased and be multiplied and rule over the fishes.

Therefore, who [is] the one able to rule beasts or fishes or birds of heaven? For we should understand that whatever rules is of authority, such that someone commanding may be lord. {19.} Therefore, if this is not in effect now, then it has flowed to us already, whensoever with them we might be perfected to become heirs of the covenant of the Lord.

{VII.} Do you not, therefore, observe, children of joy, that the good Lord prerevealed everything to us so that we might know to whom we all should praise by giving thanks? {2.} Therefore, if the Son of God, being the Lord and the one coming to judge the living and the dead, suffered so that his wound would cause us to live, we might believe that the Son of God was not able to suffer except because of us. {3.} But he was even crucified. He was given to drink vinegar and gall. Listen how concerning this the priests of the sanctuary have revealed from the written commandment:

> Whosoever might not fast the fast [is] to be exterminated utterly to death.

The Lord commanded even as he, on account of the days of sins, was about to, [as] the vessel of the Spirit, offer sacrifice so that also the type established in Isaac of the one being offered on the altar might be fulfilled.
{4.} What, therefore, does it say in the prophet?

> And they ate from the goat offered in the fast on behalf of all of the sins.

Give heed diligently:

> And all the priests alone ate the entrails unwashed with vinegar.

{5.} Why?

> Since to me, who am about to offer my flesh on account of the sins of my new people, you are about to give gall and vinegar to drink

> You eat alone while the people fasts and laments on sackcloth and ash.

In order that he might show that it is necessary for him to suffer under them {6.} note what he commanded:

> Take two he-goats excellent and alike and offer [them], and let the priest receive the one as a whole-offering for sins.

{7.} But the [other] one— what should they do [with it]? "Accursed," he says, "the one." Observe how the type of Jesus is manifested:

> {8.} And all of you spat upon and stabbed, and you put on the scarlet wool around his head and in this manner into the desert let be cast [out].

And when things happen this way, he leads, the one carrying the he-goat into the desert, and he removes the wool and lays it upon a twig which is called Rachia, which also the sproutings we are accustomed to munch in the country [when] finding. Thus, only from the Rachia thornbush is the fruit sweet.

{9.} What, therefore, does this mean? Observe:

> One upon the altar, the one accursed.

And that the accursed having been crowned, because they will see him then on that day the gown having scarlet around the flesh, and they will say: "Is this not whom we once crucified and scorned spitting upon? Verily, this was he then saying himself to be the Son of God. {10.} For how alike to that one!" Regard this:

> the goats similar, excellent, equal

so that when they might see him then coming, they model exactly upon the likeness of the he-goat. Do you not, therefore, behold the type of Jesus about to suffer?

{11.} But what [about] that they set the wool in the middle of the thorn bushes? He is the type of Jesus that was established for the Church, because whosoever may take up the scarlet wool, it is necessary for him to suffer much because the thornbush is terrible and being pressed upon to become lord over him. Thus he says:

> Those intending to behold me and to attach themselves to my kingdom, they should, being pressed upon and suffering, claim me.

{VIII.} However, what do you think a type to be that has been commanded to Israel to bring a heifer, the men in whom sins are perfected, and sacrificing to consume, and then the children to carry the ash and cast into an urn and tie the scarlet wool upon a post (behold! again the type of the cross and the scarlet wool) and the hyssop, and in this way the children sprinkle the people one by one, so that they are purified from sins? {2.} Understand how in simplicity is said to you: The calf is Jesus. The men offering, sinners, who offered him at the slaughter. Thereupon no longer men, no longer the glory of sinners. {3.} The children purifying, those proclaiming to us the remission of sins and the purification of the heart, to whom he gave the authority of the Gospel, being twelve for a testimony of the tribes (because twelve tribes of Israel), in order to proclaim [it].

{4.} But why are three children the sprinklers? For testimony of Abraham, Isaac, and Jacob, because these [are] the great ones of God. {5.} Then, that the wool [is] on the post? Because the kingdom of Jesus [is] upon the post, and the ones hoping upon him will live forever. {6.} Then why the wool and the hyssop together? Because in his kingdom the days will be evil and squalid, during which we will be saved, because the hurting flesh by means of the foul sap of the hyssop heals. {7.} And because of this it becomes thus to us on the one hand it is apparent, on the other obscured to those because they did not heed the voice of the Lord.

{IX.} Furthermore, he says about the ears how he did circumcise our heart:

> In a hearing of the ears they obeyed me

and again,

> In a hearing they far away will hear what I did, they will understand.

And, "be circumcised," says the Lord, "your heart." {2.} And again he says:

> Hear O Israel, because these things says the Lord your God. Who is the one willing to live forever? In a hearing let him hear the voice of my servant.

{3.} And again he says:

> Listen O Heaven, and hear O Earth, because the Lord uttered these things for a testimony. (Isaiah 1:2)

And again he says:

> Listen to a word of the Lord O rulers of this people. (Isaiah 1:10)

And again he says:

> Listen, O children, to the voice of one crying out in the wilderness. (Isaiah 40:3)

{4.} Did he not, therefore, circumcise our ears so that, on hearing a word, we will believe? But also the circumcision upon whom they have persuaded has been annulled, for circumcision he has commanded to become not of the flesh. But they violated because an evil angel deceived them. {5.} He says towards them:

> These things says the Lord your God,

here I find the commandment,

> Do not sow among thorns, circumcise to your Lord. (Jeremiah 4:3-4)

And what does he say?

> Circumcise your hard heart, and your neck do not stiffen. (Deuteronomy 10:16)

Take again:

> Behold! says the Lord, all the nations [are] uncircumcised, but this people [is] uncircumcised of heart. (Jeremiah 9:26)

{6.} But you will say also: "Surely the people was circumcised into a seal." But also [are circumcised] every Syrian and Arabian and all the priests of idols. Are we to believe that they also are of the covenant? And also the Egyptians are in the circumcision.

{7.} Learn, therefore, children of love, about everything abundantly, because Abraham gave the first circumcision in the spirit foreseeing up to Jesus. He circumcised receiving precepts from three letters. {8.} For he says:

> And Abraham circumcised of his house 18 and 300 men. (Genesis 17:23)

What, therefore, was the gnosis given to him? Learn, that the "eighteen" first and an interval was made [then] he says "three hundred." [In] the eighteen [I = 10 and H = 8] you have Jesus [IHSOYS]. Then because the cross in the "T" was to have grace, he says "three hundred."

{9.} Therefore, [it is] evident: Jesus in the two letters and in the one, the cross. He knows the implanted gift of His covenant placed in us. No one learned from me a word more sincere; but I know that you are deserving.

{X.} However, because Moses says:

> Do not consume swine nor eagle nor falcon nor raven nor any fish that has not scales on itself.

Into the understanding he received three ordinances. {2.} Furthermore, he says to them in Deuternomy:

> And I will set forth for this people my righteous decrees.

Hence, therefore, it is not a commandment from God to not eat, but Moses spoke [in the] spirit. {3.} Therefore, "swine" with this in mind he says, "do not adhere," he says, "to such men as these— whosoever is like a swine." This is when living in luxury, they forget the Lord. But when they are lacking in knowing the Lord, like also the swine: when he eats he does not know a lord; but when he hungers, he cries out and, receiving again, quiets.

> {4.} Neither might one eat the eagle nor the falcon nor the kite nor the raven.

By no means, he says, will you be adhered to nor will you resemble men such as these— whosoever they do not know how through trouble and sweat to supply themselves nourishment, but they seize upon the things of others in their lawlessness. And they are on the look-out for one in innocence walking about, and they look around [for] who they will strip because of covetousness, as these birds alone do not supply themselves with nourishment. Rather, sitting idle, it seeks for how the flesh of otters it may eat being pernicious in their evil.

{5.} "And he should not eat," he says, "sea eel nor octopus nor cuttlefish." By no means, he says, will you resemble men such as these— whosoever to the very end are impious and already having been sentenced to death, as also these three accursed fishes alone swim in the deeps, not swimming like others, but in the dirt beneath the deeps it dwells.

{6.} Moreover:

> And the hare by no means should one eat.

Why? By no means might he become a corruptor of boys, neither will you resemble such as these, because the hare yearly takes advantage of the anus. For as many years it might live, so many it has holes.

{7.} Moreover:

> Nor the hyena should he eat.

By no means, he says, might he become an adulterer nor a seducer, neither will you resemble such as these. Why? Because this animal throughout the year transforms nature, both when male then when male female, it becomes [the other].

{8.} Furthermore, the weasel he hated properly. By no means, he says, were you made such as these— whosoever we hear making lawlessness in the mouth because of uncleanness. Neither will you adhere to the unclean women making lawlessness in the mouth. For this animal conceives in the mouth.

{9.} While Moses received three ordinances about foods just as in spirit he uttered, those according to the lust of the flesh so about food took [them]. {10.} But David receives gnosis from their three ordinances and he says:

> Blessed [is] a man who does not pass into the counsel
> of the wicked.

Even as also the fishes pass in the dark into the depths:

And in the path of sinners he did not stand.

Just as those presuming to fear the Lord sin like swine:

And upon a seat of pests he did not sit.

Just as birds sitting for prey. You understand completely now about food.

{11.} Again Moses says:

Consume every divided-hoof animal and ruminant.

What does he say? The one receiving food knows the one feeding him, and on him resting to feast, he thinks. Properly, he speaks seeing the commandment. What, therefore, does he say? Adhere with those fearing the Lord; with those meditating who received a special meaning of the declaration into the heart; with those knowing that meditation is a work of rejoicing and ruminating the word of the Lord.

However, what [about] the cloven-hoofed animal? Because the righteous man both walks in this world and in the holy aeon he receives. Look how Moses imposed law properly. {12.} Then whence [will it be] to them [for] these things to perceive or understand? But justly we are understanding the commandment we uttered as intended the Lord. Through this, he circumcised our ears and heart so that we may understand these things.

{XI.} However, we might pursue if it was a concern to the Lord to reveal about the water and about the cross. About the water it has been written against Israel how the baptism bearing a remission of sins by no means do they admit, but they will build a house to themselves. {2.} For says the prophet:

> Be astonished O Heaven! and on this shudder long O Earth! because two things both evil did this people: They abandoned me, the fountain of life, and for themselves [are] digging a cistern of death. {3.} A desert rock is my holy mountain Sinai? For you will be as young chicks of a bird, fluttering about, stolen away from the nest.

{4.} And again says the prophet:

> I will pass before you, and mountains I will level and gates of bronze I will shatter and bars of iron I will break to pieces and I will give to you treasures, dark, hidden, invisible, so that they will know that I am the Lord God.

Also:

> You will dwell in a lofty cavern of mighty rock.

{5.} And:

> His water [is] unfailing: a king with glory you will behold, and your soul will meditate upon the fear of the Lord.

{6.} And again in another prophet he says:

> And he doing these things will be as a the tree having been planted along the thoroughfare of the waters, he will give his fruit in his season and his leaf will not hesitate, and everything as much as possibly he may do, it will prosper. {7.} Not in this way [for] the wicked ones; not in this way, but rather as the dust

which the wind drives from the face of the earth. Because of this, the impious ones will not be raised in judgment, nor sinners in the plan for the righteous ones. Because the Lord knows the way of the righteous, and the way of the impious he will destroy utterly.

{8.} Understand how the water and the cross together he determined. For this he says:

Blessed those hoping upon the cross [who] descended into the water,

"For the reward," he says in his time. Then he says, "I will render." But now he says, "it will not fall the leaves." This he says because each word, provided that it shall come forth from you through your mouth in faith and love, it will be for conversion and hope to many.
{9.} And again another prophet says:

And the land of Jacob was being praised throughout the earth.

This he says the vessel of his spirit glorifies. {10.} Thereupon, what does he say?

And there was a river flowing on the right, and blooming trees arose out from it; and whoever may eat from them, they will live into the eon.

{11.} This he says because we descend into the water being full of sin and squalid, and we arise bearing fruit in the heart, having in the spirit the fear and hope towards Jesus. "And whoever may eat from these will live into the eon." This he says, "whoever," he says, " may hear from these speaking and might believe; he will live into the eon."

{XII.} Similarly again about the cross he explicates in another prophet saying:

> And when these things [happen] it will be consummated, says the Lord: when he might fall and might raise up a tree, and when from a tree blood might drip.

You have again about the cross and the one destined to be crucified. {2.} But he speaks again to Moses, when Israel was embattled by the foreigners. And in order that he might remind them [who were] battling that because of their sins they were delivered unto death, the spirit says into the heart of Moses that he should make a type of cross and of the one destined to suffer, because unless, he says, they will hope upon him, until the eon they will be battling. Therefore, Moses set one upon one weapon in the middle of the fist, and standing above all, stretched out [his] hands, and in this way again Israel conquered. Thereupon, whenever he let down [his hands], they were being put to death. {3.} Why? So that they might know that they are not able to be saved unless upon him they will hope. {4.} And again in another prophet he says:

> The whole day he stretched forth my hands towards the people [which] was disobedient and speaking against my righteous way.

{5.} Again Moses makes a type of Jesus, because it is necessary for him to suffer, and he will make live [the one] whom they will believe to have been utterly destroyed in a sign of the falling of Israel. For the Lord made every serpent to bite them, and he was putting [them] to death (since the deviation through the snake was made in Eve) so that he might test them, because through their deviation into the pressure of death they will be delivered.

{6.} Furthermore besides, Moses himself was commanded:

> It shall not be for you neither cast-metal image nor
> carved image unto God for you.

He does [this] so that a type of Jesus he might show. Therefore, Moses makes a brazen serpent and sets [it] prominently, and by proclamation he calls the people. {7.} Therefore, those coming together were being assembled by Moses so that about them he might offer up a petition for the healing of them. But Moses says towards them:

> Whenever (he says) might be bitten someone of you,
> let him come upon the serpent which [is] lying upon
> the tree, and let him hope, believing that he being dead
> is able to enliven, and immediately to be saved.

And they doing just so, you have again also in these things the glory of Jesus, because all things [are] in him and unto him.

{8.} What does Moses say again of Jesus to the son of Naue [Nun], setting upon him this name, being a prophet, so that all the people might listen to [him] alone because the Father manifests all things concerning the son, Jesus? {9.} Therefore, Moses says of Jesus to the son of Naue [Nun], setting upon him this name, when he sent him [to be] a surveyor of the earth:

> Take a scroll into your hands and write what the Lord
> says, because the son of God in the last days will cut
> off from the roots all the house of Amalek.

{10.} Behold again Jesus, not the son of man but the son of God, yet a type in flesh being manifested.

Since therefore they are to say that Christ is the son of David, David himself prophesies fearing and understanding the delusion of sinners:

> The Lord says to my Lord: Sit on my right until I might set those hated by you a footstool for your feet.

{11.} And again in the same way, Isaiah says:

> The Lord says to the Christ my Lord, for whom I vanquished, by his right hand, nations to listen before him, and the strength of kings I will break.

Behold how David calls him "Lord" and he does not say "son."

{XIII.} However, we might see if this people inherits or the first, and [if] the covenant [is] unto us or unto those before. {2.} Hear therefore about the people what scripture says:

> But Isaac was praying about Rebecca his wife, because she was barren, and she conceived. Thereupon, Rebecca proceeded to ask from the Lord, and the Lord says towards her: "Two nations in your stomach and two peoples in your belly, and a people will rise above a people, and the greater will be slave to the younger."

{3.} You should understand who [is] Isaac and who [is] Rebecca, and by what things he has shown that this people is greater than the former.

{4.} And in another prophecy Jacob says more clearly towards Joseph his son saying:

> Behold! the Lord did not deprive me of your face. Lead me to your sons, so that I will bless them.

{5.} And he lead Ephraim and Manasseh, Manasseh intending that he might be blessed because he was the elder. For Joseph lead [him] to the right hand of the father Jacob. But Jacob saw in the spirit a type of the people yet to come. And what does he say?

> And Jacob crossed his hands and he set the right hand upon the head of Ephraim, the second [son], and he blessed him. And Jacob says towards Joseph: "I know, child, I know. However, the greater will be slave to the younger, and this will be praised.

{6.} Look by what things he has set this people to be first and of the covenant, the heir. {7.} If, therefore, still also through Abraham was remembered, we have in full the completion of our gnosis. What, therefore, does he say to Abraham, when alone believing he was appointed for righteousness?

> Behold! I have appointed you, Abraham, a father of nations believing in God through the foreskin.

{XIV.} Verily. But we might see [if], the covenant which he pledged to the fathers to give to the people, if he has delivered. He has delivered; but they became unworthy to receive [it] because of their sins. {2.} For the prophet says:

> And Moses was fasting on Mount Sinai, to receive the covenant of the Lord for the people, forty days and forty nights, and he received from the Lord the two tablets having been written by the finger of the hand of the Lord in the spirit.

And taking [the tablets], Moses carried down towards the people to give [them]. {3.} And says [the] Lord towards Moses:

> Moses, Moses, descend quickly because your people which you lead out of [the] land of Egypt transgressed.

And understood Moses that they made themselves again metal-cast images and he hurled [the tablets] out from [his] hands and shattered the tablets of the covenant of the Lord. {4.} Therefore, Moses received, but they became unworthy. But how did we receive? Learn ye: Moses being a servant received, but the Lord to us, he gave unto a people of an inheritance, because of us, enduring. {5.} But he was manifested in order that even they might be perfected in sins and we, through him inheriting the covenant of the Lord Jesus, we might receive, who because of this was prepared in order that he will shine in our hearts— [our hearts] already having been exhausted to death and having been given over to the lawlessness of the wandering— ransoming [our hearts] out of darkness. He has established in us a covenant in the word.

{6.} For it has been written how to him the Father commanded ransoming us out of darkness to prepare himself an holy people. {7.} Therefore the prophet says:

> I, the Lord your God, called you in righteousness and I will conquer by your hand and I will strengthen you, and I gave you for a covenant of a people, a light unto nations, to open the eyes of the blind, and to lead out of bonds, having been bound, and out of the guardhouse, sitting in darkness.

We know therefore whence we were liberated. {8.} Again the prophet says:

> Behold! I have set you for a light of the nations, that you become a deliverance until the end of the earth. Thus says the Lord God liberating you.

{9.} Again the prophet says:

> The spirit of the Lord [is] upon me, on account of whom he cast me out to evangelize the lowly, he has sent me to heal the broken-hearted, to proclaim to

prisoners a deliverance and to the blind a recovery of sight, to call an acceptable year of the Lord and a day of reward, to encourage all those lamenting.

{XV.} Therefore and besides, about the sabbath it has been written in the ten words, in which he uttered on Mount Sinai to Moses face to face:

> And make holy the sabbath of the Lord with clean hands and a pure heart.

{2.} And in another it says:

> Whensoever my sons might watch over the sabbath, then I will rest my mercy upon them.

{3.} He describes the sabbath in the beginning of creation:

> And God made in six days the works of his hands and he finished on the seventh day and he devoured on it and made it holy.

{4.} Be attentive children, what it says:

> He finished in six days.

This he says because in six thousand years the Lord will finish all things. For the day [was] to him a thousand years. But he himself witnesses to me saying:

> Behold! a day of the Lord will be as a thousand years.

[Is it] not therefore children, "in six days" [meaning] "in six thousand years" he will be finished with all things?

{5.} And he rested on the seventh day.

This he says when his son coming will nullify the time of the lawless one and he will judge the impious and he will transform the sun and the moon and the stars, then properly it will be restrained on the seventh day.
    {6.} Furthermore besides, he says:

> You will make it holy with clean hands and a pure heart.

If therefore [it is] the day which God made holy, who now, being pure in heart, is able to make holy, having been lead astray in everything? {7.} But if therefore consequently then, being properly restrained, we will make it holy when we will be able, those being approved and being rewarded the thing promised, no longer [the day] being of lawlessness, but all things having been created anew by the Lord, then we will be able to make it holy, those being made themselves holy first.
    {8.} Furthermore besides he says to them:

> Your new moons and sabbaths I do not support.

See how he says:

> Now the sabbaths [are] not acceptable [to me] but the one which I have made, on which I will restrain all things. I will make a beginning of the eighth day which is a beginning of another world.

{9.} Wherefore also we celebrate the eighth day into the rejoicing, on which also Jesus arose from the dead and being revealed he ascended to the heavens.
    {XVI.} But still more concerning the temple I will say to us how, being lead astray, the wretched ones hoped unto the building and

not upon their God making them as being a house of God. {2.} For almost as the nations they consecrated him in the Temple. But how does the Lord nullify it? Learn:

> "Who has measured the heaven by a hand-span, or the earth by hand-stretch? Did I not?" says the Lord, "heaven to me [is] a throne; the earth a footstool for my feet. What kind of house will you build for me? Or what resting place for me?

You have known their hope [is] vain. {3.} Furthermore besides again, he says:

> Behold! those pulling down this temple, they will build it.

{4.} It is done. For, because they quarrel, it was cleansed by the enemies. Now, also servants of the enemies themselves will rebuild it. {5.} Again, just as he was intending, the city and the temple and the people of Israel to be given over, it was manifested. For scripture says:

> And it will be upon the last days, and the Lord will give over the sheep of the law and the fold and their tower unto destruction.

And it occurred according as the Lord uttered.
    {6.} However, we might pursue if there is a temple of God. There is where he says to make and prepare. For it has been written:

> And it will be, the seventh [day] being completed, a temple of God will be built gloriously upon the name of the Lord.

{7.} I find therefore that there is a temple. How therefore will he build upon the name of the Lord? Learn ye. Before we believed in God, our abode of the heart was corruptible and weak, just as the temple actually built by hand, because it was full of idolatry and it was a house of demons, because of doing whatsoever was against God.

{8.} But he will build upon the name of the Lord.

However, be attentive so that the temple of the Lord might be built gloriously. How? Learn ye. Receiving the remission of sins and hoping upon the name we were born anew, again out of the beginning being created; wherefore in our habitation God truly dwells in us. {9.} How? His word of faith, the call from him through the gospel, the wisdom of his righteous judgments, the commandments of the instruction, he in us prophesying, he in us dwelling, those in death having been enslaved opening in us the entrance of the temple which is the mouth, giving to us repentance to lead unto the imperishable temple.

{10.} For one desiring to be saved looks not unto the man but unto that within him dwelling and speaking, at no time ever being amazed because of him, neither of him speaking the words heard out of the mouth nor when he impels [one] to listen. This is a spiritual temple being built to the Lord.

{XVII.} Upon as much as there was in power and simplicity to make known to you, my soul hopes not to have neglected anything. For, if possibly about things present or things impending I write to you, by no means would you understand because of that to be laid out in parables. Indeed, just as these things [were].

{XVIII.} However, let us pass on to another gnosis and instruction. There are two ways of teaching and of power, not only that of the light but also that of the darkness. But [there is] much difference between the ways. For in the first there are having been appointed light-bearing angels of God; but in the second, angels of the Satan. {2.} Indeed [not only] is he both the lord from the eons and unto the eons but the ruler of the present time of lawlessness.

{XIX.} Therefore the way of light is this: if someone [is] intending to travel the way on to the place having been determined, they should hasten in his works. Therefore is the gnosis given to us to walk in such like this: {2.} You will love the one making you. You will be afraid of the one forming you. You will glorify the one ransoming you out of death. You will be single of heart and rich in spirit. You will not be joined with those being carried on the way of death. You will hate all that is not acceptable to God. You will hate all hypocrisy. By no means should you depart from the commandments of the Lord. {3.} You will not take upon yourself glory. You will not accept evil counsel against your neighbor. You will not admit shamelessness into your soul. {4.} You will not fornicate. You will not commit adultery. You will not corrupt boys. By no means from you shall the word of God proceed in uncleanness of some. You will not accept partiality to convict someone because of transgressions. You shall be meek. You shall be peaceful. You will be trembling at the words which you are hearing. You will not remember evil against your brother. {5.} By no means might you doubt whether it will be or not. By no means should you take in vain the name of the Lord. You will love your neighbor over your soul. You will not expose a child into corruption; neither again will you destroy a begotten. By no means might you withhold your hand from your son or from your daughter, but from youth you shall teach fear of God. {6.} By no means might you start coveting that of your neighbor. By no means should you become greedy. Neither should you be joined in your soul with haughty ones; rather with humble and righteous ones you will abide. The things happening to you as good you should accept, knowing that without God nothing exists. {7.} You will not be of two purposes nor of two tongues. You will subject yourself to masters like to a type of God in shame and fear. By no means might you command your slave or maiden in bitterness, to those who are hoping upon him [who is] God, lest ever they cease to fear the God over both [of you]; because he came to call not according to appearances but on those whom the spirit prepared. {8.} You will share in all things with your neighbor and you will not say "mine to be." For, if in the incorruptible sharers you are, how much more in the corruptible. You will not be talkative, for the mouth is the snare of death. As much as able you will be pure for the sake of your soul. {9.} Do not become, with respect to receiving outstretching the hands, but with respect to giving drawing in [the hands]. Love as the apple of your eye everyone uttering to you the word of the Lord. {10.} You will remember the day of judgment night and day. And you will seek out every single day the faces of the holy ones, either through the word toiling and proceeding to encourage and attending to save a soul by the word, or through your hands he might work unto a ransom of your sins. {11.} You will not hesitate to give; neither, giving, will you grumble. But you will understand who [is] the paymaster of the rich reward. You will keep safe that which you accepted, neither will you add to nor be removing from. To the very end you will hate the evil one. You will judge justly. {12.} You will not make a schism, but you will make peace with those disputing at gatherings. You will confess about your sins. You will not approach prayer in evil conscience. This is the way of light.

{XX.} But the way of the black one is crooked and full of doom. For the way is from the eon of death with the punishment, in which there is the things destroying their souls: idolatry, audacity, powerful rank, hypocrisy, duplicity, adultery, murder, plundering, arrogance, transgression, fraud, malice, willfulness, use of potions, magic, grasping, fearless of God, {2.} Persecutors of the good, those hating truth, those loving falsehood, those not knowing of the reward of righteousness, not being joined to the good, not a righteous judgment of widows and orphans, those not being attentive, keeping watch not unto fear of God but unto evil, those from whom gentleness and patience [are] far-off and distant, those loving vanity, following recompense, not being compassionate of the beggar, those not toiling upon becoming weary, easy in slander, not knowing the one making them, murderers of children, corrupters of God's form, those rejecting the needy, oppressors of the afflicted, advocates of the wealthy, of the poor lawless judges, altogether sinful.

{XXI.} Therefore, pleasing it is, the one learning the ordinances of the Lord, whatsoever has been written, to walk in them. For the one doing these things in the kingdom of God will be glorified. He choosing the former things, along with his works, will be annihilated. Because of this, a raising up; because of this, a recompense.

{2.} I ask those excelling, if from my good purpose you receive some counsel: Keep among yourselves, unto those whom you might work good; do not neglect [them]. {3.} Near [is] the day in which will be destroyed together all things by evil. Near [is] the Lord and reward of him. {4.} Moreover besides I ask you: Become yourselves good lawgivers. Remain yourselves faithful advisors. Remove out of you all hypocrisy. {5.} But [pray that] God, he ruling over all the world, might give you wisdom, intelligence, knowledge, gnosis of his ordinances, endurance. {6.} Become God-taught seeking out what the Lord seeks from us, and do, so that you might be found on the day of judgment. {7.} But if there is remembrance of good, remember me meditating upon these things, so that the longing with vigilance unto what is good might succeed. I ask you, requesting a favor: {8.} As long as the excellent vessel is among you, do not neglect anything of yourselves, but continually seek out these things and fulfill every commandment. For it is worthwhile. {9.} Whence the more I hurried to write from what things I was able in order to gladden you. Be saved, children of love and peace. The Lord of glory and of all grace with your spirit.

Acknowledgments

I want to thank my friends from the National Writers' Union, especially my generous readers Alison P. Martinez and David Ray, for their support. I also want to thank my son Ryan LaFond for his conversation and insights. Also, I want to thank Simcha Jacobovici and the many other scholars in this field who have done much thoughtful research and writing. Although my conclusions may differ from theirs, this book could not have happened without their challenging work.

Index

Abel, 215
Abraham, 99, 170, 171, 206-7, 213-14, 230
Acts of the Apostles, 13-16, 32, 47-69, 77, 82-83, 99, 211-212
  on James, 118, 123, 127
  on Jesus, 123
  Paul's journeys in, 258-65
  vs. 3 John, 148
Adam, 207
Adoptionist doctrine, 144, 149-50, 163, 171, 184, 236-37
Albinus, 117
Alexander, 33, 178, 181
Ananus, 117
Andronicus, 190
Angels, 156, 161, 162, 213, 229
Antichrist, 6, 151, 159, 161
Antioch, 43, 50, 51, 69, 98
  Paul vs. Peter at, 19-20, 44, 53-55, 62, 102-3, 106, 220
  split from Barnabas at, 133
Antioch, Council of, 234
Apocalypse, 8, 115, 160, 202
  Paul on, 205, 216
Apocalyptic symbology, 115, 121, 209
Apocrypha, 222, 269-313. *See also specific books, as* Barnabas, Epistle of.
Apollos, 176, 200
Apostles, 34, 98-100, 108, 133, 136, 142, 148, 177, 178
  livelihood of, 199, 230
  requisites for, 121, 140.
  See also Paul, authority of; Twelve apostles.
Aquila, 33-34, 58, 62
Arabia, 19, 41-43, 97, 183
Arabs, Paul on, 171
Areopagite, *see* Dionysius.
Aretas, 43 n. 68
Arian doctrine, 149-50, 223
Aristarchus, 35-36
Aristotle, 80
Ascension doctrine, 164, 202, 218-19
Asceticism, 92, 179
  of Docetists, 150
  of Essenes, 221
  of James, 116-17, 130, 202
  of John the Baptist, 91
Ashkelon, 237
Assos, 59
Assyrian Church, 150, 223
Athens, 22, 45, 58, 62, 109, 110, 220
Attalia, 51

Babylon as Rome, 135
Babylonian conquest, 77-80
Baptism, 81, 170, 175, 188, 200, 208, 214, 218
  by Jesus, 200
  of Jesus, 41, 144
  of John the Baptist, 220
  of Essenes and Mandeans, 94
Barbarians, 169. *See also* Pagans.
Barnabas, 44, 50-55, 62, 69, 70, 98-100, 103, 133-34, 136, 141, 142, 189, 226
Barnabas, Epistle of, 134-35, 170, 229 text of, 280-313
Benjamin, Bishop of Jerusalem, 126
Benjamin, tribe of, 19, 39, 76-81
Beroea, 58, 127
Bible, *see* Gospels; Paul, library of; Scripture
Bodhisattva, 218
Byzantium, 45, 104, 105

Caesarea Maritima, 61, 68, 226
Cairo (Geniza) Document, *see* Zadokite Document.
Cauda, 61
Cenchreae, 29
Cephas, *see* Peter.
Chios, 59
Christology, 7-8, 111, 128, 148-51, 184
  of Clement, 236-37
  of John, 143, 146, 149, 155-57, 159-60, 171
  of Paul, 23, 82, 114, 143-44, 161-64, 171, 180-84, 198-204, 213-19
  of Peter, 230
Church
  as body of Christ, 187, 217
  as brothers and sisters, 213
  leaders and organization of, 10-11, 106-8, 146-47, 176-78, 190-91, 218

Circumcision, 44, 51-53, 62, 82-86, 94, 100-1, 132, 139, 170, 188, 202
  allegorical, 135
  importance of, 99, 126, 202-3
  Mandeans refusing, 93-94
  of Timothy, 56
  sexual morality and, 137
  spiritual, 206, 218
  "the circumcision," 85, 101
Clement, 167, 226, 233-36
Clementina, 167-68, 222, 226-29
Cleopas, *see* Simeon Clopas.
Cletus, 167-68
Cnidus, 61
Collection for Jerusalem Poor, 24-25, 28, 30, 46, 62, 104, 141, 165 n. 218, 236 n. 252
  Didache on, 230
  motivations for, 50, 101, 103, 164, 179, 183, 190
Colossians, Paul's Epistle to, 35-36, 47, 134, 188-89, 218,
  Paul's journeys in, 254-55
Communion, 65, 180, 201
Corinth, 21-25, 45-46, 58, 62, 132, 133, 137, 142, 173-74, 220
Corinthians, Clement's Epistle to, 235-36
Corinthians, Paul's 1st Epistle to, 22-25, 46, 124, 132-33, 199-201
  Paul's journeys in, 245-47
Corinthians, Paul's 2d Epistle to, 22-25, 46, 139-43, 203-5
  Paul's journeys in, 248-50
Corinthians, Paul's lost epistle to, 24, 46
Council of Seven, 65-67, 152
Covenants
  with Jews, 99, 101-2, 175
  with Noah, 52, 54, 56
  new, 215
Crescens, 234
Crete, 32, 46, 60, 61, 62, 175, 176, 220
Crucifixion, 171, 200, 201, 204-5, 229
  Peter as witness, 147
  Peter on, 229-31
  Revelation on, 160
Cyprus, 51, 60, 69

Damascus, 19, 40-43, 62, 97, 220
  Paul's escape from, 43, 49
Damascus Document or Rule, *see* Zadokite Document.
David, descent from, 11, 119-25, 127, 229
  of Jesus, 91, 155, 161, 182, 216, 235
Day of the Lord, 118, 120, 183, 198-99
  imminence of, 188, 189, 219
Dead Sea scrolls, 40, 72, 77-78, 80-81, 90-92, 98, 111, 146, 215
  apocalyptic symbols in, 115, 137
Demas, 35-36, 181
Demetrius, 147
Derbe, 51, 56
Diaspora, *see* Gentiles.
Didache, 118, 121-22, 124, 134, 181, 229-30
  text of, 272-79
Dionysius, 173, 236
Diotrephes, 147
Docetic doctrine, 143-44, 148-51, 162, 164, 171, 213, 226
Doctrines
  development of, 194-95
  Jewish Christian, 179
  modern, 2, 12, 194, 202, 237
  Paul's basic, 175, 214
  secret, 92, 93, 111, 174, 198
  See also specific doctrines, as Trinity.
Domitian, 125
Dositheans, 72
Dositheos, 227
Dragon, 153, 159
Drower, E. S., 93
Druze, 223
Dualist doctrine, 121

Ebionites, 130, 149, 185-86, 190, 195, 203, 218, 220
Elect, 185-86
Elect Lady, 144-46
Elijah, 183
Enoch, 215
Enoch, Secret Book of, 205
Epaphras, 35
Ephesians, Paul's Epistle to, 33-34, 47, 86-87, 185, 187-88, 217
  Paul's journeys in, 253

Ephesians, Paul's message to in Acts, 62 n. 142
Ephesus, 25, 26, 31-34, 58, 60, 62
  Paul's troubles at, 46, 139-40, 148, 151-52, 154, 176, 220
  Revelation and, 152-53
Ephres, 126
Epiphanius, 10, 11, 72, 73, 90, 92, 222
  on schism, 127-28
Epistles, 136, 222, 228. *See also specific addressee or author.*
Erastus, 29
Eucharist, *see* Communion.
Essenes, 40-41, 72, 89-91, 94, 97-98, 111, 220-22
  monks, 185-86
  on Temple, 190
  priests, 146
Eusebius, 103, 126, 222, 237
  Quoting Hegesippus, 116, 120, 124-25, 238

Faith vs. law
  James on, 130-31
  Paul on, 130, 139-40, 169, 173, 175, 176, 181, 184, 203, 206-10, 214
  See also Grace.
Flavius Josephus, *see* Josephus.
Fornication, *see* Moral behavior.
Fortunatus, 234

Gaius, 147
Galatia, 44-45, 62, 103-7, 220
Galatians, Paul's Epistle to, 26-28, 46, 50-56, 58, 118, 136, 139, 158, 202-3
  Paul's journeys in, 247-48
Galatians, Paul's lost epistle to, 28, 46
Galatians, Peter's epistle to, *see* Peter, 1st Epistle of.
Gaudentius, 167
Genealogies, 176, 179, 216. *See also* David, descent from; Jews and lineages rediscovered.
Gentiles
  defined, 83-88, 104, 187, 220, 237-39
  Paul and, 67-69, 206, 210, 217
  See also Gospel for all.

Gnostics, 73, 92, 111, 179. *See also* Manicheans, Pleroma, Secret knowledge.
Gorothenes, 72
Gospel for all, 94, 100, 104-5, 171-72, 180, 239
  political, 11, 195-96
Gospels, canonical, 13, 82, 90-91, 221, 222
Gospels, early, 193-94
  on Day of the Lord, 111
  on Jesus as Messiah, 122-24
  See also specific gospels as John, Gospel of.
Grace, 209-10, 217

Heathens, *see* Pagans.
Heaven, Third, 205
Hebrews, Paul's Epistle to, 28-31, 46, 174-75, 210-15
  Paul's journeys in, 251
Hegesippus, 116-17, 120, 124-25, 238
Hellenistic culture, 87
Hellenists, *see* Gentiles.
Hemerobaptists, 73
Heresy, *see* Doctrines. *See also specific doctrines as* Arian doctrine.
Hermogenes, 181
Herod Antipas, 42
Herodians, 72, 90
Historiography pitfalls, 12, 71, 76. 104, 197
Holy of Holies, *see* Temple.
Holy Spirit, *see* Spirit, Holy.
Homilies, *see* Clementina.
Hymenaeus, 33, 178, 181, 183

Iconium, 51, 56
Ignatius, 103, 157. 189, 217, 233-35
Image worship, 157

Jacobovici, Simcha, 145 n. 210
James, 6, 91, 116-21, 126-31, 154, 168 n. 220, 176, 201
  assassination of, 237
  gospel of, 202-3, 220-32
  See also David, descent from; Jewish Christians
James, Epistle of, 130-31, 136, 170, 230

and Didache, 121 and Stoic influences, 188
Jerusalem
　Christians outside, 127
　Christians outside metaphorically, 215
　Paul's arrest at, 60-61, 63
　Paul's trial at, 60-61, 63, 165
　Paul's visits to Jewish Christian authorities at, 19, 32, 42-44, 47, 49, 52-53, 62, 63, 98-101
　vs. Arabia, 41-43
　vs. Damascus, 40
Jerusalem, Bishops of, 120, 126
Jesse
　Branch of, 119, 155
　Essenes named for, 91
Jesseans, 127
Jesus Christ 3, 6-9, 90-95, 112
　Clementina on, 227
　family of, 142, 144
　marriage of, 145
　mission of, 10-11
　tomb of, 145 n. 210
　See also Christology; David, descent from; Paul, revelations to; Resurrection of Jesus Christ; Revelation of John.
Jewish Christians, 70, 81-83, 101-2, 144, 176, 195, 209, 220-21
　Ebionites in, 185-86
　obstacles for, 131, 135
　reflected in Qur'an, 223-26
Jewish Revolt, 6, 129
　Christian role in, 237-38
Jews and lineages rediscovered, 77-81, 105, 207
　by Essenes, 220
Jews of 1st century
　beliefs and sects, 8, 11, 72-73, 87-90, 222
　congregations of, 106-8
　defined, 73-83
　persecuting Christians, 19, 39-40, 64-66
　Roman, 166-67. *See also* Hebrews, Paul's Epistle to.
Jews post Temple, 72, 222
John, Bishop of Jerusalem, 126
John called Mark, *see* Mark.
John, Gospel of, 82-83, 85, 122-23, 143, 162

John of Patmos, *see* John of the Twelve.
John of the Twelve, 42, 148, 237
　writing Revelation, 152
　See also Jewish Christians.
John the Baptist, 40-42, 72, 73, 90-95, 97, 186, 200, 220, 227
　on Messiah, 123
　Qur'an on, 223
John the Elder, 148-49, 151
John the Elder, 1st Epistle of, 143-44, 146
John the Elder, 2d Epistle of, 143, 144-47
John the Elder, 3d Epistle of, 143, 144-48
John the Essene, 237
Jordan River region, 41-42, 92, 93, 223
Joseph, Bishop of Jerusalem, 126
Josephus, 40, 72, 76, 78-80, 89, 91, 117, 212 n. 242, 256 n. 252, 237-38
Judas, Bishop of Jerusalem, 126
Judas called Barsabbas, 52
Judas Iscariot, 77, 82
Jude, Epistle of, 138-39, 176, 205
Judgment Day, *see* Day of the Lord.
Judgment eternal, 175, 199, 214
Justin Martyr, 87
Junia, 38, 146, 190
Justus, 126

King of Israel, 104, 123 n. 200, 180, 195, 207
　obedience to, 107-8, 115, 196
Kingdom of God, 119, 195, 198. *See also* Messianic age.
Koran, *see* Qur'an.
Kosher rules, *see* Mosaic law.

Lamb of God, 123 n. 200
　in Revelation, 155, 156, 159, 160, 161, 162, 163-64, 171
Laodiceans, 153, 218
Laodiceans, Paul's Epistle to, 18, 35, 47, 188-89, 218
　Paul's journeys in, 255
　text of, 270-71
Law, *see* Mosaic law.
Levi, 126
Levites, 78-81
Linus, 167-68
Logos of God, 213

Luke, 36, 47-48, 103, 189
Luke, Gospel of, 212
Lycaonia, 51
Lystra, 51, 56

Magnesia, 234
Malta, 61
Man of Lawlessness, 115-17, 137, 138, 199
Mandeans, 73, 92-94, 117
Manicheans, 222. *See also* Gnostics.
Mark, 35-36, 51, 54-55, 69
Mark of the Beast, 157-59
Marsh Arabs, *see* Mandeans.
Mary Magdalene, 145, 153
Mary, mother of Jesus, 145
Matthew, Gospel of, 122-23, 229
Matthias, 126
Melchizedek, 213-24
Messiah, 99, 111-12, 183, 217
   Ebionites and, 186
   James as, 6, 118-21, 155, 161
   Jesus Christ as, 6, 9-10, 30, 119, 122-24, 160-62, 194
   priests and, 146
   Simon bar Gioras as, 238
Messianic age, 81, 87, 146. *See also* Kingdom of God.
Midrash, 78
Miletus, 59
Mishnah, 83, 91, 222
Mitylene, 59
Money, *see* Collection for Jerusalem Poor; Schism.
Moral behavior
   Paul on, 110, 112, 132, 169-70, 173, 198, 200, 206, 216
   Peter on, 136-37
   sexual, 54, 137, 208
Mosaic law, 44, 127-29, 139
   agreement on, 52-54, 99-103
   allegorical view of, 135
   difficulties of, 54, 82-88
   James and, 52, 117, 130-31
   John on, 153
   Paul on, 39-40, 140, 169-70, 178, 206-9, 216
   Peter on, 138
   Peter's vision on, 69, 105
   See also Circumcision, Covenants, Gentiles.
Moses, 200, 213, 215
Myra, 61

Nasareans, 92
Nasrani, *see* St. Thomas Christians, 223
Nathaniel, 123 n. 200
Nations, *see* Gentiles.
Nazareans, Nazarenes, Nazoreans, 9-10, 42, 72-73, 90-92, 94, 98, 127-29, 222
   and Docetism, 150-51
   and Jesus as angel, 161
   and Qur'an, 225
Nazareth, 10, 91-92
Nazarites, 60, 91, 180
Nero, 154, 159
Nestorian Church, 150-223
Nicolaitans, 66, 152, 153, 164
Nicolaus, 66
Nicopolis, Epirus, 132; Illyricum, 177
Niger of Perea, 237-38
Noah, 215. *See also* Covenants.
Number, *see* Mark of the Beast.

Onesimus, 36, 189, 217, 234
Onesiphorus, 33, 181

Pagans, 84-85, 110, 207. *See also* Gospel for all.
Pamphylia, 51
Paphos, 51
Patmos, 152
Paul
   authority of, 26-27, 42-43, 52, 56, 59-60, 63-64, 68, 96-101, 118, 140, 141-42, 194-95, 216
   chronology of, 154, 266-68
   evangelization method of, 21, 24, 27, 45, 70, 103-9, 166, 191, 199, 200-
   failures and worries of, 6, 25, 26, 28, 33, 44, 51, 55, 96, 110, 175-79, 191, 220
   faith, forgiveness, and hopes of, 33, 54, 82, 100-101, 103, 132, 133-34, 140, 164-65, 169, 172-73, 181-83, 209-10

final sufferings and death of, 31-37, 47, 61, 185-86, 191, 233
gospel of, 87-88, 103, 166, 175, 182-84, 187, 193-210, 212-19
health, appearance and persuasive power of, 56, 96, 103, 121, 140-42
Jerusalem arrest and trial of, 60-61, 63, 165, 216
Jerusalem Jewish Christian authorities visits of, 19, 32, 42-44, 47, 49, 52-53, 62, 63, 98-101
Jerusalem trial of, 176, 181-82
Jewish upbringing and zeal of, 19, 39-40, 60-61, 62, 96, 220, 227
journeys of as in Acts, 47-54, 258-65
journeys of as in epistles, 19-20, 39-47, 52-70, 244-57
lasting influence of, 70, 131, 135, 192, 237, 239
library of, 193
opponents of, 109-10, 112-20, 126-30, 151, 191
Peter and, 136-37, 139, 167-74, 184, 205-6, 226-31
revelations to, 19, 25, 40, 44, 52, 96-97, 100, 112, 142, 160, 183, 201, 205
See also Antioch, Paul vs. Peter at; Christology of Paul; Revelation of John.
Paul, epistles of
Acts and, 13-16, 47-50
authenticity of, 37-38
historical value of, 12-16, 37, 49
order of, 18-38
structure and contents of, 16-20, 30
Pella, 127, 212 n. 242
Perea, 128, 237-38
Perga, 51
Pergamum, 153
Pesher, 78
Peter, 124, 226-30
and James, 118, 226-29
death of, 186-87, 233
in Rome, 58 n. 122, 136, 167-68
not bishop, 126, 167-68, 173-74
Paul and, 136-37, 139, 167-74, 184, 205-6, 226-31
puns on name, 136, 172, 201, 209

vision on foods of, 69, 105
See also Antioch, Paul vs. Peter at; Simon Magus.
Pellegrino, Charles, 145 n. 210
Peter, Epistle to James of, 226
Peter, 1st Epistle of, 135-36, 147, 162, 176, 230-31
Peter, Gospel of, 150-51, 161
Peter, 2d Epistle of, 50, 115 n. 192, 136-39, 176, 231
Petra, 42
Pharisees, 41, 72, 82-83, 89-90, 97-98, 195, 209, 220, 221-22
as priests, 79
Paul as, 19, 39
Philadelphia, 153, 234
Philemon, Paul's Epistle to, 35-36. 47, 189, 217, 253-54
Philetas, 181, 183
Philip, 126
Philippi, 45, 57, 59, 62, 106
Philippians, Paul's Epistle to, 36-37, 47, 190-91, 218, 255-57
Philippians, Polycarp's Epistle to, 235
Philo, 8, 72, 81, 89, 135
Phoebe, 29, 190
Phoenicia, 60, 69
Phygelus, 181
Pilate, 123, 180
Pleroma doctrine, 218
Polycarp, 233, 234, 235
Poor, *see* Ebionites. *See also* Collection for Jerusalem Poor.
Predestination doctrine, 187, 207, 217
Pre-existence doctrine, 187, 217
Presbyters, 146-47
Priests, 94, 146-47
genealogy of, 76-81
James as High, 91, 128-29
Jesus Christ as, 214-15
Logos as, 213
Prisca, 33-34, 58, 62, 153
Priscilla, *see* Prisca.
Purity rules, *see* Mosaic law.
Puteoli, 61

Qur'an, 150, 223-26

Rapture, 111, 137. *See also* Day of the Lord.
Recognitions, *see* Clementina.
Resurrection of Jesus Christ, 143, 187, 198, 202, 203, 206
   Christ after, 124, 160, 162-63, 219, 230-31
   Peter on, 230
   Revelation on, 156, 160, 162-63
   tomb of, 145 n. 210
Resurrection of the dead, 21, 110-12, 133, 145, 175, 183, 195, 198, 202, 214
Revelation of John, 66, 111, 148, 152-64, 231
   Qur'an and, 225-26
Rhegium, 61
Righteous One, 128-29
Roman emperors, 153-54. *See also* Nero.
Roman persecution at Jews' behest, 106, 108, 129, 178, 234. *See also* Satan, consignment to.
Roman rule, 8, 117, 178, 212
   collaboration with, 43
   Paul on, 180
   Peter on, 136
Romans, Ignatius' Epistle to, 235
Romans, Paul's Epistle to, 28-31, 46, 84-85, 166-74, 205-10, 250-51
Rome
   as Satan, 178
   bishops of, 167-68
   burned, 129
   Jews expelled from, 58
Rome, Paul's imprisonment and death at, *see* Paul, final sufferings and death of.
Rufinus, 167-68, 227
Rufus, 234

Sacraments, *see* Baptism; Communion.
Sacrifice, 201, 207-8, 214-15
   1st Peter on, 230
Sadducees, 72, 89, 98, 133, 143, 195, 209, 221-22
St. John Christians, *see* Mandeans.
St. Thomas Christians, 223
Saints, 185-86
Salamis, 51
Samaritans, 72, 76, 89-90, 104-5, 123, 222
Samos, 59
Sanhedrin, 117, 178
Sanity and cultural norms, 8-10
Sardis, 153
Satan
   apocalyptic struggle with, 153-54
   attribution to, 140, 142, 153, 162
   consignment to, 33, 108, 115, 178
   Rome as, 178
Saul, alleged name of Paul, 63-64
Saul, King of Israel, 80
Schism, 65-67, 152-53, 181-82, 190
   by baptizer, 200
   violence in, 139, 142
   See also Satan, consignment to.
Scholarship, critique of conventional, 2-4, 7-12, 37. *See also* Historiography pitfalls.
Scoffer, 137
Scribes, 90
Scriptures, holy
   of early church, 90
   of Jewish sects, 89-90, 222
   of Mandeans, 92-93
   reinterpretation of, 135, 221
   See also Gospels, Dead Sea Scrolls, Qur'an.
Sebuacans, 72
Secret Book of Enoch, *see* Enoch.
Seneca, Bishop of Jerusalem, 126
Sidon, 61
Silas, *see* Silvanus.
Silas of Babylonia, 237
Silvanus, 20-22, 44, 52, 57-58, 62, 103, 107, 135-36, 137, 167, 205, 237-38
Simeon Clopas, 120, 124, 126, 212, 237, 238. *See also* Simon bar Gioras.
Simeon Niger, 238
Simon bar Gioras, 212 n. 242, 238
Simon Magus, 226-27
Simon the Cyrene, 150
Sin
   atonement for, 151, 161, 164, 206, 237
   forgiveness of, 204-8
   Paul defining, 208-9
   purification from, 213
   redemption from, 170, 180-81
   See also Moral behavior.
Slave of Christ, 158-59

Slavery, 179, 189, 217
Smyrna, 153, 234
Son of David, 123-24, 160, 183, 184, 229, 230
Son of God, 123 n. 200, 160, 161, 163-64, 171, 184, 195, 199, 213
Son of Man, 123 n. 200
  in Revelation, 154
Spirit, Eternal, 215
Spirit, Holy, 194, 207, 210, 216
  adoptionist doctrine of, 149
  finding lost Jews, 77-81, 105
  in Acts, 51, 56, 57, 59, 63, 69, 77
  Jesus on, 139, 140, 170
Stephen, 64-65, 235-36
Stoic philosophy, 188
Suetonius, 58 n. 122
Symeon, *see* Simeon Clopas.
Syracuse, 61

Tabor, James D. 145 n. 210
Talmudic scholarship, *see* Mishnah.
Tarsus, 50
Temple,
  after destruction of, 84
  Clement on atonement at, 237
  James in, 116-17, 129, 221
  Paul's arrest at, 60-61
  rejection of, 190, 215, 220
Textual emendations, 177, 179, 181, 197
  Colossians, 134
  Corinthians, Paul's 1st Epistle to, 201
  Hebrews, 30, 211-12
  James, 130-31
  Peter, 2d Epistle of, 137
  Revelation, 152
  Timothy, Paul's 1st Epistle to, 178
Thecla, 153
Therapeutae, 72
Thessalonians, Paul's 1st Epistle to, 20-23, 106, 109-12, 118, 198-99, 244-45
Thessalonians, Paul's 2d Epistle to, 20-23, 114-16. 198-99, 245
Thessalonika, 21-22, 45, 58, 62, 106, 220
Thyatira, 153
Timothy, 20-23, 26, 30-37, 44, 46, 56, 58, 59-60, 103, 107, 177, 185-87

Timothy, Paul's 1st Epistle to, 31-33, 47, 51, 177-81, 215, 216, 251-52
Timothy, Paul's 2d Epistle to, 33-34. 47, 115, 165 n. 218, 181-82, 185, 216, 252-53
Titus, 31-32, 44, 46, 48, 52-53, 60, 100-1, 103, 107, 140, 141, 181
Titus, Paul's Epistle to, 31-32, 47, 60, 175-77, 216, 251
Tobias, 126
Trallia, 234
Transjordan, *see* Jordan River region.
Translation issues, 34, 55, 83
  Hebrews, 26-27, 274, 210-12
  "jealous/zealous," 172
  "Mark of the Beast," 157-58
  "presbyter," 146-47
  "sin," 204-5
Travel conditions, 45
Trinity doctrine, 162, 198, 201, 202, 213, 216, 218
Troas, 45, 46, 57, 140, 193, 220
Troy, *see* Troas.

Twelve apostles, 128, 160
  not bishops, 126
  replenished by lot, 77
  See also Didache.
Two Ways, 134, 229
Tycbicus, 32, 34, 35, 185, 187, 189

Virgin Birth, 128
Vine, 122, 123 n. 200, 155
Vine of David, 119, 121-22

Wine, 179-80
Wolf, 83-84
Women
  in Revelation, 153, 159
  Paul on, 29, 34, 38, 133, 146, 177, 178
  See also Elect Lady.

Zacchaeus, 126, 168
Zadok, sons of, 78
Zadokite Document, 77-78, 221
Zadokites, *see* Sadducees.
Zarathustra, 3-4
Zealots, 72, 89, 195, 217

Zenas, 176
Zoroastrian religion, 3-4, 94

Printed in Great Britain
by Amazon